THE TERRORIST ALBUM

The Terrorist Album

Apartheid's Insurgents, Collaborators, and the Security Police

JACOB DLAMINI

Harvard University Press

Cambridge, Massachusetts
London, England
2020

First printing

Library of Congress Cataloging-in-Publication Data

Names: Dlamini, Jacob, 1973– author.

Title: The terrorist album : apartheid's insurgents, collaborators, and the security police / Jacob Dlamini.

Description: Cambridge, Massachusetts : Harvard University Press, 2020. | Includes bibliographical references and index.

Identifiers: LCCN 2019049259 | ISBN 9780674916555 (cloth)

Subjects: LCSH: Anti-apartheid movements—South Africa. | Anti-apartheid activists—South Africa. | Apartheid—South Africa. | Police—South Africa. | Post-apartheid era—South Africa.

Classification: LCC DT1757 .D585 2020 | DDC 305.800968—dc23

LC record available at https://lccn.loc.gov/2019049259

For Simanga Tsotetsi and Khaya Lynn

Who are you who will read these words and study these photographs, and through what cause, by what chance, and for what purpose, and by what right do you qualify to, and what will you do about it?

—JAMES AGEE, *Let Us Now Praise Famous Men*

If I open my old photo albums, my companions from the past, most of them dead now, look back at me. Some days it gives a sad kind of pleasure, and then other days, the same activity brings me face to face with nothingness. So many of the men, the women, were young and charming, truly beautiful. They will never be old. Soon it becomes intolerable to realize that they're in a tomb or reduced to ashes. I close the album.

When I look at those photos from the past, I have the impression that the present is a foreign country. I live here in exile.

—ROGER GRENIER, *A Box of Photographs*

CONTENTS

CONTENTS

PROLOGUE

In October 2018, I met two former members of the South African Security Police to ask for their help in solving a number of archival puzzles. I was working with files, remnants of the apartheid security archive, and wanted to know, among other things, why the police gave their agents, informers, and sources in the anti-apartheid movement codes that began with the prefixes HK, RS, and OTV. What exactly was the difference between agent HK 619 and agent RS 195—both of whom seemed to be spying on the same meetings of the exiled African National Congress (ANC) and whose reports were synthesized into one report? Was it a difference in kind? If so, what and how?

My helpers, a lieutenant-general and a brigadier (both long retired from the South African police), were veterans of the Security Police, having joined in 1963 and 1964, respectively. Each had participated in every major Security Police mission, from the smashing of domestic opposition to apartheid in the 1960s, to South Africa's paramilitary misadventure in Rhodesia in the late sixties, and to the repression of extraparliamentary political activity in the 1970s, 1980s, and early 1990s. Each had risen through the ranks of the Security Police at the height of the fight against what the South African government called terrorism.

I had known the brigadier, a fellow historian and the unofficial chronicler of the apartheid police, for some four years at this point. A shared interest in the history of policing and politics in South Africa had brought us together. As so often happened in my meetings with former members of the Security Police, discussion soon turned to the destruction of South Africa's security archive shortly before the formal end of apartheid in 1994. That memory purge was so extensive that some commentators have called it a "paper Auschwitz."

Why, I asked the two men, had the Security Police destroyed their records? The brigadier's answer caught me by surprise. "The greatest form of terrorism," he said, "was to destroy our documents." Coming from a man who had dedicated his professional life to fighting terrorism, this was strong stuff indeed. Warming to his theme, the brigadier relayed an argument that he had recently had with the general who was in charge of the South African police when apartheid ended (and had likely given the order for the memory purge). The brigadier said he had told the general that, rather than destroy their archives, the Security Police should have used their slush funds to send those records to their allies in Israel and Taiwan for safekeeping. "Today we need these things, because so many guys come and say 'I was a freedom fighter.' And he wasn't! . . . Now we can't prove it," the brigadier said.

I did not share his positivist faith in archives as bearers of the truth, which is why I was not interested in the identities of the police agents, informers, and sources whose code names I had found. But I was interested in what each code meant. If his indignation revealed the passions aroused by the memory purge, it also crystallized the historical and political significance of the object that is the subject of this book.

This object, a secret compendium of mug shots that the Security Police called the "Terrorist Album," was among the documents marked for destruction. This was arson, thundered the brigadier. His thunder was, at one level, a historian's lament over the loss of an archive. But it was also a partisan's dirge over the loss of advantage in South Africa's wars over the country's unsettled history. He was angry about the loosening—unintended, to be sure—of the past's grip on the present. If I had been in any doubt about the necessity of sifting through the remnants of the apartheid security archive in contemporary South Africa, the brigadier's anger (and his reasons for it) revealed the stakes of the historical inquiry essayed here.

The brigadier believed in the moral and political correctness of what the destroyed material had done in the past (which was to document individuals and their actions) and in its potential to act in the present (to unmask spies and blackmail former apartheid agents). His anger helped me realize that the album that frames this study is important not simply for what it was (its materiality, if you will) but also for what the police made it do and expected of it during the most violent period in the history of modern South Africa. If the brigadier's indignation surprised me, however, his assumptions about what the Security Police could and could not do did not.

In the years it had taken me to conduct the research presented by this book, I had become used to former security policemen believing in their own omniscience. I had heard enough policemen tell me how efficient they had been—so good at keeping an eye on their enemies, some said, that they could read in real time every fax sent from and to the ANC's head office in Lusaka, Zambia, and could tell you what each ANC leader had for breakfast on any given day. So beholden were these men to this myth of efficiency that they had come to believe that it had extended to the destruction of their records. They believed that, because they had set out to destroy every record, they must have done exactly that.

Ironically, scholars of South Africa's contemporary political history (myself included) have lent this myth credence by taking claims of Security Police efficiency at face value and, worse, neglecting the relics of the apartheid security archive that dot different parts of South Africa—from the tormented bodies of its inhabitants, to the dusty storerooms of its contested archives, to the landscapes scarred by some of the worst political violence recorded in the twentieth century. This book gives the lie to that myth. My presence in the brigadier's living room that October day disproved the idea of a police force so efficient it had destroyed every record it had ever held.

There I was, after all, not just working with physical objects (an album, confidential police correspondence, informer reports, photographs, secret memoranda) that had survived the memory purge but asking these men to decipher for me the bureaucratic hieroglyphics that marked these relics. This book bears testimony to the failure of the Security Police and, by extension, the apartheid state to obliterate the past. The album at the heart of this book matters because of what it was and because of how the police used it. But it matters also for what it tells us about how those sections of the apartheid bureaucracy charged with the exercise of its monopoly on violence worked. This is not to say that this book treats the thousands of mug shots in the album as straightforward evidence of history or, to use the words of Martha Sandweiss, as self-evident transcriptions of fact. They are not. As John Tagg reminds us, photographs are themselves the historical. They are not mere illustrations.

Like the tons of records that the Security Police and other apartheid operatives fed into industrial furnaces in Johannesburg and Pretoria in the early 1990s, the album bore a taint of criminality that these agents sought to erase. They failed. This book records that failure. It also records the pain of those whom the album branded *terrorists*. It documents the tragedy of households torn asunder by men who did not hesitate to destroy families (by turning father against son in two cases documented in the following pages) even as they claimed to be acting in the interest of *volk en vaderland*. The album was no mute prop in the South African drama but itself an actor. This book documents that drama, and does so at a perilous moment in how we remember the history of apartheid. It comes at a time when memories of the apartheid past and its depravities threaten to disappear forever—unless we, taking inspiration from Walter Benjamin, recognize and seize them in the present.

If the men who invented the Terrorist Album had had their way, this book would not exist, for there would be no album to look at. But it does exist. So does the album, even if as nothing more than a remnant. It is probably for the best that we have only remnants—slivers of what was once a massive physical archive. Unlike the men who tried to reduce this archive to ashes, we cannot afford the luxury of assuming that only a total archive could tell us how apartheid corrupted individuals, ruined lives, and destroyed a country. We cannot assume that our understanding of South African history would be different if we had the total apartheid security archive (assuming there is such a thing as a total archive) to explain to us what the prefixes HK, RS, and OTV meant, and to tell us who the individuals were who operated under the cover of these codes. Even if we did have access to the lost archive, we could never ask it direct questions and hope to receive straight answers about the past. We could never ask the album, even if every copy of the 500 made still existed, to tell us something definitive about the past. Archives cannot do that. This is why we should not despair that all we have left are relics. They still have a lot to say. Writing in a different context, Theodore Adorno makes an observation that applies just as well here: "One should never begrudge deletions. The length of a work is irrelevant, and the fear that not enough is on paper, childish. Nothing should be thought worthy to exist simply because it exists, has been written down."

THE TERRORIST ALBUM

Introduction

IN AUGUST 1912, *The State,* a journal dedicated to the establishment of South Africa as a nation-state, published an article extolling the virtues of fingerprinting.[1] The article, carrying the byline "W" and headlined "On the Track of the Criminal," was of a piece with other efforts by the journal to invest South Africa with the accoutrements of statehood, while at the same time promoting a shared sense of nationhood among South Africans. The author said that, while those responsible for the country's systems of identification and surveillance had accepted the infallibility of fingerprinting, the public was still ignorant about how this new technology worked. This was not because South Africa, only two years old at this time and still a year away from having a national police force, was some colonial backwater isolated from the latest developments in criminology and policing. On the contrary, said W, the country was at the cutting edge of these developments.

Natal, one of the four constituent provinces of the new nation, led the world in fingerprinting and boasted a collection of prints more extensive than Scotland Yard's. There was one problem, however, explained the author: the fact that the other provinces (Cape, Free State, and Transvaal) were not as far along as Natal was in the use of fingerprinting. This undermined its dependability and national reach. This lack of uniformity only compounded other problems caused by lack of knowledge; in one case, a police sergeant in a rural town substituted one man's fingerprints for another man's, thinking that all prints were the same, especially if taken from Africans. Such was the technology's efficacy, however, that even Africans found it uncanny. The author implied that if Africans were sold on fingerprinting, so should be the general (meaning white) public. To illustrate the author's point, the article told the story of Fayedwa, an African ventriloquist who had discovered the art of making easy money by taking advantage of "superstitious, childlike" Africans.

Fayedwa led his victims to believe that he could make their ancestors speak through him and that he had the power to summon evil spirits that only he could chase away—for a fee. The illustration came with two mug shots of Fayedwa, one showing his face and shoulders and the other his side profile. The article made sure to draw the reader's attention to the "peculiar formation" of Fayedwa's throat, the key to his particular ability to commit fraud. But the author added reassuringly that, even though Fayedwa traveled the country defrauding gullible Africans, he could not escape the attention of the colonial state. "Over and over again Fayedwa has been punished for this crime," the author said, "and although he is found under all sorts of disguises in all parts of the country, yet his fingerprint record stands as his accusation." Although Fayedwa could remake himself with all kinds of costumes, he could not erase the impression the state had of him. That impression was fixed. As the article made clear, his fingerprints and his mug shots saw to that. This was the first national display of mug shots in South Africa.[2] The

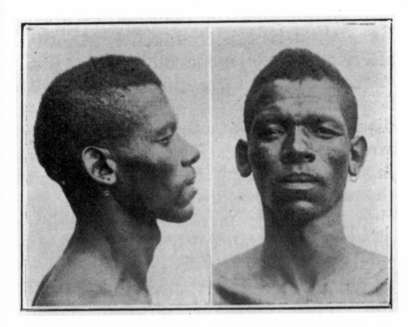

FIGURE I.I Fayedwa's mug shots. *The State*, August 1912.

article marked the first public dissemination of mug shots to an audience imagined to be truly national, meaning South African. This did not make Fayedwa a national subject. Nor did it mean that questions about the constitution of the South African nation had been settled. Far from it. The article sought to portray a young country fast gaining confidence in its ability to track criminals. But it gave the impression of a state unable to keep up with those criminals. Here was Fayedwa, despite his fingerprints and his mug shots, showing up all over the place. The state had punished him over and over again for his crimes. Yet there he was, making the state play catch-up. The article tried to use Fayedwa's story to demonstrate the realization of the state's ambitions to broadcast its authority. But all it did was expose the chasm between what the state thought it could do and what it was in fact able to do.[3]

Apartheid Objects and the Object of Apartheid

Between the fantasy of what the South African state thought it could do and the reality of what it was able to do lay the roots of the album that is the subject of this book. In that breach between fantasy and reality was to be found the hubris—a hallmark of white rule in South Africa—that begat the Terrorist Album.[4] This book is about this album: an object made up of a thick, grey cardboard cover that measures twelve inches in length by nine inches in width. Inside the covers are glossy, cream-colored pages, each measuring eleven inches in length by eight inches in width. Each page contains nine black-and-white mug shots, each of which is two inches in length by 1.7 inches in width. Scholars of contemporary South African history have neglected this object.[5] But it deserves attention because it speaks like no other relic from the apartheid past of the ambitions of South Africa's Security Police to document every known enemy of the state.[6] The police created the album in the early 1960s. They used this small object for a big project devoted to the provision of a list of all South Africans who had fled the country because of opposition to apartheid.[7] Onto its pages went accountants, blue-collar workers, doctors, journalists, students, teachers, writers—individuals united by nothing more than that they were, first, South African and, second, opposed to apartheid.

The police only made it to about seven thousand mug shots by the end of apartheid in the 1990s but, in the course of putting those portraits together, they assassinated individuals, tortured thousands and, in at least two cases recounted here, turned fathers into informers charged with spying on their sons. But, as this book makes clear, an individual did not have to do much—did not have to do anything at all, in fact—to be branded a terrorist. For this was no ordinary rogues' gallery, a pictographic presentation of criminals and their crimes. It was a special object

FIGURE I.2 Copy of the Terrorist Album in National Archives, Pretoria, South Africa. Photograph by the author.

imbued with the menace as well as the political and racial anxieties of apartheid. This book tells the story of how this particular collection of mug shots came about and why, how it was used and by whom, how it acted in the world, and how it came to be called the Terrorist Album. The book shows how, by looking at the album after the end of apartheid, the individuals whose portraits were frozen within its covers opened it up to new meanings. The book uses the album and associated objects (confidential police correspondence, informer reports, photographs, secret memoranda) to examine the history of apartheid violence. It does not treat the album simply as evidence of history but as an artifact—an object with a social life—whose material history also deserves examination.[8] By recounting the history of apartheid violence through objects, this book does not minimize the effects of that violence, or spread moral and political culpability for it so widely that even objects stand accused. As Hannah Arendt says, where all are guilty, nobody is.[9] When everything is guilty, nothing is.

The book treats the album and linked objects as cracks through which to look afresh at the ruins of apartheid. Rather than offer a grand theory of photography and surveillance in South Africa, it asks that we look to see if the perspectives gained through these cracks—compromised, crooked, and limited as they may be—might allow for new understandings of apartheid. The book argues that, by looking at the album as both an instrument of violence and a material object with a life of its own, we might come up with richer accounts of what apartheid's object (meaning its aim) was and of the role of objects (meaning artifacts) fabricated by the police to manage the "bureaucracy of everyday life" in South Africa.[10] By looking at the album as a crack through which to peer into the past, scholars might also come up with historically grounded and ethically sound protocols for the treatment of the thousands of remnants from the apartheid security archive that scholars have yet to explore. These protocols might help us avoid the temptations of positivism and to shun the false comforts of complexity.[11]

Looking at the Album

By tracking the history of apartheid violence through objects, the book also shows the arbitrariness and extent of political repression in South Africa. As was the case with all authoritarian governments in the twentieth century, notably in Eastern Europe and in Latin America, apartheid South Africa actively produced the stock figure of the dissident and then used objects such as the album to implicate individuals in the commission of all sorts of political and social crimes. Like the fingerprinting system of which colonial officials were so proud, the album symbolized the scale of the ambitions of the apartheid state. Just like the colonial officials who thought they could keep track of Fayedwa, the apartheid Security Police believed they could use the album to track every exiled South African branded an enemy of the state. They thought they could contain the likeness of every person labeled a terrorist within the covers of the album. To be sure, there was no straight line connecting Fayedwa's mug shots and the estimated seven thousand photographs that constituted the Terrorist Album.[12] The colonial state founded in 1910 did not turn seamlessly into the apartheid state in 1948, when Afrikaner nationalists won power and gave the world one of the most odious words in any language. But each state harbored bureaucratic ambitions designed to hide their lack of political legitimacy. Each regime refused to see black South Africans as deserving of political rights and reacted to struggles for such rights with violence. The album was one instrument of that violence.[13]

If Fayedwa was an anthropological curiosity whose social deviance issued as much from his cleverness as from his anatomy (notice the odd formation of his throat, said the article), the men and women—black and white, young and old, communist and liberal—reduced to two-dimensional figures in the album were, to the state, sociological oddities whose political deviance stemmed from their refusal to live by the verities of apartheid. If Fayedwa was a racial type, the seven-thousand-odd individuals in the album were political types. That is, to colonial officials, Fayedwa represented a type of human (the native) whose cunning remained politically harmless even as it required the constant attention of the state, while the so-called terrorists in the album were political actors who posed a danger to the state precisely because of their insistence that the apartheid state recognize them as individuals and not as members of racial or, to use apartheid-speak, population groups. This does not mean that Fayedwa was an apolitical actor. Neither is it to suggest that he existed beyond the colony's political pale.

But it does alert us to the fact that different logics governed Fayedwa's mug shots and the photographs in the album—even if their basic composition followed the same rules of police photography, unchanged since the establishment of the genre in the second half of the nineteenth century. To colonial officials, Fayedwa was a petty criminal whose schemes did not threaten the state. He was a figure of fun who colonial officials could use to show the utility of fingerprinting (so effective that even simpleminded Africans were charmed by its uncanny qualities) while also displaying their paternal care for the hapless natives duped by Fayedwa. The so-called terrorists, on the other hand, posed an existential risk to the apartheid order. While it would not have occurred to colonial officials to label Fayedwa an enemy of the state (though he was certainly a public nuisance), no such official qualms existed about the individuals in the album.[14] They were enemies of the state and, as such, could be subjected to all forms of violence, from assassination to detention to torture. To be in the Terrorist Album was to live in the shadow of death. It was to live constantly with the knowledge that apartheid assassins might strike at any time and that they might do so for no better reason than that the target was in the album.

When human rights lawyer George Bizos asked apartheid operative Craig Williamson in 1998 why, in 1982, he killed anti-apartheid exile Ruth First, despite knowing she was not involved in the armed struggle against apartheid, Williamson said it was because "she was in the Terrorist Album."[15] This meant, Williamson told me years later, that First was "fair game."[16] But he was adamant that the album was not a book filled with "targets of elimination."[17] He insisted that it was "essentially a book used as part of an intelligence-gathering process."[18] Officially, the police used the album to do nothing more than keep track of people who left South Africa without the permission of the state.[19] But to be in the album was to be a terrorist. As Williamson told the Truth and Reconciliation Commission during his amnesty application for a string of murders, "The only people who were in the Terrorist Album were people who were external [in exile] and about whom there was information that these were active at a high level, either militarily or at a high political level. These were terrorists."[20] But we should hesitate before we take Williamson at his word. The question of what made one a terrorist is easy to answer: any form of opposition to apartheid. Harder to answer is the question: Who made one a terrorist? Among the people in the album is novelist Bessie Head, who left South Africa for Botswana in 1964 to escape the "fatal feeling of doom" that pervaded apartheid South Africa.[21] The police had detained Head in 1960, making her one of the estimated two thousand individuals taken into custody shortly after the Sharpeville massacre on March 21, 1960.[22] That massacre opened a new chapter in the history of political violence in South Africa. It led to the banning of the African National Congress (ANC) and the Pan Africanist Congress (PAC); saw the introduction of systematic torture by the police; resulted in the adoption of violence by the ANC, the PAC, and other groups as a legitimate form of struggle; and drove thousands of South Africans into exile as the government unleashed a wave of repression that swept many, including Bessie Head, into the clutches of the Security Police.

Bessie's Head

The Security Police forced Head to inform on friends in the PAC, and she suffered a nervous breakdown and tried to kill herself because of this.[23] When the police were done with her, they let her leave South

Africa on an exit permit—a one-way ticket to statelessness whose holders had to renounce their South African citizenship. The permit, a piece of paper designed by the apartheid government to rid itself of individuals considered to be political problems, was a provision of the Departure from the Union Regulation Act, introduced in 1955 to give government control over the mobility of its citizens. The law gave the Minister of the Interior the power to decide who could receive a passport or travel document.[24] Any person who left South Africa without a valid passport or exit permit faced between three months and two years in jail.[25] Having granted Head her exit permit, the police included her in their album, thereby branding her a terrorist.

As an indication of the mix of bureaucratic meanness and callous indifference that defined the album, Head's terrorist portrait was not, in fact, a formal mug shot (certainly not the photograph she would have submitted with her passport and exit-permit applications). It was a cut-and-paste job. The image in the album shows Head smoking, her right hand raised, and her index and middle fingers parted as she prepares to pull the cigarette out of her mouth. Her head is tilted rightward. Head, in a floral dress with an open collar, has an afro the sides of which are touched with white. Her eyes look heavy with worry. I can tell you about these details because I have a copy of the original photograph the police cut and pasted into the album (fig. I.2). George Hallett, a South African photographer famous for his portraits of African writers, took the photograph at a writers' conference in Berlin in 1979. The Security Police likely clipped Hallett's photograph and put it in the album after it appeared in a 1984 issue of *Staffrider*, an anti-apartheid literary magazine (fig. I.3). But why include Head in the album? Why brand an impecunious writer estranged from the anti-apartheid movement a terrorist?

Eric Abraham is another person whose inclusion in the compilation calls for caution in the way one looks at the album. A liberal opponent

FIGURE I.3 Novelist Bessie Head. Photograph © George Hallett. Image courtesy of Gallery MOMO.

of apartheid, Abraham earned his entry into the album by leaving South Africa clandestinely for Botswana in January 1977 to escape house arrest. The police had confiscated his passport and rejected his application for an exit permit. But who planned Abraham's daring escape? This was done by Craig Williamson and his superiors in the Security Police. In fact, the police planned every detail of Abraham's flight, from the secret code he and Williamson used to communicate once the plot to spirit him out was underway to the car and driver who took him to the border fence over which he jumped into Botswana.[26] The idea was to use Abraham (a genuine activist living in fear for his life) as cover for Williamson (an apartheid spy with his eyes set on the anti-apartheid movement abroad). Having planned all this—without Abraham's knowledge—the police then added his mug shot to the album, placing him alphabetically on the very first page. Having helped the twenty-two-year-old Abraham break the law, they then branded him a terrorist.

Odirile Meshack Maponya, a schoolteacher and talented singer, landed in the album after leaving South Africa illegally in 1977 to join the military wing of the ANC. Trained in guerilla warfare in Angola and the Soviet Union, Maponya became one of the most active insurgents in South Africa. By the time he died in 1988, killed when the bomb he was trying to plant outside a whites-only cinema in Pretoria exploded prematurely, he had been on the police's most-wanted list for eleven years. In their pursuit of him, the police turned his father Joseph Maponya into an informer paid to spy on his family, tortured his brother Japie Maponya to death in 1985 and deposited Japie's corpse on the border with Swaziland, murdered his ANC colleague Stanza Bopape in 1988 and fed that body to crocodiles, arrested and tortured his brother Itumeleng and cousin Tiro Tumane, and detained almost every member of the family after Maponya's death in April 1988.[27]

How, then, are we to look at the album? What does the album tell us about the ways in which the apartheid state pictured and framed its enemies? How are we to understand a rogues' gallery in which Abraham (journalist), Head (novelist), and Maponya (combatant) bear the same label of *terrorist*? We cannot answer these questions by looking to the album to reveal the logic of apartheid rule. We cannot turn to Williamson and the other apartheid operatives I interviewed because they cannot be trusted. But we can treat the album as what it is—a relic of repression—and use a variety of our senses to apprehend its materiality, its meaning, and its purpose.[28] By moving back and forth between the album and some of the men and women it sought to reduce to two-dimensional figures, we can examine its successes and failures, and use the object to shed light on the functioning and self-understanding of the apartheid state between 1960 and 1994—the most violent period in the history of modern South Africa.[29]

Indexing Apartheid

If apartheid was indeed a policy "born in fear, nurtured in hubris, and sustained through obfuscation," how might the album help us make sense of that fear, hubris, and obfuscation?[30] What happens when we refuse to see the album as indexing both a long list of apartheid's enemies as well as a certain technical efficiency? It is a commonplace of South African historiography to foreground the violence of apartheid, to say that apartheid was by definition coercive. But, as Ivan Evans reminds us, that coercion depended less on spectacular violence and more on bureaucracy.[31] It depended on government by paper.[32] In fact, the creation of a complex bureaucratic web to ensnare every South African in this blueprint or that program, this black spot or that whites-only area, this file or that album, was crucial to the normalization of the violence upon which racial domination was founded.

Yet we should not take this to mean that the apartheid state enjoyed a bureaucratic sophistication it did not have.[33] To see the album, for example, as pointing to a sophisticated panopticon-like capability is to take apartheid's delusions as givens.[34] As Nicky Rousseau says, South Africa's war against its enemies was "far more contingent, haphazard and depleted" than, say, a literal understanding of the album as indeed a Terrorist Album depicting dangerous individuals might suggest.[35]

It is worth recalling that the Promotion of National Unity and Reconciliation Act 34 of 1995, which gave South Africa its storied "truth commission," mandated the commission to establish as "complete a picture as possible of the causes, nature and extent of the gross violations of human rights" committed between 1960 and 1994—with the start of its inquiry being the Sharpeville massacre and the end being the advent of democracy in April 1994.[36] From the very beginning, the commission thought of its work in terms of images. It endeavored to replace the visual economy of apartheid—with its racial anxieties, criminal secrets, and moral depravity—with a new one founded on accountability, dignity, and justice. This meant seeking justice for all, finding answers to questions about what happened to loved ones, and exposing the excesses of the past. More than that, the commission set out to give voice to those silenced by apartheid. As the commission said in its final report:

> The story of apartheid is, amongst other things, the story of the systematic elimination of thousands of voices that should have been part of the nation's memory. The elimination of memory took place through censorship, confiscation of materials, bannings, incarceration, assassination and a range of related actions. Any attempt to reconstruct the past must involve the recovery of this memory—much of it contained in countless documentary records.[37]

The commission noted how, before the dawn of democracy in 1994, the apartheid government "deliberately and systematically destroyed a huge body of state records and documentation in an attempt to remove incriminating evidence and thereby sanitize the history of oppressive rule."[38] Among the archives destroyed were forty-four tons of paper-based and microfilm records held by the National Intelligence Service (NIS). Anthony Turton, a senior NIS official who participated in this orgy of destruction and who offers a first-hand account of it in his memoirs, says the NIS top brass called the purge a "Revaluation."[39] The destruction lasted eight months in 1993, with NIS agents such as Turton feeding the material into industrial furnaces belonging to the state-owned steelmaking company Iscor and located in Johannesburg and Pretoria.[40] The commission found that, in March 1992, the head office of the South African Security Police ordered the destruction of all operational records, including copies of the album and materials confiscated from individuals and organizations over the years. But the commission could identify neither the source nor the content of that order. "The evidence suggests that a verbal instruction was received at both regional and local levels."[41] The instruction resulted in a "massive and systematic destruction of records," with security officers using the facilities of companies such as Nampak and Sappi for the job.[42]

The commission found that, on the whole, Security Police offices "implemented the instruction to destroy records to the letter."[43] But there were exceptions. Security Police offices in Ficksburg, Kimberley, Pietermaritzburg, Pietersburg, Port Elizabeth, Potchefstroom, Rooigrond, Thaba Nchu, Thohoyandou, Tzaneen, and Welkom did not destroy their operational records.[44] In fact, the Port Elizabeth, Empangeni, and Cape Town offices also kept lists of the files sent to the Pretoria head office for destruction—in apparent violation of the verbal order issued in March 1992. It is thanks to these exceptions that we have remnants of the apartheid security archive. It is thanks especially to the office in Thohoyandou, the headquarters of the Security Police in the homeland of Venda, that copies of the album survive. Before the March 1992 order, there were five hundred copies of the album in Security Police offices around the country.[45] Only three, as far as I have been able to establish, survived the memory purge. One is in the National Archives in Pretoria; one is with the National Prosecuting Authority, and one is in private hands. For ethical reasons, you will not see the copy in the National Archives listed in its catalog. Individuals who suspect or know they are included in the album can, however, gain permission to view it.

Two of the surviving copies bear the marks of the Venda Security Police. The one I have been able to see, smell, touch, and listen to is numbered 340 V / H / K—the three letters standing in Afrikaans for Venda Hoof Kantoor (Venda Head Office). The copy is numbered 340, showing where it stood in the sequence of the five hundred copies in secret circulation before March 1992. An official stamp on the album's cover shows that the Venda Security Police received it on September 17, 1985. (The copy in private hands is numbered 339 and the stamp on its cover shows that the Venda Security Police received it September 19, 1985.) When this book talks about "the album," using the definite article, it is talking about copy 340 in both its material and digital form. I have a digital copy of the album because of the truth commission, whose investigators and researchers salvaged the surviving copies during a research visit to the offices of the Venda Security Police in the late 1990s. A researcher who took part in that visit told me that she and her colleagues found two of the copies of the album in an office in a pile of seemingly discarded documents. This salvage made possible the archival reconstruction attempted in this book.

By stating this book's debt to the truth commission so explicitly, I intend to caution against those who would have us see the commission as a failure. Critics who blame the commission for bringing about neither truth nor reconciliation fail to see the unglamorous but important work the commission did to prevent the total destruction of the apartheid archive.[46]

We know more about how apartheid functioned—who gave the orders and who did what—than we did before the commission began its work in 1996. Consider, for example, Odirile Meshack Maponya, whom the Security Police, acting out of spite, buried as a pauper in 1988. He might still be missing and the Maponya family might still be looking for his remains (as well as those of his brother Japie Maponya), but because of the commission they at least know which police officers recruited family patriarch Joseph Maponya in 1977 to spy on his family and for how much; which askaris and police operatives killed Japie Maponya and why; and how the security services operated.[47] Knowledge of these actions does not equal power and it certainly does not amount to justice.[48] Knowledge alone is not power. But, as Michael Ignatieff put it in his appraisal of the South African truth commission, the commission narrowed the range of lies that could be told about the apartheid past.[49] It is thanks to the commission that we know how the police used the album during the interrogation of detainees, and how central the album was to the transformation of apartheid opponents into collaborators. In fact, for every collaborator, the album marked both the beginning and seal of their collaboration with the police. This began with their pointing out, often under duress, their fellow comrades in the album and ended with their driving around with copies of the album on their laps, using them to identify former comrades on the streets, at train stations, and in bars for arrest or elimination.

The album was not just an intelligence tool used by the police to extract information. It was an object imbued with danger. To be confronted with the album, especially under torture, was to come face to face with the possibility of one's death. "Talk to us about the people in the album and live, or refuse to talk and die"—that was the impossible offer that police interrogators gave insurgents and other opponents of apartheid. The album came with an offer that many detainees could not refuse. This was not just a collection of photographs that one could approach in the same way one looked at a family album. Hiding behind the covers of this particular album was coercion, masquerading as choice. That is why the Security Police used it assiduously to break off the detainee's voice and to claim it as their own. These merchants of violence understood that capitulation is measured not by the quantity of the information given, but by the very act of talking itself. Detainees understood this, too. They pretended to give up only crumbs and the police pretended not to mind—until it was time to seize on a contradiction, a slip of the tongue, to pounce on the detainee. But there was more to the album than that.

Viewed from the vantage point of the twenty-first century, there is a sense in which the album—with its collection of black and white, young and old, liberal and radical—offers against itself and its compilers a collective portrait of the hope and idealism that animated the anti-apartheid movement of the twentieth century.[50] To look at the album from this vantage point is to see not the omniscience of the apartheid state, with its neat framing of dissidence, but the hopeless failure of that state to stave off its demise. Read against itself, the album offers a vivid portrait of a cosmopolitan and democratic vision for South Africa. This raises the question of how a state that defined itself as white supremacy's last hope in Africa dealt with opposition that came not in predictable black but in a rainbow of colors. How, in other words, did the album handle the question of race when opponents of apartheid's thinking about race came in so many colors? As the following chapters will explore, the South African Security Police tried to make the album conform to apartheid visions. They endeavored to make the album adhere to the logic of apartheid and its obsession with racial apartness (the literal meaning of *apartheid*). But they failed. This does not mean that the album chronicled a failure foretold. There was nothing inevitable about the end of apartheid. It took years of struggle by millions of people, including those captured in the album, to bring apartheid to its knees.

The Historian's Task

To look at the album in the twenty-first century is to be confronted with the historian's failure to make artifacts of oppression—objects from a repressive past—speak of that past and to do so in service of justice and historical redress. The album is mute. It cannot speak. It cannot represent the past in any direct and transparent way. It cannot even articulate the prose of counterinsurgency that marks its composition.[51] The men who compiled the album, however, and the individuals whose photographs populate its pages, can and do speak. It is through them that the album is made to speak in this book—through them that we are able to listen to what the mug shots have to say about the past. That, in fact, is how this book makes sense of the album and its history: through human voices. Constantly being updated, constantly on the move, constantly being opened and shut, the album was and is a work in progress.[52] It was and is constantly in production. To look at the thousands of portraits in the album, and to have them stare back at you in silence, is to remake the album. To look at it mug shot by mug shot is to produce it anew. But that is no easy thing to do because, in a number of cases, asking individuals to make the album speak entails directing them to look at photographs last seen while they were in detention or going through unspeakable torture. When I pointed out her mug shot in the album to Lumka Yengeni, an ANC insurgent tortured by the Security Police to the point of attempting suicide, she asked: "But where was I then, at which stage of my detention?"[53] The photograph not only reminded Yengeni of her torture, it also prompted her to wonder what other photographs the police took during her detention. She asked: "Where are the other photographs?" For some individuals, looking at their mug shots at my urging meant remembering the broader circumstances in which the mug shots were taken—in one case, for example, the parent who was present when the picture was taken and whose later funeral the person could not attend, as he was a fugitive and in exile when the parent died. One individual denied that the mug shot marked as hers was indeed hers, even though it bore a striking resemblance to her and was hers according to the police details that went with it. What to do, then, with memories that cannot recognize their own reflection in the album?

To help me make sense of the album and of their presence in it, some of the individuals interviewed for this book gave me access to the secret files kept on them and, in one case, on a dead husband by the apartheid security services.[54] The truth commission and the post-apartheid government made these files available to individuals so they could know what the apartheid state had said about them and, more often than not, had used as justification for their harassment. This posed a number of ethical questions. How, for example, does the historian deal with a declassified file filled with content that was obviously intended at its origin to slander the file's subject? How does one deal with the prudishness of undercover police operatives who thought nothing of passing judgment on the private lives of their targets, even as they themselves were violating the privacy of those targets in the most intrusive ways possible?[55] How, in short, should one read the apartheid security archive in the post-apartheid period? This books grapples with these questions. It does so in an attempt to settle its debt to the truth commission and, hopefully, to remind South Africa and the world of the forms of knowledge about the past that the commission made possible.

Archives of Terror

It is not surprising that, in its mission to uncover the secrets of the past, the truth commission thought in terms of pictures. It had to. The apartheid state was obsessed with how individuals, places, and things looked. Take its definition of racial identity, as laid out in the Population

Registration Act of 1950, a piece of legislation that served as the bedrock of apartheid by providing for the classification of every South African according to distinct racial categories. The act said:

> A White person is one who is in *appearance* obviously white—and not generally accepted as Colored—or who is generally accepted as White—and is not obviously Non-White, provided that a person shall not be classified as a White person if one of his natural parents has been classified as a Colored person or a Bantu. . . . A Bantu is a person who is, or is generally accepted as, a member of any aboriginal race or tribe of Africa. . . . A Colored person is a person who is not a white person or a Bantu.[56]

The act introduced a population register, with each African, Colored, and white South African male over sixteen issued with a national identity number and classified "according to the ethnic or other group to which he belongs."[57] (Because South Africans of South Asian descent were not considered South African citizens until the 1960s, the original act excluded Asian / Indian as a distinct racial category. It was only after South Africa became a republic in 1961, having severed ties with the British Commonwealth, that the government created a separate racial category marked Asian.)[58] The particulars of each registered male had to include a "recent photograph of himself," his identity number, and "in the case of a native who is not a South African citizen," fingerprints. In fact, this register and the photographic archive it spawned provided the foundation for the album, generating the majority of its mug shots. As Keith Breckenridge notes, however, the police use of the register to compile the album was illegal.[59] It violated the terms of South Africa's census laws, which said that personal information gathered through the census could not be used for any other purposes, even by the state. Yet, the Security Police treated the register as a source to be used at their whim. In some instances, the Security Police planted their own officers in the bureaucracies charged with handling the register. Masquerading as regular public servants, these undercover officers plundered the register for information and kept track of applications for exit permits, passports, and other travel documents.

Apartheid in Global Context

South Africa was not unique in its obsession with the repressive use of documents and photographs to make citizens legible. Scholars such as Michelle Caswell on Cambodia, Kirsten Weld on Guatemala, Katherine Verdery on Romania, and Tina Rosenberg on Czechoslovakia, Germany, and Poland have explored the bureaucratic and ideological obsession of authoritarian states with the documentation of their own excesses.[60] Even the Khmer Rouge, which banned clocks and turned the country's National Library and Archives into a pigsty in a bid to obliterate all signs of Cambodian history before its takeover in 1975, still saw fit to generate extensive records, including torture logs and mug shots.[61] As Caswell informs us, 5,190 mug shots remain from the Khmer Rouge's bloody archive, "the last trace of victims before their executions."[62] In Guatemala, where a thirty-six-year civil war claimed more than two hundred thousand lives, the military dictatorship responsible for most of those deaths generated what Kirsten Weld calls "paper cadavers"—a mountain of archival records made up of about eighty million pages.[63] This included a quarter of a million personal identity cards that came with the obligatory mug shots.

But, as Weld reminds us, these cards and mountains of paper are not the sum total of the lives they tried to discipline and, in many cases, punish. As she puts it, "one must not confuse the rich life of a person with its thin archival record—its paper cadaver."[64] One way to avoid that confusion, Weld argues, is to resurrect these paper cadavers by recalling their lives beyond the gaze of the state and its machineries. Individuals are never simply what the state tells us they are. Resurrecting paper cadavers is a crucial step in any attempt to reconstruct the past by recovering lost memory. As Katherine Verdery says, in her ethnography of the archive of Romania's authoritarian regime, Nicolae Ceausescu's secret police not only classified individuals as enemies of the state, they actively manufactured those enemies.[65] Verdery has examined the files, complete with surveillance photographs, compiled by the Romanian secret police during their fabrication of her as an enemy of the Socialist Republic of Romania. "The files were a principal means," she says, of branding someone an enemy: "a repository containing the tracks of that process. Somehow the materiality of the file guarantees the reality / identity of the person produced through it."[66] In the South African context, we only have to think of Bessie Head and Eric Abraham, two of the cases cited above, to appreciate the validity of Verdery's observation. Odirile Maponya, with his bomb and intention to cause mass civilian casualties, might be a more complicated case to read along the lines suggested by Verdery and Weld. But even he deserves a less condemnatory reading, one that moves critically beyond his mug shot. As Ian Hacking observes, "Even the dead are more than their deeds, for we make sense of a finished life only within its sphere of former possibilities."[67] Likewise, Jonathan Finn warns that treating mug shots as though they were objective "presupposes the existence of the criminal body."[68] Readers attuned to the complexities of archives cannot afford such a presupposition. Like the partial files from Romania's secret police archives, photographs are by definition "fragmentary and incomplete utterances."[69] They need captions and context for their meaning to reveal itself.[70] They cannot, for this reason, stand in direct relation to the truth. They need interpretation and a critical attitude towards their source and archive. This means paying heed to the call by Antoinette Burton for scholars to challenge the claims of objectivity associated often with the so-called traditional archive, and to do so by "telling stories about its provenance, its histories, its effects on its users, and above all, its power to shape all the narratives which are to be 'found' there."[71]

By using a small object to tell a big story about South Africa between 1960 and 1994, I intend to cut apartheid down to analytical, moral, and political size, thereby challenging the myths that continue to surround popular understandings of apartheid. As the dream of a democratic and egalitarian South Africa disappears into a twenty-first-century hellhole of corruption and increasing economic inequality, apologists for apartheid have taken to saying something along these lines: "The apartheid state might have been authoritarian and brutal but at least it was efficient"; or "Blacks were better off under apartheid"; or "the apartheid police were murderous bastards but they at least knew what they were doing."[72] Such revisionist claims are similar to the arguments made in defense of Italian fascist Benito Mussolini, under whose dictatorship the trains supposedly ran on time.[73] We give the apartheid state too much credit, however, by assuming that it was efficient. It was not. This did not make it less brutal. But efficient it was not. It could not always tell its friends from its enemies, its Indians from its whites. We only have to look at the album, feel its pages, and listen to its voices to know that.

ONE

From Racial Types to Terrorist Types

ON NOVEMBER 4, 1863, German anthropologist Gustav Fritsch landed on Robben Island armed with guns and a stereoscope camera.[1] The following day, Fritsch photographed a group of Xhosa leaders imprisoned on the island.[2] The men had been on the island since 1858, exiled there by the British as punishment for their role in the Xhosa Cattle-killings of 1856–1857.[3] The killings grew out of a millenarian movement that sought to expel the British from Xhosa lands by laying waste to those lands through the destruction of cattle and crops. Fritsch photographed the men, whom he had to bribe with cash and tobacco to sit through the twenty seconds necessary for each exposure, in both front and side profile.[4] Thus began a photographic tradition in southern Africa that, while not strictly within the bounds of prison photography, hewed nonetheless to the protocols of that genre.[5] Fritsch, a medical doctor and budding scientist with an interest in the racial types of southern Africa, had set out to collect portraits of the natives of southern Africa.[6]

Fritsch began on Robben Island with his reluctant sitters and, over the next three years, visited different parts of the Cape Colony, Natal, the Orange Free State and Bechuanaland. By the time he sailed back to Germany in 1866, Fritsch had photographed more than a hundred Africans.[7] To be sure, Fritsch did not introduce photography to southern Africa. The first daguerreotype had arrived in South Africa in 1846, seven years after scientist Dominique François Arago unveiled artist Louis Daguerre's invention before the French Academy of Sciences.[8] By 1851, three daguerreotypists were active in the Cape.[9] In 1852, Scottish missionary David Livingstone sat for a portrait in Cape Town before embarking on his journey to central Africa.[10] In 1858, photographer John Kirk accompanied Livingstone on a missionary expedition up the Zambezi River, making this the first Christian mission into central Africa to use photography as a scientific tool.[11]

In 1871, linguists Wilhelm Bleek and Lucy Lloyd photographed a group of so-called Bushmen imprisoned in Cape Town's Breakwater Prison.[12] But the first racial-type photograph in southern Africa was that of a "Native woman of Sofala," taken in 1845 by French daguerreotypist E. Thiesson in Mozambique.[13] Thiesson's photograph is marked by a pronounced lack of interest in its sitter's subjectivity. We learn nothing about the sitter other than that she was a woman, from Sofala, and about thirty years old when she sat for the photograph. Thiesson sought to capture not the person herself but the racial type he believed she represented. He was not alone in his fascination with racial types. Even though the genre of racial-type photography was established in the 1860s and 1870s, its antecedents were much older. They went back at least to 1850, when Harvard scientist Louis Agassiz commissioned photographs of African-born slaves in Columbia, South Carolina.[14] Agassiz wanted to use the photographs to support his claims about polygenesis—the theory that humans had descended from different evolutionary ancestors. Fritsch himself had come to Africa looking for pure racial types but his search had been stymied by constant encounters with diversity. The Africans he met and photographed came in a variety of hues. Even among the Zulu, whom he considered the noblest Africans, "external appearance is so diverse that it is difficult to fix an exact type," he said.[15] By the time he published his images in Europe in 1872, however, he had removed all evidence of this diversity.[16] He excluded pictures of people of mixed descent and of Malays to present a picture of racial purity that bore no relation to reality.[17] Ironically, the Malays were the very first subjects that Fritsch had photographed upon his arrival in Cape Town in September 1863. Fritsch used his published photographs to emphasize physical and racial differentiation.[18] He shifted his interest from the individual sitters and their cultural diversity to the bodies and heads of his African subjects.[19]

Still, Fritsch's Robben Island daguerreotypes, the first we have of any political prisoners on the island, have retained their historical value because they alert us to the earliest coexistence of politics and photography in southern Africa.[20] As Patricia Hayes says, "It seems that as political captives filtered to Robben Island prison or exile elsewhere, they were also filtered by the camera."[21] But how did the camera come to play this filtering role? How did photography itself come to serve an explicitly political role in the service of the colonial and apartheid state? To ask these questions yet another way: How does the history sketched out above explain the origins of the so-called Terrorist Album? It is worth recalling that when police forces around the world began using photographs in the 1870s, it was more to symbolize scientific policing than to detect criminals.[22] Drawing on the new sciences of anthropology, biology, criminology, eugenics, and medicine, and on the methodologies spawned by these fields, police forces developed a keen interest in finding reliable means of capturing criminals. Photography, with its cloak of scientific objectivity and technical infallibility, offered state functionaries from the 1840s onward what looked like a ready solution to the problem of how to recognize and record criminals. But, as Jens Jäger points out, the process by which police forces around the world came to adopt photography was halting and long. When the police finally adopted the technology, the adoption was reluctant. It was only after 1870 that there emerged rogues' galleries, and these—collections of photographs used to identify perpetrators of witnessed crimes—classified their mug shots by crime.[23] This form of classification grew out of assumptions about the biological nature of criminal behavior, which held that criminal conduct was so fixed that, as one South African policeman put it, criminals could be "classified under the crimes they follow."[24] This policeman was among those who assumed that biology begat criminal conduct.[25]

But these early rogues' galleries were not systematic and, in fact, most police forces continued to rely on old-fashioned methods of detection to solve crime. If the police used photographs at all, it was as a "memory aid in the broadest sense."[26] This reminds us that photography was not designed from its start to serve only repressive ends. It could function both honorifically and repressively.[27] When Louis Daguerre and his British counterpart Henry Fox Talbot invented the daguerreotype and calotype, respectively, they did not set out to develop a means of surveillance. That the camera became such is a function of contingent histories in different contexts. As Jäger says, "It is well worth recalling that the common photographic portrait was a sign of respectability, and the arrangements in the studio represented, or hinted at, a respectable environment."[28] By the time Fritsch undertook his Africa expedition in 1863, however, portrait photography was beginning to change its social role in Europe, from the honorific function associated with bourgeois respectability to the repressive task connected to a growing state interest in population control.[29] In practice, this meant that when scholars such as Fritsch took photographs of their native sitters, they were drawn more to the purported scientific value of their subjects than they were to their biographies. But when a state institution used a portrait, it was interested precisely in the biography—the individuality—of the person represented by the portrait. "This resulted in a tension between the social function of portrait photography as a proof of respectability and its administrative function, as a means of recording, identifying, and detecting."[30] For the respectable classes, the problem was that nothing distinguished the portrait of a respectable member of the bourgeoisie from that of a criminal. It also did not help matters that in late nineteenth-century Europe, commercial photographers took both elite portraits and criminal mug shots as a matter of course.[31]

The unsystematic use of photography by the police changed after 1871 following the Paris Commune, a short-lived experiment in radical rule. In its brutal repression of the commune, the French government introduced a photographic register of political radicals, thereby ushering in the camera as an instrument used to capture those who had participated in the uprising.[32] The French army used the register systematically to eliminate the communards. The creation of the register followed an instruction by the minister of the navy and the colonies that every person sentenced by maritime courts to more than six months in jail be photographed before the start of their sentence. In 1874, the Prefecture of Police in Paris established its own register. After that, every person sent to jail had to have his or her photograph taken. In 1876, the Berlin criminal police began collecting photographs. By the following year, they had collected 764 portraits and these were classified by crime in nine albums. Still, there was yet no "discourse on criminal photography."[33] Even though most police forces in Europe maintained photographic records of suspects and criminals, they still lacked a systematic approach to photography. This changed in 1879 with the entry of Alphonse Bertillon, a police clerk in Paris. Bertillon introduced a system of identification governed by a set of measurements of the adult body.[34] He issued detailed instructions about how to measure each person and how to photograph that person. His system promised to solve two problems at once: how to identify a suspect or criminal with a great degree of accuracy, and how to organize the mountains of mug shots in police possession. Paris adopted Bertillon's system in 1882; between 1885 and 1888, it was extended to all of France. In 1892 the third international congress of criminal anthropologists recommended the system's adoption by every police force in Europe.[35] It was in this context that criminologists and police officers started discussing in earnest the merits of photography.[36]

Bertillonage, as Bertillon's system was named, called for two body measurements plus two photographs showing a neutral, standardized view of the face: one from the front, a second in profile. This has remained the standard protocol for the taking of mug shots around the world.[37] In truth, however, Bertillon did not inaugurate the use of rogues' galleries. In the United States, for example, Mathew Brady was photographing inmates of Blackwell's Island Prison in New York as early as 1846, while the San Francisco Police Department began using daguerreotypes of criminals in 1854. By the 1880s, albums made up of criminal portraits were common in police departments in North America.[38] In 1886, Thomas Byrnes, inspector of police and chief of detectives in New York City, published the most famous of these albums—and did so *pro bono publico* (for the public good), as he wrote in the preface to the album. Byrnes sought to enlist the help of the public in fighting crime. "While the photographs of burglars, forgers, sneak thieves, and robbers of lesser degree are kept in police albums, many offenders are still able to operate successfully," he noted. "But with their like-nesses within reach of all, their vocation would soon become risky and unprofitable."[39] Byrnes wanted New York families to have copies of his album, all the better to know the criminals in their midst. By taking the mug shots out of police hands and putting them in those of the public, Byrnes wanted to overcome a key weakness of mug shots—namely, that mug shots could do only so much if knowledge of them was limited to the police. But the limited circulation of mug shots among the police was not the only problem that bedeviled police pho-tography and Bertillon's system. There was also the fact that photo-graphs could not be trusted. Bertillonage itself was fallible. Despite its claims to scientific rigor, the system and its demand for precise mea-surements and strict photographic protocols were cumbersome and could not resolve the fundamental problem of any archive: volume.

Gandhi's Fingerprints

In 1900, fingerprinting—a practice developed in Bengal in colonial India and then transmitted through imperial networks to other parts of the world, including South Africa—supplanted and in some places replaced Bertillonage altogether. Although scientist Francis Galton is credited with inventing fingerprinting, more important was his unfettered ac-cess to the colonial laboratory that was nineteenth-century India.[40] As Keith Breckenridge points out, Galton invented fingerprinting with the colonial world in mind. He saw fingerprinting as a "remedy for the absence of writing" among nonliterate populations of the British empire.[41] As Galton himself said, "It would be of continual good ser-vice in our tropical settlements, where the individual members of the swarm of dark and yellow-skinned races are mostly unable to sign their names and are otherwise hardly distinguishable by Europeans, and, whether they can write or not, are grossly addicted to personation and other varieties of fraudulent practice."[42]

Edward Henry, commissioner of police in Bengal, was among those who took a professional interest in Galton's work on fingerprinting. Its many attractions included its transformation of the human body into a text that government bureaucracies could read and track over time.[43] Henry, who had introduced Bertillonage to the police force in Bengal in the early 1890s, began corresponding with Galton in 1894 and visited the latter's London laboratory that same year. But it was Henry's subordinates Azizul Haque and Chandra Bose who refined Galton's project and gave the world the fingerprinting system that came to be identified with Henry.[44] By 1897, Henry's system was compulsory in prisons across India. By 1900, Henry was back in London advising the British government about the use of his system.

That same year, British Colonial Secretary Joseph Chamberlain dispatched Henry to the Witwatersrand, South Africa, to develop a new police force for the Transvaal Colony.[45] When Chamberlain appointed Henry, the South African War was still underway; it would not end for another two years.[46] But the British government had identified the resumption of mining on the Witwatersrand and the prevention of gold theft as urgent needs requiring the expertise of someone like Henry.[47] He arrived in South Africa in July 1900 and within six months had laid the foundation for a new police force, one charged as much with the control of Africans and their mobility as with the prohibition of liquor sales on the mines and the theft of gold.[48] Nothing illustrated the priorities of Henry's force better than its structure: a lightly-staffed head office at the top, supported below by a Gold Branch and a Liquor Branch.[49]

Henry's police force mixed the proscriptive (gold theft) with the prohibitive (liquor sales) in ways that made it effectively an arm of the mining industry.[50] As Breckenridge says, "Before Apartheid, it was the prohibitionist arm of the police force that cut most deeply into the daily lives of black urban residents, with hundreds of thousands of men and women convicted and imprisoned every year."[51] Henry's focus on the needs of the mining industry left him with little resources for detecting ordinary crime: "The result was a paradox: the police force designed by the most famous English-speaking advocate of forensic policing was bereft of investigative capacity in general and a working detective [branch] in particular."[52] But Henry was adamant about his force's focus on gold thefts, liquor rules, and maintenance of pass laws. His insistence on the enforcement of the pass laws was especially devastating for blacks over time, as these laws "set in place the engine of incarceration in South Africa" by providing for the unrelenting jailing of black men found on the Witwatersrand without a pass.[53]

Not surprisingly, Henry made fingerprinting the cornerstone of his new force.[54] It was Henry, says Breckenridge, who introduced to South Africa the "long-running fantasy that only a single, centralized register of the identities of Africans could solve the problems of impersonation and uttering" prompted by the demands of the Pass Laws.[55] He set up a Criminal Investigation Department (CID) and created a Records Section to run the fingerprinting function.[56] In time, colonial governments in other parts of Africa would consult the CID about their plans to develop similar systems of identification.[57] In 1916, for example, W.C. Burgess, a member of the CID, created a Military Labor Bureau in Nairobi to fingerprint Africans recruited to serve in the British war effort in German East Africa.[58] Henry returned to England in 1901 to a senior position at Scotland Yard, having set a standard for policing in South Africa that would last more than a century.[59] This standard began with the assumption that, as a rule, Africans could not be trusted.

Before 1907, however, it was Chinese workers on the Witwatersrand mines and Indian men in the Transvaal who constituted the main target of fingerprinting.[60] The British brought about sixty-four thousand Chinese to South Africa between 1904 and 1910 to cover a labor shortage caused by the South African War.[61] Within five years of the first arrivals, the British had fingerprinted every Chinese and Indian adult male in the Transvaal.[62] In fact, Breckenridge says, Gandhi wrote his anticolonial manifesto *Hind Swaraj* after a six-year struggle against colonial plans to fingerprint Indians in the Transvaal.[63] That struggle marked Gandhi's loss of faith in the idea of progress; it showed him the repressive ends to which a progressive technology like fingerprinting was put in South Africa. Gandhi initially supported the state's bid to collect fingerprints of Indian males in the Transvaal.[64] He even told his readers that "in England they are all the rage."[65] But he changed his mind when the state failed to distinguish between the Indian elite and hoi polloi.[66]

The police force that Henry set up in 1900 was a provincial body for the Transvaal. The country known as South Africa did not yet exist in 1900. It would not come into being until the union of the four provinces (Cape Colony, Natal, Orange River Colony, and the Transvaal) in 1910. But Henry helped sow the seeds for a national policing culture by gearing his force to the needs of the mining industry. This created a bias that found its way into the national police force that South Africa later set up, in 1913. By 1919, for example, 25 percent of all fingerprint searches conducted by the police's Central Identification Bureau were for the mining industry. C.G. MacPherson, the officer in charge of the bureau, said that the "matter of these . . . searches is one of prime importance to the gold industry, as the knowledge of a native's criminal history prevents his being employed on reduction works and the possibility of the leakage of gold is prevented."[67] MacPherson could not have been clearer about the presumed overlap of race and crime.

If each province brought to the union a different policing culture, all four cultures were united by the fact that they were colonial by definition. This meant that police officers served the government—not the law.[68] It also made policing a "conjuring trick of enormous proportions" as colonial authorities sought to mask the thinness of their blue line by putting together civil, judicial, military, and political administration under one umbrella.[69] This helps explain why the colonial and the apartheid police soon acquired a reputation for brutality.[70] These colonial roots meant that the police forces in the provinces combining to form the Union of South Africa were white-led, and that they saw their jobs as primarily the protection of white power and the associated economic order. It is important to understand these colonial roots of policing in South Africa, as such understanding shields us from the false assumption that authoritarian policing and the wholesale criminalization of political dissent came with apartheid.

April Fools?

The South African Police (SAP) came into being on April 1, 1913, with Theodore Truter, a former magistrate in the Transvaal farming town of Standerton, as the first national commissioner of police. In addition to establishing a national force out of the different city, municipal, and provincial police forces in South Africa at the time, Truter set up a national CID modeled on the Indian Police and founded in part on the already-existing CIDs of Natal and the Transvaal.[71] By 1916, the CID had 341 men, 97 of whom were "native detectives."[72] The CID—whose tasks included the handling of immorality cases, naturalization, immigration, enemy subjects, the registration of Asians, and identifications—housed a Central Identification Bureau (later renamed the South African Criminal Bureau). The bureau had three departments: fingerprints, photographs, and drawing.[73] The bureau also handled the printing and circulation of police materials. It is here, in the bureau, that the roots of the album are to be found.

By 1916, out of the 45,749 photographs and negatives held by the bureau, 30,187 belonged to black individuals.[74] The SAP's original mandate to police South Africa's urban areas was rendered dual from the start by the needs to police whites and to keep blacks under control.[75] Because of its commitment to the maintenance of the social order, with the mining industry at the center of that order, policing in South Africa developed a negative interest in radical politics and trade unionism from early on. With radical white workers resorting to strike action in 1913, 1914, 1917, and 1922—largely in defense of white privilege on the mines—the SAP used spies and plainclothes detectives to check the spread of radical ideas within the industrial working class.[76] A bigger fear was that these ideas might find their way to black workers, thereby threatening the entire economic and social order.[77]

As Prime Minister Jan Smuts told South Africa's parliament, in response to the white-led 1922 Rand Rebellion, "the fear that obsessed me above all things was that owing to the wanton provocation of the revolutionaries, there might be a wild, uncontrollable outbreak among the natives."[78] To forestall this, the SAP kept tabs on radical activism. For example, of the 284,745 cases reported to the police in 1915, 1,480 concerned what the police classified as offenses against the state; of these offenses against the state, 1,459 led to arrests, with 662 blacks and 511 Europeans convicted.[79] In 1916, offenses against the state accounted for 565 (0.18 percent) of the 309,617 cases reported that year.[80] Even though the category of serious crimes (in which offenses against the state fell) saw a 77.35 percent jump between 1921 and 1927, offenses against the state accounted for only .39 percent—or 1 in 254 of all serious crimes reported in the period.[81] Nevertheless, the SAP took subversion seriously enough that it set up a section in 1929 to monitor radicals.[82] It was only in 1939, however, that the SAP established a special unit, with Hendrik du Plooy as commander, to monitor a Nazi-supporting Afrikaner organization called the Ossewa Brandwag, most of whose members came from the police and the defense force. This organization opposed South Africa's participation in the Second World War. Du Plooy's unit recruited Afrikaner policemen who could infiltrate the Ossewa Brandwag with relative ease.[83] In time, the branch's origins as a unit that had been set up to combat pro-Nazi activities by Afrikaners would be forgotten, and the unit would be presented as a force established specifically to combat communism.[84] Du Plooy visited the Metropolitan Police in London shortly after his appointment in 1939 for advice on how to combat subversion.[85] His visit to London was part of an imperial project designed to help police forces in British colonies and dominions acquire the latest training from Scotland Yard.[86] This project sought to instill a policing common sense throughout the British empire.[87]

By the 1940s, these visits had become the norm. Du Plooy seems to have visited Scotland Yard again in 1947, shortly after his appointment as commander of the newly-established Special Branch (forerunner to the Security Police).[88] As South African Police Commissioner Robert J. Palmer told Sir Harold Richard Scott, commissioner of police at Scotland Yard, in August 1947, Du Plooy's visit would give the South Africans a "special opportunity of studying and gaining knowledge of the Police methods of your department generally."[89] Palmer wanted Du Plooy to study the "methods of police duties and criminal work generally but principally . . . the system and methods employed by your Special Branch."[90] In May 1948, Palmer sent Du Plooy, together with colleagues who included a fingerprinting and photography expert as well as a head constable responsible for indexing files and classifying suspects, to Scotland Yard for further training.[91] The links between Britain and South Africa would only grow from there. In October 1949, British Prime Minister Clement Attlee offered Daniel Malan, his South African counterpart, help in setting up a proper Security Police. Britain wanted to recruit South Africa to the anti-communist cause but worried that the South Africans did not have a security apparatus fit for purpose. A senior British Intelligence officer had visited South Africa on three occasions between 1948 and 1949 but found the South African Police's Special Branch not yet "equipped for tackling security work."[92] Attlee offered to send Percy Sillitoe, director-general of MI5, to give the South Africans advice. Although couched in the language of fraternal benevolence, Attlee's offer was in fact an act of *realpolitik* intended to ensure "disciplined anti-communism" on the part of the South Africans.[93] Sillitoe was an old hand with regard to Africa and his mission to South Africa had two aims: to persuade the South Africans to accept British training in the latest techniques of national security and counterespionage, and to encourage them to allow the Special Branch to focus solely on counterespionage. That is, the British government wanted the Special Branch to become a technically proficient force capable of thwarting Soviet activities in southern Africa, rather than yet another police division constantly running after blacks for violating some petty apartheid law. But Sillitoe and his political masters knew that petty apartheid went with grand apartheid. They understood that whatever security agency they helped the South Africans build would be used to keep blacks down. They were concerned that their help might lead, in Sillitoe's words, to the "creation of a Gestapo."[94] Still, they reasoned, the benefit of making South Africa a secure member of the western alliance outweighed the risk that South Africa would indeed turn authoritarian. But the British need not have worried about the anti-communism of the South African state and its police force. In fact, so eager were the South Africans to display their pro-Western credentials that they even tried to join the North Atlantic Treaty Organization in 1950.[95] The United States demurred.[96] But the British were more than happy to help cement South Africa's ideological positioning, with Sillitoe asking the South Africans to continue to send their officers to London for training.

Apartheid Crimes

As John Brewer points out, the apartheid era did not lead to a qualitative change in policing in South Africa. But it saw a major increase in the powers of the police to regulate race relations.[97] In 1949, a year after the National Party came into power on the back of its promise to enact apartheid, the state introduced a new category of crime called *Crimen Laesae Majestatis,* meaning high treason. Between 1952 and 1960, the state brought twenty-eight cases to trial (with thirty-one individuals prosecuted) for this crime.[98] This was part of a raft of new crimes that included blasphemy and suicide.[99] It was also at this time that it became a serious offense to promote hostility between blacks and whites. This gave the state the power to interpret any challenge to the status quo as promoting racial hostility. It also resulted in the criminalization of most forms of opposition politics. Between 1952 and 1960, the state brought twenty-eight cases of promoting racial hostility to trial, resulting in the prosecution of thirty-one people.[100] In 1950, Parliament passed the Suppression of Communism Act. The act not only banned the Communist Party of South Africa but offered a definition of communism so broad that one did not have to be a communist to fall foul of the law.[101] Between 1951 and 1960, the police and state prosecutors used the law to bring successful prosecutions against 107 individuals.[102] This rise in offenses against the state was concomitant with an increase in the ability of the Special Branch to go after perceived enemies of the state. By 1960, the Special Branch had the means to keep tabs on South Africans leaving the country without the permission of the state. By 1970, the Special Branch had the legislative apparatus and the political muscle (not to mention official sanction to use torture) to brand opponents of the apartheid state *terrorists*. The branding did not require much proof.

Still, offenses against the state did not account for the bulk of the criminalization of black South Africans. Accounting for the mass criminalization of Africans were the pass laws, regulations against the brewing of African beer, violations of the Masters and Servants Act, the flouting of so-called native labor laws, and failure to pay taxes targeted specifically at Africans.[103] The pass laws, for example, which dated back to 1760, were used extensively by colonial and apartheid governments to regulate the movement of Africans, as a way of asserting control over the supply of African labor.[104] In 1952, Parliament passed the Native Laws Amendment Act. The act limited the number of blacks allowed to reside in so-called white South Africa and gave the police the power to expel so-called surplus populations to rural reserves.

The act was in keeping with the ideology of the National Party, which had come to power promising to curb black urbanization.[105] Even as government was introducing such laws and extending pass laws to black women, however, black urbanization continued apace, driven by the industrializing country's demands for cheap labor. Between 1951 and 1960, black urbanization grew by 47.9 percent to represent 31.8 percent of the total African population by 1960.[106] Tellingly, the increasing modernization of the South African Police (such as the use of technology) went hand in hand with the constant resort to crude forms of policing, such as collective punishment and torture. In 1954, South Africa recorded its first publicized use of electric shock to force a confession, when a policeman named Niewenhuis admitted to torturing a suspect in a cattle-rustling case.[107]

In 1957, a nineteen-year-old policeman named Willem Johannes Spence killed an unarmed African by shooting him at point-blank range. Asked why he killed the man, Spence said: "I threatened to shoot him and he said 'shoot then,' so I shot him. He was cheeky."[108] But the police could not always be trusted to know their natives, cheeky or not. In 1959, policeman Andries van Rensburg and a colleague drove around Cape Town's black townships assaulting Africans for fun. Van Rensburg and his friend attacked a man who turned out to be white. Asked why he had assaulted the man, van Rensburg said he had mistaken the man for an African.[109] This periodization of police brutality and torture is worth recording for it goes against police claims that it was only because of the Cold War, and in the face of a communist onslaught against Protestant South Africa, that members of the South African Police had no choice but to dispense with legal niceties and to take off their gloves in a war to save the country.[110] The Cold War did not force the South African Police to adopt torture. They chose torture because they could do so. More than that, they chose torture because they believed it worked for them.

An Ordinary Atrocity?

The biggest turning point in the history of politics and policing in South Africa came in 1960. On March 21, 1960, the police killed sixty-nine residents of Sharpeville, a township forty-two miles south of Johannesburg, during a peaceful protest against the pass laws.[111] The government followed up the massacre by, first, declaring a state of emergency and, second, passing a law granting the police retroactive immunity for the massacre. On April 8, 1960, it banned the ANC and the PAC, which had organized the protests. The ban, as well as the detention of an estimated two thousand individuals, drove thousands of South Africans into exile. More importantly, the ban led to the adoption by the ANC and the PAC of violence as a form of struggle.[112] Because the turn to violence coincided with the decolonization of Africa, the apartheid government saw it as a major threat that necessitated a change of focus from looking for enemies within the country's borders to finding them without.[113] This change of focus also led to an increase in police powers, as well as to the adoption of new training methods in riot control and counterinsurgency.[114]

In 1963, Parliament introduced the General Law Amendment Act, which gave police-station commanders the power to put detainees in solitary confinement for as many as ninety days without interference from a judge. To give the police sufficient cover for their actions against political opposition, Parliament in 1965 introduced a new Official Secrets Act. The act exempted the police from media scrutiny. In 1967, Parliament passed the Terrorism Act, which offered such a general definition of terrorism that any act that called the status quo into question could be considered an act of terrorism. These policing and legislative moves brought in train the militarization of white South African society, with the police providing firearms training to public bodies and private companies.[115] In 1965, even white postmen received firearms training from the police.[116]

Given the SAP's obsession with the threat posed by South Africans driven into exile by the state's reaction to the events of 1960, South Africa's long borders came in for special attention.[117] In 1961, SAP members began operating along South Africa's border with Bechuanaland

and Namibia's border with Angola. In 1964, the SAP established thirty-five border posts, through which SAP members conducted passport control, crime prevention, and intelligence duties. In 1966, the Security Police took over the running of the border posts on the Lesotho and Swaziland borders. Together with the Bechuanaland border, these were the major conduits for political exiles leaving South Africa between 1960 and 1990 (fig. 1.1).[118]

In 1967, the South African government announced that SAP units were operating in Rhodesia against Zimbabwe's nationalist guerillas. That incursion was as much about black guerillas threatening white rule in southern Africa as it was about divisions within the South African security establishment. The SAP had succeeded in having its members fighting in Rhodesia only because the police had the ear of the prime

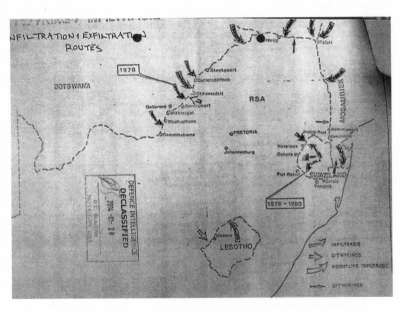

FIGURE 1.1 Declassified map from South Africa's Defense Intelligence Archives showing insurgents' infiltration and exfiltration routes. Image courtesy of Dave Fell, who had the material declassified.

minister, John Vorster. As Constand Viljoen, then a senior officer in the South African Defense Force, said: "We resented it when Vorster . . . used the police in Rhodesia. We felt it was a military task."[119]

Despite the military's displeasure, the Rhodesian operation, which lasted until 1974, became a rite of passage for SAP members. In fact, the policemen who were to play prominent roles in South Africa's counterinsurgencies and death-squad activity between the 1960s and the 1990s first saw action in the Rhodesian bush. As Viljoen said, "I believe it was because of their involvement in Rhodesia that the police became a type of militia using crude methods not within the principles of the Geneva Convention."[120] For their part, the ANC, the PAC, and the African Resistance Movement (ARM)—a predominantly white and mostly liberal outfit that was, in fact, the first organization to take up arms against apartheid—certainly tried to take the battle to the apartheid state.[121] Between 1960 and 1974, South Africa recorded fifty-five guerilla attacks.[122] But these guerilla groupings, whose actions were largely symbolic terror attacks, were no match for the South African security forces. The police knew that their adversaries were amateurs, idealists playing at revolution. But the police blew the threat posed by these amateurs out of proportion. As far as the police were concerned, "The threat was an external and military one, emanating from northern borders."[123] The SAP also refused to see the political nature of the South African conflict, thereby foreclosing the possibility of a negotiated political solution for four decades.

Putting the Album in Context

It was in this context that the album emerged as a tool of state power and surveillance. This is not to say that the album marked the first use of mug shots by the South African Police. As we know from the story of Fayedwa told in the Introduction, the police in South Africa were using mug shots by the first decade of the twentieth century. At the same time, prisons were, as a rule, taking photographs of certain categories of inmates.[124] The South African Police were also no strangers to the use of photographic albums and posters bearing the identikits of suspects. In 1916, for example, the police produced 8,091 police albums and twenty-seven wanted posters.[125] They had 45,749 mug shots and negatives on file.[126] The police also issued daily circulars (three thousand a day by 1919) to inform different parts of the police force about crimes committed, suspects wanted, and property missing.[127] But these circulars were not "elastic enough," complained C.G. MacPherson, the inspector in charge of the police's Central Identification Bureau, meaning that they could not serve as a dedicated rogues' gallery.[128] In fact, as early as 1916, the bureau was lobbying government for a special gazette to be used as a rogues' gallery. As A. Pinto Leite, the inspector in charge of the bureau at the time, put it:

> It would be of inestimable assistance in dealing with the criminal classes if this office could be equipped so that it could issue monthly or periodically a confidential photographic circular of criminals— expert forgers, burglars, swindlers, etc. Each station in the Union [of South Africa] would be supplied with a copy. The police would thus be in possession of separate files of photos of criminals classified under the crimes they follow. The photos would bear an identification number and could be shown to complainants calling at a Police station for the purposes of reporting a crime.[129]

Leite's plea must have fallen on deaf ears, because he repeated it in his report for the year 1917, adding: "A Gazette such as this is exchanged between nearly all European police forces."[130] C. G. MacPherson, who replaced Leite in 1918, took up the crusade, saying that such a publication would leave all police stations "better posted with criminal intelligence."[131] It was only in 1921 that the government finally agreed to the publication of a confidential *Police Gazette*.[132] By 1926, the police were publishing the gazette in the two official languages (English and Afrikaans) three times a week. The gazette was an instant hit with the police. Theodore Truter, the commissioner of police, said it had "proved a most effective means of bringing about the arrest of persons wanted for serious offenses and supplying general information in regard to crime. The special photographic supplements and indexes issued with the gazette constitute a valuable permanent record for all police stations in the Union."[133] In 1927, the police issued 155 copies of the gazette and these—which contained 2,044 mug shots of wanted persons plus photographs of lost or stolen animals and property—came out three times a week.

The gazette was South Africa's first experiment with something approximating a rogues' gallery. It was also the precursor to the Terrorist Album. But it was only after the passage of the Suppression of Communism Act in 1950 and the Terrorism Act in 1967 that the labeling of political opponents as terrorists took on the ominous connotations that would fill the Terrorist Album with such peril for three decades. To be certain, the laws passed between 1950 and 1967 did not produce the Terrorist Album as such. They merely provided the framework within which the album came to acquire its status as a confidential compendium of state enemies and to mark those caught within its covers as fair game. As Chapter 2 will show, the album emerged incrementally during the course of the 1960s. It took shape gradually as the South African Police and the Special Branch, in particular, began taking an interest in individuals fleeing South Africa for political reasons. This interest in political exiles coincided with the entrenchment in South Africa's security establishment of attitudes refracted through the prism of the Cold War. Convinced that black South Africans were a contented lot, the South African government refused to acknowledge the economic and political grievances that fueled black discontent. Instead, it blamed increasing levels of protest against apartheid in the 1950s on Soviet meddling. When it did acknowledge the local nature of the protests, it blamed Indian and white communists for misleading Africans who were said to be otherwise content with their lot. In fact, one reason for the introduction of the Departure from the Union Regulation Act of 1955 was to shield South Africans from supposedly harmful foreign influences. The act, which gave government control over the international movement of South Africans, earned thousands of people automatic entry into the album after 1960.

This is because, while Clement Attlee was offering the South Africans British expertise, Interior Minister Eben Dönges was complaining to South Africa's parliament about his lack of powers to deport communists. When Parliament considered the bill that would become the Departure from the Union Regulation Act, Dönges said the law would "prevent Communists or fellow travelers from visiting Iron Curtain countries and on their return spreading Communist propaganda."[134] Dönges might have been inspired by the United States, which had adopted the McCarran Act in 1950.[135] The McCarran Act made it difficult for US communists to obtain passports or for international communists to enter the United States.

As is always the case with apartheid, however, one cannot leave matters simply at the level of the ideological by assuming that the Cold War provided all the justification needed to understand apartheid machinations. To do that would be to miss the malevolence and petty racism that fueled apartheid. In 1955, for example, the South African government used the new law to deny Stephen Ramasodi, a sixteen-year-old high school student, a passport so he could take up a scholarship at the

Kent School, an Episcopalian private school in Connecticut. "Frankly, Stephen Ramasodi would be taught things he could never use when he came back to South Africa," a government spokesman said. "Why should we let the boy be frustrated by being led to hope for things he can never have in this country?"[136] The Special Branch refused to give Ramasodi, whose father was headmaster of a state school in Pretoria, the certificate of good character that he needed to obtain a passport. Father Trevor Huddleston, the anti-apartheid Anglican priest who had, together with writer Alan Paton, secured the Kent scholarship for Ramasodi, criticized the decision: "This can be due to only one thing, namely, malice, for there can be no possible political reason for preventing a boy leaving [South Africa] in order to complete his education in a Christian school."[137]

We should be careful, however, not to assume that the history of police photography in South Africa went in a straight line, with one development leading seamlessly to another. The evidence shows that the career of police photography in South Africa was messy. We have only to look at the disjuncture between the police's embrace of photography and the courts' more reluctant acceptance of photographs and their evidentiary powers. For example, in 1916, while the Central Identification Bureau was processing more than 71,772 fingerprints and amassing thousands of photographs to go with those prints, the courts were still reluctant to accept both fingerprints and photographs into evidence.[138] It took the 1917 Criminal Procedures and Evidence Act to make fingerprints and photographs admissible as evidence.[139] Even then, the courts were reluctant to go along with the legislature.

In 1921, the Johannesburg High Court heard *R v. Mbulela,* the first court case in South Africa in which a photograph was submitted as evidence.[140] The case concerned a mineworker named Fatini Mbulela who had stabbed to death a mine guard named Samuel Madoda. The judge rejected the photograph submitted as evidence by the prosecution on the grounds that it constituted a leading question. The judge did not reject photographs in principle. But he said prosecutors "should take care that the photographs simply show the locus in quo unadorned. The stage should not be set so as to be suggestive to witnesses."[141] The photographs tendered in court were different from those tucked into the pages of the *Police Gazette* and, later on, the Terrorist Album. They served different purposes.

But the gazette engendered a set of practices that led to the Terrorist Album. By the time that album formed part of the police's arsenal against political opponents, South Africa had come a long way from Gustav Fritsch and his racial types. Instead of racial types, the album depicted terrorist types, individuals who held no scientific value but posed a political threat to the state. This gradual shift from racial types to terrorist types came against the backdrop of a number of developments key to the story of political violence in South Africa. These developments included the hardening of the SAP's view that South Africa's problems were driven externally by communist stooges; increasing support for apartheid among South Africa's white electorate; the cementation of Cold War geopolitics in the world; and the SAP's growing reliance on torture and experience in bloodletting, thanks in part to the police's involvement in Rhodesia. These terrorist types had to be in the album because they were terrorists; they were terrorists because they were in the album. In time, that small object would lead to mayhem. The next chapter will explore how this small object was used, by whom, and when.

TWO

Apartheid's Mismeasure

What was the album's official title?

SGT. EUGENE FOURIE: We called it the Terrorist Album.

No official title?

FOURIE: The Terrorist Album.

So, someone in Ermelo would call you and say, "I need the latest version of the Terrorist Album?"

FOURIE: On that name, yes. That was the official name for it.[1]

The object that came to be called the Terrorist Album did not spring fully formed into the world. It was the product of accretion: a slow process of accumulation driven by the deeds of countless actors over the course of three decades. These deeds—which ranged from the bureaucratic to the banal, the political to the petty—did not go in a straight line, but each one added a layer of sediment that, over time, resulted in the object called the Terrorist Album. If these acts fixed the album in time, by making it a peculiar artifact of the apartheid police, they did not fix it in place. Right up to the end of apartheid in the early 1990s, the album was constantly in production—continually in the making as mug shots were added and subtracted, apartheid opponents arrested and killed. In 1964, after first denying writer Bessie Head a passport, then kicking her out of South Africa on an exit permit to stateless-ness, the Security Police appended her photograph to the album. In October 1965, Police Commissioner J. M. Keevy gave the South African Criminal Bureau instructions regarding the investigation of 302 indi-viduals who had fled South Africa for exile.[2] The group, whose ranks included Chris Hani and Thabo Mbeki (two men who would go on to play leading roles in the struggle against apartheid), was part of the political exodus that had followed government's banning of the ANC and PAC in April 1960.

The Security Police and the bureau had initially investigated the group's flight as one case but, said the police commissioner, they were to be treated as 302 individual cases and each case was to be handled by the police in the magisterial district from which the suspect came. In December 1973, ANC defector Gladstone Silulami Mose, identified only as a source codenamed HK 87 in a secret police report, said the following about an ANC member named Matsibe Samuel Maimela: "Having perused the official photograph album of terrorists, I am able to state that . . . I never came into contact with or heard of the person whose photograph appears on the middle right-hand side of page 53 of the official Terrorist album."[3] (This is one of the earliest archival traces we have, not only of the album being used but being referred to as the "official Terrorist Album.")

These deeds—police pettiness towards Bessie Head, the police com-missioner's orders about the investigation of political fugitives, an ANC defector's failure to identify a former comrade—may appear disparate.

But each was, in fact, a building block used to construct the album. Each act was connected to the others in ways that ensured that, at the very least, the album was constantly being made and remade. Take Gladstone Mose, the ANC defector who perused the album—at the behest of his new masters in the Security Police—to identity former comrades. Mose was, in fact, one of the most important curators of the album. From 1972, when he defected to the Security Police, through at least 1976, Mose fleshed out, likely under duress, the skeletons that populated the Terrorist Album. He made sure that each identikit had a biographical point of reference. During the 1970s, it was Mose, more than any other person, who helped the Security Police put names to the faces in the album. He was able to do this in part because he had been among the 302 fugitives identified by the police commissioner in 1965. So had Matsibe Samuel Maimela, the man whose mug shot Mose did not recognize.

A Branding Exercise

When I asked Eugene Fourie, a retired member of the Security Police, in August 2015 what the official name of the album was, I was trying to establish its place within the apartheid security apparatus. Given that this was a system in which every document had a name and number, and aware that Fourie was one of the policemen responsible for its upkeep, I assumed that the album, too, had an official title. The copy of the album I had seen did not have a title on its cover, but every time a police officer referred to it, he called it the Terrorist Album. When I examined Mose's police debriefing reports for the years 1973 to 1977, I found lots of references—in Afrikaans and in English—to the "official Terrorist Album" but nothing that suggested that this was in fact the official name. So I wanted to know if this was the album's real name or just a nickname—shorthand that policemen used among themselves in the way they might use an acronym. I was trying essentially to grasp the album's operating logic. I thought that comprehending such logic might help me understand the album's composition and to see who was in the album, who was not, and why. I was trying to understand how the album functioned—not simply the reason for its existence. The policemen I interviewed had told me enough times that the album was a record of individuals who had left South Africa illegally. But why call it a *Terrorist Album* when, as these policemen well knew, most of the people who left South Africa illegally between 1960 and 1990—not to mention the majority of those in the album—did not take up arms against the apartheid state? More than that, why have in the album someone like novelist Bessie Head, who had left South Africa on a state-issued exit permit?[4] As I examined the album, however, looking for patterns that might reveal an organizing logic, I realized I was making a mistake common among scholars of violence in apartheid South Africa.[5]

I was assuming that the album was subject to some higher purpose, that it served some well-defined reason of state.[6] But as I looked at many of the individuals in the album, it dawned on me that the Security Police called this the Terrorist Album for no better reason than that they could. They labeled it the Terrorist Album because they had the power to do so—not because it apprehended terrorists as such. This power to name, to jail, to hound, to terrorize, to kill, was central to the operation of apartheid. It was there, in its projection of the power of the apartheid state to do all of the above, that the album's operating logic was to be found. This made me realize that, rather than look to the Afrikaner's existential fear of getting swamped by black hordes, or to white South Africa's divine mission to save Africa from the communist onslaught, scholars needed to examine the quotidian operation of power under apartheid to comprehend the history of political violence in South Africa.[7] Such an approach would not diminish the ideological frame around apartheid or dismiss the stories that apartheid apparatchiks and supporters told themselves. It would also not mean privileging the spectacular violence of apartheid at the expense of its slow, structural violence.[8] But it would give us the conceptual tools to understand apartheid both at its most grandiose and its most prosaic. By locating the album and its operating logic within these two levels, scholars could understand both the power that gave the album its name as the Terrorist Album, as well as the commonplace violence to which the album bore testimony. When members of the Security Police tortured captured insurgents and then roasted them to death over a spit braai, while roasting meat and drinking beer nearby, they were not serving any higher purpose.[9] They were doing that because they could. They were not bad apples fallen off some tree.[10] The Security Police damned individuals as terrorists and then placed their mug shots in the album—because they could.

Indexing Apartheid

How, then, are we to look at the album? How are we to make sense of its cultural biography?[11] Let us first recall its physical qualities. The album, which measures twelve inches in length by nine inches in width, has a grey cover made up of a thick cardboard, with black binding running along the spine. Inside are glossy pages held together by metal screws, for ease of updating. Each page contains nine mug shots, each with a number below it. The photographs are in black and white. The Security Police printed the album at a press inside their

Pretoria headquarters. Police printers chose the look, from the thickness of the cover to the glossiness of the paper stock. Most of the mug shots in the album assume the pose of formal portraiture and show the suspect's head and shoulders, "as if those parts of our bodies were our truth."[12] Some of the photographs, however, lack this formal pose. This is because they were yanked from another context—say, a family album—and inserted into the police album. As a matter of course, the Security Police would ask families for the latest photographs of suspects or confiscate family albums during raids. Police spies would also take photographs of suspects and these would end up in the album, especially if the police did not have a formal mug shot. On the face of it, the album did not follow any logic, except to line up the photographs numerically. There were no racial hierarchies on the page. The first page starts with Eric Abraham's mug shot. Of the nine photographs on the first page, two are Colored women and two are Colored men; there is one white woman and there are two white men (including Abraham). The remaining two are African men. But how does the viewer know that these individuals are indeed African, Colored, or white? How can the viewer glean this information from two-dimensional photographs in black and white, when photographs are by their nature "fragmentary and incomplete utterances?"[13]

Furthermore, how can one answer these questions without falling into the historicist and positivist trap that, as Allan Sekula argues, haunts historical narratives that rely on photography?[14] I identify these nine individuals by race to reveal something of the album's operating logic. To call these individuals African, Colored, or white is to see them as the police saw them. It is to reflect the police's own assumptions. For, key to making the album comprehensible and its subjects legible to the police was an index that was kept separate from the album itself (fig. 2.1). Without the index, the album was nothing more than a

FIGURE 2.1 Copy of Index at Wits Historical Papers, Johannesburg, South Africa. Photograph by the author.

collection of photographs that could not be made to speak with any coherence. If the mug shot was a signifier floating in the apartheid ether, the index was the anchor that grounded it in a historical context so that each image became one of this person and not of that person. Thanks to the index, the album dispensed with racial types, but only to give us a political type: the terrorist. The index gave us the name behind a mug shot as well as a series of numbers—bureaucratic hieroglyphics—freighted with peril. Let us take Eric Abraham as our example. His mug shot is numbered one (1); then follows his national identity number; then comes a column telling us which region in South Africa he hails from (Western Province); then comes the number (77 / 35391) which tells us the year (1977) in which the Security Police and the South African Criminal Bureau opened a case against him for leaving the country illegally, plus the case number (35391). The last number is S1 / 56094. The Security Police gave this last number to their classified files on Abraham. The S in the prefix S1 stands for Security while the number 1 gives Abraham's racial designation. White suspects were S1, Indians S2, Coloreds S3, and Africans S4. It is here that we see the racial management of dissidence. It is in the index that we see the police grappling with how to police racial boundaries when opponents of apartheid covered the racial spectrum.

The letter S marked not just the security threat that the police believed each person so designated posed, but also a number (1, 2, 3, or 4) that sought to nail down the jelly that was the suspect's race. For the police, as for the apartheid state in general, race was as fixed as were the numerals 1, 2, 3, and 4.[15] To call a person a 1 was to state a natural fact; to place the letter S before the number 1 was to state a political fact. That is how the police used the album. But how exactly did individual police officers encounter the album? How did they use it and, most importantly, to what end? This was, after all, their cultural object and it is important to hear them explain in their own words how they encountered it, used it, and understood its mission and place in the world.

Johann van der Merwe, who joined the police in 1953 and commanded the Security Police in the late 1980s, recalled seeing copies of the album in the 1960s. "I know that border posts were in possession of a full album by 1966, with full details of names, aliases, organization, and South African Criminal Bureau references. I do not know how the album originated."[16] Jac Büchner, who joined the South African Police in 1955, told me: "If I remember correctly, the photo album was compiled and printed by Police Headquarters in Pretoria in the early 1960s, possibly 1962 or 1963. The photo album contained photos and personal particulars of all the members of the various banned organizations that had left South Africa clandestinely or were known to be politically active abroad."[17] Büchner, regarded as one of the best interrogators in the Security Police, said that while he could not say who at police headquarters was responsible for the album, he knew for a fact that it was in use by 1964, updated periodically and distributed to all police divisions around the country. But, as I show below, Büchner was not being entirely forthcoming. Hennie Heymans, who joined the police in 1964, explained how the album worked.

When the police received a report—usually from a concerned family member or an informer—that a person had disappeared, they opened an investigation. If it looked like the missing person was involved in the anti-apartheid movement, the Security Police took over the search and, depending on the race of the person, mobilized various branches of the apartheid bureaucracy for birth records, tax returns, pass and passport applications, and mug shots. As Heymans said: "Now we start looking for you. We *brandmerk* you. We brand you. We put a little flag on this and we . . . do research and it goes into the album. Or it lies there until we catch Mr. Mehlomakhulu from Mkhumbane and we show him all the photos. 'Ah, he was with me . . .' Now you go into the album."[18] Going into the album meant more than just having your photograph pasted on its pages. Heymans said: "They open a docket, a criminal case, you've left the country. Then they check, 'did he leave the country legally?' No. Then they open a docket."[19]

That, in fact, is what Police Commissioner J. M. Keevy was refer-ring to in October 1965 when he wrote to the South African Criminal Bureau about the 302 individuals who had gone into exile. The Secu-rity Police head office in Pretoria had opened a docket numbered ROM 478/6/63. ROM was an Afrikaans acronym for Register of Charges In-vestigated. The register was a monthly report that documented every docket opened for investigation at a police station. Once the investiga-tion was complete, the detective would then proffer charges and if the charge office sergeant approved the charges, he would enter them into the Register of Charges Accepted.[20] Because Keevy wanted the inves-tigation of the flight of each of the 302 fugitives devolved to their places of origin, he ordered the bureau to give each case a unique ROM number. As Heymans pointed out, the police took full advantage of the Departure from the Union Regulation Act of 1955, which made it a crime to leave South Africa without government permission.[21]

By 1974, however, South African security services were doing more than monitoring enemies of the state. On February 1, 1974, they killed activist Abraham Tiro in Gaborone with a letter bomb. Tiro had fled to Botswana a year earlier following his expulsion from the University of the North. On February 12, 1974, they killed ANC exile Adolphus Boy Mvemve in Lusaka, Zambia, also with a letter bomb. (Mvemve was one of the 302 individuals listed in the police commissioner's 1965 letter). Tiro and Mvemve were the first South African exiles to be killed by the South African state.[22] They would not be the last. We cannot say for sure that Tiro was in the album but, judging by how the album worked, we can assume that he was. Here, the album served not so much as a reason for the elimination of the two men but as a frame through which to understand their assassinations.

Tiro incurred the wrath of the Security Police by asking why the University of the North, at which he was a student leader, was not being faithful to the apartheid mission it was founded to serve.[23] The apartheid government set up the university in 1959 to cater exclusively to so-called Bantu from the Sotho, Pedi, Tsonga, and Venda ethnic groups. Yet its administrators and key members of its professoriate were all white, Afrikaner apparatchiks of the apartheid state. In a 1972 commencement address that marked him for death, Tiro asked why his father had to stand in the back at his own son's graduation while white strangers were allowed to monopolize the seats in the front. He also asked why all the business contracts issued by the university went to white businesses when, according to the logic of apartheid, they should have gone to black businesses. Such questions brought Tiro to the attention of the Security Police. When Tiro fled South Africa a year later to avoid imminent arrest, he likely walked straight into the album. Thus Tiro was branded a terrorist.

Subject and Object

To call the object a police album is, in some ways, inaccurate. Properly speaking, the Terrorist Album belonged to the Security Police, a smaller, elite, subsection of the South African Police. It was a secret object whose circulation was limited to members of the Security Police. To understand how it functioned, we must understand the structure of the Security Police. The Security Police (initially called the Special Branch) came into being as a fully-fledged elite organization within the South African Police in 1947. Over time, the branch was made up of fourteen sections, with each section named after a letter of the alphabet.[24] Section C was responsible for fighting terrorism. The section was divided into units C1, C2, and (later) C3, with C1 serving as the operational arm, C2 responsible for identifying and monitoring suspects, and C3 taking on the research job of keeping statistics on acts of terrorism around the country. While members of C1, which housed police death squads, saw themselves as the strike arm of the police force, members of C2 and C3 prided themselves on being analysts and researchers whose work relied on brains. Colonel Johannes Viktor founded C1 in 1979 on the back of South Africa's growing involvement in counterinsurgencies in southern Africa.[25] Viktor was part of the South African Police contingent that saw action in Rhodesia. He had learned from the Rhodesians that captured insurgents could be turned into counterinsurgents and then used against their former comrades. The Rhodesians had, in turn, discovered this from the British during the Mau Mau insurgency in Kenya.[26] At first, Viktor presented C1, which he housed on a farm outside Pretoria called Vlakplaas, as a re-habilitation unit for turned terrorists.[27] In time, however, these turned terrorists became the spearhead of the police's counterinsurgency force and were used to eliminate their erstwhile colleagues. C2 emerged at about the same time as C1, but its base was the police headquarters in Pretoria.[28]

It was at police headquarters in Pretoria that members of C2 set about identifying suspects and conducting research that could be used by their colleagues in C1. Eugene Fourie joined the Security Police in 1977 immediately after graduating from Police College. His first posting was to John Vorster Square, a police station in Johannesburg respon-sible for a number of deaths in detention. In 1981, Fourie transferred to Namibia; in 1982, he moved to C1, where he worked with turned in-surgents to look for guerillas who had entered South Africa. In 1983, the Security Police sent Fourie to C2. It was there that he saw the album for the first time. "But it was an old album and then in '83 we decided to make a new album."[29] When Fourie joined C2 in 1983, the unit had four members, including its founders, Jac Büchner and Trevor Baker. The unit grew over time to eight members, however, including Major Martin Naude, Captain Jan Meyer, a warrant officer from the railway security branch, and two young officers. When C2 began updating the album, the album was thin and had only about two thousand mug shots.[30] By the time C2 was done, Fourie said, the album had increased in size to 4,800 photographs. It is possible that Fourie misremembered the date of the update or that there were two major updates. We have a secret letter to the Security Police from Büchner, dated July 30, 1985, announcing a major overhaul of the album and giving instructions about how both the album and the accompanying index were to be handled. The letter, written in Afrikaans and with each point num-bered, bears quoting at length. Büchner wrote:

1. All photo-albums and indexes are provided with serial numbers and a register is kept at the Security Police head office, Pretoria, indicating the distribution of the albums and the indexes according to serial numbers. Changes will be made only to albums with serial numbers. The index is up to date and an asterisk must be used to indicate individuals whose names have been deleted.

2. The index is no longer divided alphabetically but an alphabetical compendium will be sent to all sections for control purposes.

3. Please check for any defects and errors and report them to Unit C2. In cases where poor prints appear, attempts must be made to obtain better photos from families and friends.

4. The photo-album and the index must be kept separate and not bound together. All changes related to persons to be deleted must be done only on the index. No photos may be scrapped or taken from the album and there are to be no notations on photos.

5. Sections that provide albums to the national states [i.e., bantustans] will be held responsible for those albums and must ensure that they are kept safe and up to date.

6. All photos to be placed in the album must be sent to Unit C2.[31]

When I first corresponded with Büchner about the album in November 2016, he downplayed its significance and minimized his involvement in its development. He made it sound as if the album were nothing more than an *aide-memoire*, a simple tool used by the police to monitor fugitives, and that he had nothing to do with it. He said:

> I am afraid you have been wrongly advised with regard to my involvement in the establishment of the police photo album which became known as the "Terrorist Album." If I remember correctly, the photo album was compiled and printed by Police Headquar-

ters in Pretoria in the early 1960s, possibly 1962 or 1963 . . . I do not know who [was] responsible for compiling the album, and there was no indication in the album who [did] it. After publication, the albums were distributed to all police divisions in South Africa and [were] used by [Security Police] members as an aid in monitoring the movements and activities of the persons whose pictures appeared in the album. Although I do not know the precise date of the publication of the album, I do know that it was already in use during 1964. The album was updated from time to time.[32]

But we know from his letter dated July 30, 1985, that Büchner was more than a bit player in the development of the album. The letter, which Büchner wrote at the height of the Security Police's offensive against political opponents, comes from an index that belonged to a former security policeman and was donated in 2018 to Wits University in Johannesburg.[33] This is the only extant copy of the index we have. It is possible that Büchner thought his letter had disappeared in the memory purge that preceded the end of apartheid. But that letter is not the only archival trace we have that bears, as it were, Büchner's fingerprints. We also know from testimony that Büchner gave in July 1997 to a Section 29 investigation of the Truth and Reconciliation Commission (TRC) that he was intimately connected to the album. Section 29, a provision of the Promotion of National Unity and Reconciliation Act of 1995, gave the commission power to subpoena individuals implicated in political crimes to appear in-camera before an investigative inquiry. As Büchner, who described himself as a "reasonable or a good interrogator," told the inquiry:

> . . . my job . . . was identifying, let's use the word terrorists because that was the word in use at the time, and making sure that I knew who was the enemy and how many there were outside the country,

and these were people who had left the country for military training and were going to be posted back into South Africa, and we compiled long lists of every person that had left the country, with photographs, with his personal history, with his background or her background, and every time I did a debriefing or interrogation we had photographs of all these people—6000 photographs or something like that—and the idea was, establish where is this trained person, what is this person doing, what is the threat that this person holds for South Africa on the terrorism front.[34]

The Exodus

As Büchner's Section 29 testimony makes clear, part of the explanation for the increase in the number of mug shots in the album and for Fourie's transfer to Unit C2 in 1983 was that, as more South Africans were leaving the country illegally for military training abroad and more were getting arrested upon their return, the Security Police needed to beef up its capacity to keep up. The album was crucial to the interrogation of suspects. As Fourie told me, "What happened is that, when people got arrested, we were sent to them with the set of photos, the same photos [as] in the album."[35] Fourie was adamant that members of C2 were not responsible for the torture for which their colleagues in C1 were notorious. In fact, C1 and C2 followed the "bad cop, good cop" routine, with C1 torturing a suspect to within an inch of his or her life for on-the-spot tactical intelligence, and C2 coming along later for what Fourie preferred to call a conversation. Describing his approach to interrogations, Fourie said:

You had to be able to work with people, you know. You can't be aggressive. I'm trying to think of a nice word. If you work with people nicely, if you talk to them nicely, don't scream at the people. Must be very human, that's why I'm saying we didn't get involved in the initial interrogation where they hit the people. You had to be very human. Then the people appreciated it because they've just gone through this rough interrogation and now you get the nice man who gives you a cold drink and take-away [food] and talks nicely to you. That's how we got good cooperation.[36]

Fourie was keen for me to understand that he did not interrogate suspects but merely conducted research. "It wasn't interrogation, just part of the system that people [who] were arrested went through [the album] and that was to identify these photos. We would sit there for a week or two weeks and we would show him every single photo. . . . Normally, [these debriefing sessions would take] about two weeks and then if the person identified [a mug shot] we would make notes. We wrote reports . . . we wrote a big thick report of every photo that this man identified."[37] That is how Fourie and his colleagues sought to make the mug shots speak; that is how they tried to make these two-dimensional images reveal their secrets. By portraying this as a friendly conversation between a detainee and his police interrogator, Fourie cast it as a dialogical process, a three-way conversation featuring a police interrogator, a suspect, and the album. But this was anything but a dialogue. In one notable case, Fourie spent two months going over the album with an ANC insurgent named Glory Lefoshie Sedibe, kidnapped from a jail in Swaziland by a South African police death squad in August 1986.[38] To give a sense of how the Security Police scripted and controlled the dialogue between Fourie, Sedibe and the album, presented below are four excerpts from the 152-page report that Fourie wrote after spending two months with Sedibe in 1987. We do not hear Fourie's voice in these excerpts, only Sedibe's (in the third person).

But we can imagine Fourie showing Sedibe a mug shot, asking him to identify the person in the photo, and writing furiously in Afrikaans as Sedibe told on his former comrades. The telling purports to come from Sedibe but it is in truth through Fourie's pencil and voice. Fourie, who always used a pencil for ease of erasure and correction, ventriloquizes Sedibe's voice. Here is Sedibe (through Fourie's pencil and voice) responding to the photograph of fellow ANC insurgent Barry Gilder:

> He went to live with the [ANC military's] special operations group in the Terror Nest residence . . . [in Mozambique]. The group planned the attack on Sasol. Rashid was commander of the group. He moved between Swaziland and Mozambique and had an affair with [the wife of a comrade].[39]

Here is Sedibe talking about the mug shot of an ANC colleague named Sue Rabkin:

> She drives a white Golf and lives next to the police station on Julius Nyerere Avenue in Maputo . . . she keeps the codes for decoding secret [ANC] messages on her.[40]

And here is Sedibe describing Ray Lalla, another ANC colleague:

> Sedibe . . . met him [in 1981] in the diplomatic shop in Maputo after he [Lalla] asked [Sedibe] to explain the shop's pricing. During that same week, [Sedibe] saw him driving with [another ANC comrade] in a Datsun 120Y. The car was called Mugabe [after the Zimbabwean president] because it looked like the salted meat that Mugabe donated to the ANC. The meat had a lot of bones.[41]

And here is Sedibe talking about Joe Slovo, a senior member of the ANC and leader of the South African Communist Party:

> He got the wife of another comrade pregnant, after which she divorced the husband and moved to London, where she now lives.[42]

Listen to how Fourie not only ventriloquizes Sedibe here but makes him fluent in the language of torturers. Notice, for example, the mix of the strategic with the salacious, the significant and the silly: this was a blend of Security Police neuroses made to sound real by having Sedibe mouth them. Sedibe moved, through Fourie's pencil, between talking about which of his comrades held the ANC's secrets to talking about the secret lives of his comrades, including affairs. He not only described where each person was perched in the ANC hierarchy, he also talked about where they lived and the color and type of cars they drove. Such was the rawness of the encounter between Fourie and Sedibe that, more than a decade later, Fourie would remark to the truth commission's amnesty committee about Sedibe's body odor.[43] What Fourie did not tell the committee, perhaps because he could not without implicating himself in Sedibe's torture, was that Sedibe had been kept in solitary confinement for almost six months without access to ablution facilities or a change of clothing.

Given that a suspect's meeting with Fourie or other members of C2 was often preceded by torture, which left the suspect disoriented at best, Fourie learned early on not to use the album itself when debriefing a suspect. Instead of using the album itself, Fourie used individual photographs stored in a steel filing cabinet with three drawers. In each drawer would be loose photographs, matching those in the album, with a card attached to the back. On these cards would be whatever information the police had about the person in the mug shot. So while Fourie, who as a rule sat across from a suspect with a table between them, held up a mug shot before the suspect, he could see what the police knew, "so if this guy talks rubbish to me then I know. I don't even write it down." The loose photographs were bigger than the mug shots in the album. As Fourie said, "Easier to use the boxes for each photo than sitting here next to a person and showing them [the whole album]. They get confused if they see fifteen people on one page. So you show them one by one and it's easier for them to identify these people."[44] When I asked Fourie how long it took to go through each photograph, he answered: "It depends on if he knows the person or not and how long he knew the person. Sometimes, he knows him from home and then he tells a long story—you can write forty-five minutes on one person."

> **How would you organize the photos?**
> They are numbered from one to seven thousand.
>
> **You would go through the whole stack?**
> Yes, the whole cabinet.
>
> **What's the longest session you ever had?**
> Normally, it takes three weeks. That is the normal . . . but if you get a guy like Glory Sedibe, two months.
>
> **Why two months?**
> Because he knew so many people and he knew so much about MK that he had a lot to say.

Fourie knew the ANC so well that suspects would think that he had been in exile himself. "My strength is that I was calm and collected . . . I knew my job. If someone started talking about Caculama [an ANC military camp in Angola], I could tell them exactly where was the trench, where's [the] radio control room, where's this. If they talked about Quatro [an ANC prison camp in Angola], I could tell them how many cells there were, where's the pigsty, where's the coffee trees."[45] This would leave the detainees feeling like they were in the presence of an omniscient force. Fourie said while he did not receive any specialist training in interrogation or psychology, his inquisitiveness helped him build enough experience that, by 1985, he was one of the top interrogators at C2.[46] Asked to describe his interrogation techniques, Fourie said: "I would talk to the person as if he was my brother, talk about his family, talk about my family, make him feel at home, comfortable, keep him out of the cells for as long as possible. They were always in solitary confinement so they would like to get out. [I would] buy food from the restaurant for him."[47] When the family line did not do the trick, Fourie would try sports or women. Fourie sought to portray himself as a regular guy. He tried to present himself as a regular guy who, under different circumstances, would be at a bar enjoying a drink with the detainee. But he was not.

Looking at Race

In one case, the Security Police mistook Barry Gilder, a white insurgent mentioned above, for an Indian insurgent named Aboobaker Ismail, who went by the nom de guerre of Rashid. Instead of seeing this mix-up as an intelligence failure and an illustration of the limits of the police's own powers, however, Fourie saw the episode instead as a lesson about the immutability of race. He said: "We knew [Rashid] was an Indian and we knew he was born on Christmas day. . . . But . . . if we showed a photo of Barry Gilder [to captured insurgents], then they said 'this is Rashid—commander of [ANC] special forces.'"[48] Fourie blamed this case of mistaken identity on supposedly innate racial differences. He explained: "You see, the people that identified [Gilder and Ismail] got mixed up. They were not very good with white people and Indian people—they couldn't identify them very well."

> **Why is that? You found that was common?**
>
> Ja. They couldn't identify white people and Indian people like they did with black people. They got confused between the white people.
>
> **But there were so few Indians and whites in the ANC. Surely, they should have been easier to identify?**
>
> I don't know. I think it's just that black people, they don't mix with white people and they don't stay with them in the [ANC military] camps so much.[49]

Keep in mind, however, that of the four excerpts above taken from Fourie's 1987 debriefing of Glory Sedibe, three of the people that Sedibe identified for Fourie were classified white and one Indian. For Fourie, however, the failure of the insurgents to identify their comrades by race lay not with race-thinking itself but with the lack of racial awareness, even among those purporting to be fighting for a nonracial South Africa. His explanation fed on the logic of apartheid, which sought to naturalize racial difference. Africans could not, according to this logic, identify white people as individuals, and vice versa. With no room for mutual comprehension, how could blacks and whites say that they were fighting for the same thing?

> **So who did captured white insurgents identify?**
>
> Only white people and Colored people and Indian people. For us [meaning whites] black people's features are mostly the

same. I don't want to sound racist. I don't know why, that I have realized for many years, we cannot identify black people. You ask a black man, "identify these few whites," and they can't. I think it's got something to do with our features, I don't know, never gone deeply into that.[50]

Despite his insistence on racial incomprehensibility, Fourie developed close, even personal, connections with some of the (black) mug shots in his charge—not with the individuals depicted by the mug shots, but with the photographs themselves. Fourie, who retired from the South African Police on medical grounds in 1994, could recall from memory the names and aliases of some individuals, as well as the numbers of their mug shots. One of these photographs belonged to Muziwakhe Boniface Ngwenya, an ANC operative who used the alias Thami Zulu. Ngwenya died in Zambia in November 1989 after the ANC accused him of being an apartheid agent. Fourie brought up Ngwenya's name during our first interview in August 2015: "I can remember his photo number was 4036 . . . Muziwakhe Boniface Ngwenya, that is Thami Zulu."

What makes you remember his name?
We had a photo of Thami Zulu [but] we could never identify him.

Why?
We didn't have his real name; we only had Thami Zulu. We knew he was a Zulu. We knew he was a commander. . . . [Then] we got information from Swaziland. They gave us a new photo of him and his real name and that is why I remember so well.

So how much of this do you remember?
Not much. After the reconciliation . . . I just wrote everything off. I decided now I'm finished, the TRC . . . I don't want

anything to do with it anymore. I want to start a new life. I forgot a lot of things. I don't dream about it anymore. I don't think about it anymore.

You used to dream about it?
I used to.

Regular dreams or nightmares?
Not really nightmares, just dreams about . . .

Would you dream about the album?
Sometimes but not very often but, anyway, then we kept this thing up to date.

With that change of subject, Fourie dropped the matter of dreams. I did not push, as he had told me that his medical discharge from the police was due to a diagnosis of post-traumatic stress disorder. When I asked him about his symptoms, Fourie said: "Bad dreams, tend to forget a lot. Drinking too much, things like that."[51] When I interviewed Fourie a second time, in July 2016, he brought up Thami Zulu again. "A person like Thami Zulu, I can picture him."[52] Keep in mind that Fourie and Ngwenya likely never met and that, while Fourie knew a lot about his quarry, it is unlikely that Ngwenya even knew that Fourie existed. Ngwenya certainly knew about the album, as did many ANC operatives.[53] In truth, Fourie grew attached to Ngwenya's mug shot because a lot of his work was by hand: pulling the photographs out of his filing cabinet, sorting through stacks of photographs, arranging them on a table, touching them, turning them over, writing on their backs, putting them back in order in his filing cabinet. This was personal. Through that haptic experience, Fourie was able to get not only a feel for a photograph itself but a sense of his suspect's being. This did not make Fourie less of a bureaucrat.[54] He was still a functionary, but his expertise in pushing pencil and paper and in getting information from detainees came from his intimate access to the police's photographic archive. Fourie was allowed this haptic experience with the mug shots by the fact that the South African Police came late to the world of computers.[55] The delay in the adoption of computers by the police was itself part of a national lag by South Africa itself, despite the country's status as the most industrialized in Africa.[56] South Africa received its first computer only in 1959 and, while the 1960s saw an exponential growth in the number of computers available in the country, by 1970 the country still had only four hundred computers nationwide—with the vast majority of them in government hands. The Security Police, especially C2, began using computers only in the late 1980s. That is when the index was computerized. Before that, "Everything was written down. . . . We had ladies who just typed our reports. . . . The ladies would type it and we'd make copies and send to different divisions."[57] The late computerization meant that, for years, Fourie tended his collection of photographs by hand. This helped him develop the emotional connections that allowed him to retain vivid memories of the photographs. In addition to the interrogation of suspects, Fourie's unit was responsible for maintaining the album. Every six months or so, C2 would update the album, always adding new mug shots from the back. Fourie explained: "Our unit, C2, all the information came from [police] divisions in the country and we compiled the album ourselves. We kept it up-to-date. It was our job as the research unit."

> How did you ensure that the album was updated every six months?
>
> Depends on how many photos we got in. Got a lot of photos, print them, add them to the album. Each division had maybe five albums and we would send all the updates to the divisions and then they would add it on the bottom, on their

albums. . . . Everybody had a terrorism unit and that person, that commander, was supposed to make sure that it's up-to-date.

How many pictures did you have by the time you left the police?
When we destroyed them, there was about 5000 pictures. We destroyed them at Iscor, in the furnaces there.

What year?
It must have been around '92–'93.

Why did you destroy them?
It was an instruction from the politicians.

What did they say?
"These things must be destroyed. The ANC is a legal organization now. We are not allowed to have this information about them anymore. They're not the enemy."

Do you remember how many copies you took to the furnace?
No.

Did you destroy a whole stack or a roomful?
No, we didn't have a lot at head office. Each of us had our own album. There were eight copies there and the most important, what we used, because it worked better for us, was these cabinets with the single photos. We didn't use the album a lot because it was easier and better to use them. There were four of these sets of photos and they were destroyed with the albums that we had.

How did you feel, this was your lifetime's work?
It was quite sad because we'd put a lot of work [into] . . . the system [the] individual photos. We really put a lot of work into that. . . . It was quite sad when they were destroyed.[58]

Does the album have any historical value?

If you take the identifications we did, that is part of our history. The album is just photos. Nobody knows who they are, why the photos were taken. I don't think [the album] tells us much about the history of our country if you just know there was an album of people who left, who went into exile. If you put the album down there now, it won't mean anything to anybody. It's just photos. Might be photos of a political party. It can be anything.

So it's just photos?

If you don't tell somebody . . . what the meaning of them is, where they come from and why they were used, then it's just a book lying there with photos—nobody will know what it's about.[59]

But this was not just a collection of photographs. Each mug shot came with a history. Behind each photograph was a person whose biography shaped his or her entry in the album. The following chapters examine these biographies and, in the process, show the byways, alleyways, and paths that individuals took into the album. This examination, however, does not and cannot end with the mug shot. To do that would be to cede the last word to Fourie and to his colleagues, and to arrest these images, not to say the individuals behind them, at a time in history. There is always more to a photograph than what lies within its four corners. But, first, how did Fourie and his colleagues know what lay behind each photograph? The following chapter addresses this question.

THREE

The Uncertain Curator

THE TERRORIST ALBUM was a creature of context, deriving its meaning only within an ensemble of other apartheid objects.[1] That is, for the album to make sense, it needed objects such as an index, police memoranda, informer reports, and photographs to place it in its proper environment. More than that, it needed police officers such as Jac Büchner, Trevor Baker, and Eugene Fourie to give it its status. But these men were themselves creatures of context—meaning that, for their work to make sense, they needed collaborators. They needed men such as Gladstone Mose to curate the album for them. As members of C2—a small unit within the Security Police—Büchner, Baker, and Fourie had to make themselves appear larger than life. Their worth depended on their capacity to know their enemy and to make the enemy believe that they knew everything there was to know about him or her. As Büchner told the truth commission, "my job at that stage was identifying . . . 'terrorists . . .' and making sure that I knew who was the enemy and how many there were outside the country."[2] Recalling his interrogation by the Security Police, ANC defector Mwezi Twala said, "It was mindboggling to listen to their exposition. They knew more about me than I did."[3] Hugh Lewin, a captured insurgent, remembered his police interrogators "telling me all about myself, precisely so. It was eerie."[4] But the police did not come naturally by this information. They needed the likes of Mose and Twala to tell them everything that these men could remember about people's names, places of interest, and everything that might be of use in an interrogation. Büchner, Baker, and Fourie collected strips of information and used these to sketch composite portraits of their targets. Just as painters constantly look at the subjects whose likenesses they are trying to reproduce on canvas, these men and their charges referred constantly to the album as they went about collecting their strips of information.

This chapter examines how Mose helped to put the album together, and indeed, came to be one of the most important curators of it. To tell the story of how Mose came to occupy this key position in apartheid's security apparatus, the chapter draws on Mose's file from the apartheid security archive. This, too, is a remnant. It is a fragment of what once was but is no longer. It, too, should have been reduced to ashes but was not, leaving it stranded in that indeterminate zone called the post-apartheid period. But Mose's file does not lend itself to easy readings. It is, after all, an intelligence file, stamped in red with the word *geheim*, Afrikaans for secret. It was not meant for our eyes. This raises the question: with what set of eyes, then, are we to read this file? How are we to look at it? As Peter Jackson says, intelligence documents do not speak for themselves—and some, in fact, dissemble and lie.[5] This is because, Jackson says, deception, deceit, and manipulation are central to the operation of security agencies. Rather than treat intelligence documents as keys to some hidden history, the historian must "develop a feel for how papers moved within and across departments, as well as a sense of the institutional cultures of these organizations in general and prevailing attitudes towards intelligence information in particular."[6] Gerald Hughes and Len Scott suggest three questions to guide any engagement with intelligence material: Is the document genuine? Was it written by someone knowledgeable? And why does the document exist?[7] The file in question is certainly genuine. It came from Section C2 of the Security Police headquarters in Pretoria. Trevor Baker and Mose wrote the reports that make up the file. Sometimes, Mose wrote them himself; other times, he dictated them to Baker, who then had them signed before a witness. We cannot say what role, if any, duress played in Mose's relationship with Baker. Mose's reports exist because, for reasons lost to us, the Security Police missed them when they destroyed their records in the 1990s.

Political Epistemics

To understand the thicket of details that constitutes Mose's file, we must develop protocols of reading attuned to what that thicket tells us about apartheid and its failures. Rather than point only to its lack of political legitimacy for reasons why apartheid failed, we must look to what Andreas Glaeser calls "political epistemics" for other possible reasons.[8] Glaeser's concept is designed to capture the "ways in which [a regime] produced and certified knowledge about itself." To read Mose's file—to hack our way through the forest of dates, proper names, pseudonyms, and places—is to see up close the convoluted ways in which the Security Police and the apartheid government let their anxieties about ethnicity and race guide their politics. Each time Mose blamed tribalism for strife within the ANC, he merely confirmed what the Security Police thought they knew already about their adversaries.

"That is just how the Bantu are," says Captain Trevor Baker in response to one of Mose's reports about ethnic tensions within the ANC. But, like the East German state studied by Glaeser, apartheid South Africa produced knowledge about itself that, in fact, blinded it to the ways in which its own quotidian operations undermined its basic assumptions. Smug in their assumptions about how the Bantu were, the Security Police failed to come to terms with the reality that no amount of ethnic tabulation and tribalist analysis about Xhosas and Zulus could mask the fact that South Africa's fundamental problem was, first and foremost, political—and that only a settlement that took seriously the idea of political equality could resolve the country's conflict. Mose wrote no accounts during his time as a member of the ANC, leaving us with no way of understanding how he rationalized his membership in it. The only accounts we have are those he gave to the Security Police. His voice comes to us only through his curatorship of the Terrorist Album. Often, during this process of curatorship, Baker ventriloquized Mose; sometimes Mose spoke in his own voice.

Before we consider Mose's curatorship of the album, however, we must grapple with his life story. We must retrace the steps that led him from insurgency to counter-insurgency. A notable feature of intelligence documents such as the ones considered here is that they are, by definition, autobiographical sketches. For intelligence operatives and informers to grant their reports veracity, they must first give account of who they are and say what it is about their background that gave them access to the information peddled in their reports. Mose provided one such autobiographical sketch in the form of an affidavit dated September 22, 1972. According to the affidavit, Mose was born September 29, 1936, in Engcobo, Transkei. He joined the ANC in 1959. When the government banned the ANC in April 1960, he joined the South African Congress of Trade Unions (SACTU). "On the surface,

SACTU appeared to be independent of the ANC but in actual fact was only subtly furthering the aims [of the ANC]," said Mose.[9] On May 1, 1964, he joined the military wing of the ANC and, four days later, "I clandestinely and unlawfully left [South Africa for Botswana] en route to . . . Tanzania. Our purpose was to undergo military training . . . with the object of eventually returning and overthrowing the government of [South Africa] by force of arms." Mose spent three months in Tanzania, where he acquired the first of his *noms de guerre,* Jackson Mlenze. In September 1964, the ANC sent Mose to Odessa, Ukraine, for military training. He received instruction in topography, artillery, truck mechanics, engineering, military tactics, firearms handling, radio communications, infantry drills, and politics. "Our training lasted from September 1964 until October 1965. We all wore Russian officers' and combat uniforms whilst training." After Odessa, Mose went to Moscow for a special course on intelligence, security, and secret communications taught by English-speaking Russian instructors. "Basically our course was on Russian methods."

Mose returned to Africa in January 1966. In July 1967, he and fellow members of the Luthuli Detachment, a group of ANC insurgents trained in the Soviet bloc, attempted to march to South Africa via Rhodesia's Wankie Game Reserve. But their mission fell apart following two clashes with the Rhodesian security forces. Mose fled to Botswana, "unscathed from the skirmishes." The Botswana police arrested him for illegally bringing arms and ammunition into the country. He spent eighteen months in jail in Gaborone and was deported to Zambia at the end of his sentence. The ANC sent him back to the Soviet Union for retraining in November 1969. He spent three years at different military camps in the Soviet bloc, undergoing training in guerilla warfare, underground work, and explosives handling. During his time in the Soviet Union, ANC officials gave him and his fellow trainees copies of affidavits from a 1971 terrorism trial in South Africa. These documents explained the torture methods favored by the South African Security Police. "We were instructed to study these methods and prepare ourselves psychologically should we ever find ourselves in a similar situation. . . . They wanted to impress upon us that the Security Police used methods amounting to electrical shock treatment to force statements from their victims." In February 1972, Mose and his fellow trainees flew to Mogadishu, Somalia, in preparation for a seaborne infiltration of South Africa. Here, Mose acquired his second *nom de guerre*, Sizwe Nkomo. In June 1972, he flew on a false Lesotho passport to Swaziland via Kenya and South Africa. On June 26, 1972, Mose crossed illegally into South Africa for a military mission that included, he said, the assassination of police collaborators and informers. On September 9, 1972, the Security Police arrested him at the Queenstown Post Office, in the Eastern Cape, shortly after he arrived for a meeting with an ANC contact, a white man carrying a copy of *Time* magazine. The contact turned out to be a member of the Security Police.

Mose's autobiographical sketch stops at the news of his capture. If Mose's account is to be believed, he signed the sketch on September 22, 1972, thirteen days after his arrest. He declared: "I am in my sound and sober senses and have made this statement freely and voluntarily, without having been physically compelled or influenced in any manner whatsoever, either by promises, inducements or threats to do so. I further declare myself willing to co-operate with the authorities of the State in any way deemed necessary by them." As we now know from the truth commission and from the documents examined in this chapter, what the authorities of the State deemed to be necessary cooperation by Mose ranged from his curating the Terrorist Album to his assassinating members of the ANC. Terry Bell and Dumisa Ntsebeza describe Mose as one of the "most prolific killers" in the apartheid Security Police.[10] Timothy Gibbs says that Mose defected to the Security Police after they "tortured and turned" him following his capture in 1972.[11] The truth commission found that Mose was involved in the killing of student activist Bathandwa Ndondo in September 1985.[12] Not surprisingly, Mose's handlers in the Security Police saw him differently. When Mose died of a heart attack on April 18, 1990, a police obituary lauded his "strength of character and the fact that he never complained."[13] The writer of the obituary (unnamed but most likely Trevor Baker) took credit for recommending in 1974 that Mose be admitted as a member of the Security Police. "I am only able to say that, during the eighteen years that I knew Madiba [Mose's clan name], his conduct was at all times exemplary. He was an excellent example to other members of the Force. His behavior, dedication, diligence and honesty were in the most praiseworthy and credible category." The writer said there was no better proof of Mose's excellence than the fact that, in his first fifteen years in the police, he received four promotions, rising from detective constable to captain.

The Diligent Curator

The archival remnants we have cover only the first four years of Mose's time in the Security Police, when he was first an unnamed operative codenamed HK 87, and then a Bantu detective constable assigned the police force number 161463W. In his stints as HK 87 and Bantu detective constable 161463W, Mose and his reports consistently received the grade B2, the highest evaluation the Security Police could give a defector. The letter B meant that, as a source, Mose was "usually reliable" and that the content of his reports was "probably true." The grading was part of an evaluation system that covered the spectrum: from A1, meaning the source was "completely reliable" and his or her information "confirmed by other independent sources," to F6, meaning the source and his or her information "cannot be judged." Between A1 and F6 was a range of grades, from C3 ("Fairly reliable" and "possibly true") to D4 ("Not usually reliable" and "doubtful") to E5 ("Not reliable" and "probably false"). A1, the highest grade, denoted a perfect source. But it was an impossible attainment for Mose, given his status as a Bantu and defector. Although he would go on to distinguish himself over the course of eighteen years as an apartheid killer, Mose could not shed his past as a former insurgent, a man who had spent eight years in the ANC and trained in the Soviet Union. In a country where the political order, meaning apartheid, was predicated on the perpetuation of white power, Mose could not be trusted fully—even as that order depended on black collaborators for its preservation. He could be trusted enough to kill for apartheid, trusted enough to protect apartheid. But he could not be relied upon to ignore the slights that came with being a black person in apartheid South Africa. He could not be trusted to forget what had driven him into the arms of the ANC in the first place. So he remained a B2: usually reliable and the content of his reports probably true.

To call Mose a curator is not to ignore the torture he likely endured on his way to becoming a collaborator. Rather, it is to alert us to the fact that, as David William Cohen puts it, "*Curation* is more than a set of practices defined by technical competency, professional standards and property rights. While ostensibly about the management of things produced by others, curation is itself a means of production."[14] Mose used his senses to help produce the album. To curate the album, he had to see its contents, hear the voices between its covers, and touch the object over and over again. For Mose to become a diligent curator, he had to develop a feel for the album. As Cohen says, "Curation involves tactile and cerebral engagements . . . that could include—beyond documentation, exhibition and conservation—viewing, touching, speaking of, marking, remarking and even simply finding the presumed objects of curation."[15] The earliest report we have from Mose is dated December 13, 1973. Mose's words, taken down verbatim by Baker, are about an ANC insurgent named Matsibe Samuel Maimela:

> Since leaving the Republic of South Africa on 5.5.1964 up until my return on 27.6.1972, a period of over eight years, I came into contact with many members of the ANC in various countries . . . which include . . . Zambia, Tanzania, Somalia, Botswana, Swaziland and the Union of Soviet Socialist Republics (USSR). . . . In some instances I only heard of members of the organization and never actually came into contact with them. Having perused the official photograph album of terrorists I am able to state that in all the aforementioned countries, various ANC camps and other premises abroad I never came into contact with or heard of the person whose photograph appears on the middle right hand side of page 53 of the official Terrorist Album.[16]

Notice Mose's deployment of his senses: He has heard of some members of the ANC; he has perused the album, but he has not heard of Matsibe Samuel Maimela, the subject of his report. Mose did more than look, listen, and touch. He developed an intimate connection to the album. He got to know the album well. As he said on January 22, 1974: "I have perused the Terrorist Album thoroughly on many occasions and have never come across a photograph of Kim Ndlovu."[17] Like a diligent curator, Mose developed a proprietary relationship with the album. He sought to master its contents in ways that allowed him both to care for it and to exercise custody over it. This, as Carolyn Hamilton and Pippa Skotnes point out, is a key paradox of curation and curatorship: care of the object always entails appropriation.[18] Mose mixed thoroughness with a care for detail that would be admirable in a museum curator. He says this in one report: "On 29.1.74 I was shown a photograph by Captain Baker who asked me that should I be able to identify the person appearing thereon I should inform him accordingly. After close scrutiny . . . I am unable to identify the photograph and have never seen the person appearing thereon."[19] Mose was certainly being careful. But his fastidiousness—borne by a stilted diction designed, possibly by Baker himself, to lend Mose's reports official credence—must be understood not only as the doings of a cowed man but as the actions of a man who had determined to use his knowledge to make the album as accurate as possible. Mose wanted the album to be up to date. He wanted the album to offer as much information as possible. So he made sure to confirm and identify only those photographs about which he was certain. As he said about an insurgent named Kenneth Jimmy Phambo, "I have perused the official Terrorist Album and was shown a photograph of a person appearing on the middle right side of page 135 of the album. I have neither seen nor heard of this person and cannot identify him as being a member of the ANC."[20] Mose trusted his senses and made sure his police masters knew that.

Asked to identify an ANC member named Francis Meli, Mose said: "I have seen the name . . . in the *African Communist* many times. . . . Whether the name . . . is a pseudonym or not I cannot say. . . . Should Chris Nkosana write an article . . . then it is easily recognizable as I knew him and [can] hear [him] express himself."[21] Mose knew Chris Nkosana so well, he could hear Nkosana's voice when he read anything that Nkosana wrote.[22] Mose's knowledge of people's voices extended to the ANC's radio broadcasts. In January 1974, he not only gave the frequencies used by the ANC for broadcasts (from Egypt, Russia and

Tanzania) into South Africa, he added the following tidbit: "The Moscow broadcasts were eagerly listened to whilst we were in the USSR as [they were] attractive to South Africans because of the Bantu language and the type of music reminding us of home."[23] To be an insurgent exiled thousands of miles from home was to live in foreign landscapes but sometimes familiar soundscapes.[24] Insurgents kept contact with home through sounds that came over the air. This nostalgic stimulation of the senses helped to keep insurgents rooted to some notion of home, even as their status as exiles seemed indeterminate, a purgatory without end. For Mose, exile not only stimulated the senses it also implanted in him memories that came in handy once he became a counterinsurgent. Memory became his weapon against former comrades. In two reports dated February 2, 1974, Mose says the following: "I heard over the news [meaning radio] and during formal addresses made by Oliver Tambo and Chris Nkosana that during 1970 a group of people belonging to the African Peoples Democratic Union of South Africa had been arrested. . . ."[25] In the second report, Mose says: "I first saw Nimrod Sejake during 1964 in Dar-es-Salaam. At this stage he was the ANC camp commander at the . . . Luthuli camp in Tanzania." (Baker adds in a commentary attached to the report that Sejake's mug shot appears on page 147 of the album).[26]

In a report dated March 20, 1974, Mose says the following about police confusion regarding the identities of ANC insurgents named Justice Moabi and Ben Mooki:

> The only person abroad who had undergone military training, under the auspices of the ANC, known by the name of Justice or Justice Moabi is the illegitimate son of Fish Keitsing. To my knowledge nobody else was known by this name and Ben Mooki is a

separate personality and I am adamant when I say that he [Ben Mooki] was never called Justice or Justice Moabi.[27]

Mose does not summon the album here. That falls to Baker in his commentary on Mose's report. Baker says that Justice Moabi and Bodisa Lucas Keitsing are the same person and that Fish Keitsing is also named Ntwaesele Fish Thatayaone. "Sy foto verskyn op bladsy 166 van die Terroriste-album," he writes ["His photo appears on page 166 of the Terrorist Album]."[28] Baker concludes: "Ben Mooki and Justice cannot be identical, and so the person who uses the pseudonym Ben Mooki abroad has not yet been positively identified." Baker had to comment on Mose's reports because they were considered raw intelligence— meaning unevaluated—until he had examined them for accuracy. From Baker's desk, reports such as this one went to the commanding officer of the Security Police and he shared them with other sections for further investigation. That is how such reports moved from desk to desk. Each time the Security Police arrested an ANC insurgent, they would pump that person for information about Justice Moabi and Ben Mooki and use whatever the insurgent said to develop their composite sketch. This was painstaking work that required patience and attention to detail. Men such as Büchner, Baker, and Fourie prided themselves on these qualities.

In addition to using his senses to produce the album, Mose also adopted a number of registers. In an affidavit dated April 23, 1974, he said: "On 23.4.1974 I was shown a photograph by Captain H. T. Baker who asked me whether I am able to identify the person appearing thereon. Without any shadow of a doubt I am able to categorically state that the person appearing on the photograph and the person using the pseudonym Simon Dlakiya Mandlakadlaka abroad is identical."[29]

Notice the different points of emphasis. Mose went on to detail how he knew Dlakiya when both were at school in the Transkei in 1953–1955; how he next saw Dlakiya in 1961 when the latter represented the Transkei as a goalkeeper. "I next saw him in Odessa in the Ukraine during 1964 undergoing military training under the auspices of the ANC." Mose's senses did not always work in concert, with one supporting the other. In January 1975, for example, he said the following about an ANC member named James Blackie Mtswane Molife: "I have personally never seen subject but heard that" Molife died in a skirmish with Rhodesian security forces in 1968.[30] Here, what the eyes could not do—confirm an insurgent's identity—the ears could do just fine. Mose did not need to engage every sense to give his police masters the information they needed. He did not need to know everything to become an effective defector. He simply had to know enough. He also had to become a reader, reading not just his new police masters to make sure he understood their intentions (his survival as a defector depended on that) but also his former comrades and their literature to stay informed about what they were up to. He read insurgent publications such as *Sechaba,* the official organ of the ANC, and the *African Communist,* the magazine of the South African Communist Party. (Both publications were, of course, banned in South Africa). Through the pages of these publications, Mose kept abreast of the latest propaganda offensives against the apartheid government.

He used the photographs published in these magazines to add to the Terrorist Album. On April 2, 1974, Mose identified a photograph (fig. 3.1) published in the March 1974 issue of *Sechaba.*

He said: "The big man speaking on page 12—top left hand side I can positively identify as being Zola Zembe, also known as Zola Nqaba. His proper name is Archibald Mcedisi [*sic*] Sibeko and his photograph appears on page 155 of the Terrorist Album—middle right hand side."[31]

FIGURE 3.1 Image presented to Mose by the Security Police April 2, 1974. *Sechaba* 8, no. 3 (March 1974). Courtesy of National Heritage and Cultural Studies Centre, University of Fort Hare.

Mose identified the man to Sibeko's left as Anthony Mongalo, the ANC's representative in Italy, and suggested that the ANC had paired the men to avoid accusations of ethnic bias. Mose said Sibeko was Xhosa and Mongalo Sotho.[32] On December 2, 1974, the Security Police gave Mose the August-September 1974 issue of *Sechaba* and asked him to identify the individuals depicted in one of its photographs (fig. 3.2).

Mose said, "Moses Mabhida is the grey-headed man dressed in a dark suit, tie and white shirt in the right-side foreground. In the left foreground dressed in a polonecked white garment appears Vuyisile Richard Mdala. . . . Next to Vuyisile Mdala, on his left and similarly attired appears Phillip Jezele. . . ."[33] In January 1976, Mose identified a

FIGURE 3.2 Image presented to Mose by the Security Police December 2, 1974. *Sechaba* 8, no. 8 / 9 (Aug-Sep 1974). Courtesy of National Heritage and Cultural Studies Centre, University of Fort Hare.

photograph (fig. 3.3) taken in Moscow in August 1975 at a ceremony celebrating the seventieth birthday of Moses Kotane (seated in the middle of the front row). Kotane, the general secretary of the South African Communist Party, had been hospitalized in Moscow since 1969 and would in fact die there in May 1978. Most of those in the photograph

FIGURE 3.3 Image presented to Mose by the Security Police in January 1976. *Sechaba,* 9, no. 10 (October 1975). Courtesy of National Heritage and Cultural Studies Centre, University of Fort Hare.

were ANC and Communist Party leaders already known to the Security Police.

The Security Police did not, however, know the identity of the man on the extreme left, in the black-rimmed glasses. So it fell to Mose to say who he was. "The bespectacled person standing on the extreme left hand side of the group photograph . . . is known to me by the name of Wesi Masisi." Mose had first met Masisi in Tanzania in 1969. Masisi worked in the ANC office in Dar-es-Salaam and was "actively engaged and entrusted with the compilation and preparation of travel documents" for ANC members.[34] Masisi came from the Orange Free State and was educated in Cuba, Mose said. In his commentary, Baker wondered why such a seemingly key figure did not appear in the album. Baker said: "Subject does not appear in the official Terrorist Album even though he seems to play an important role in the ANC." It is not clear if Masisi's mug shot ended up in the album.

But Mose did more than confirm people's identities and put those people in places (such as ANC military camps and the Soviet Union) that were of interest to the Security Police. He also gave the Security Police a context within which to understand people's motivations. In a report dated August 1, 1974, he said, "Should a person in the ranks of the ANC be referred to abroad by the name of Hlupa Sitole then it would possibly be Peter Sithole whose photograph appears on page 7 of . . . the Terrorist Album."[35] Mose said Sithole was the son of a priest and that he had joined the ANC in hopes of furthering his studies. That did not happen, however, so he lost faith in the ANC. "He is an embarrassment to the leadership as he does not accept . . . ANC ideology and indoctrination. . . . The leadership considered him a problem and a nuisance as he was always complaining." Playing the role of native expert, Captain Baker added, for the benefit of his superiors: "The word Hlupa means worry, bother, nuisance, etc." Like a colonial official stationed in some far-flung outpost writing to his seniors at head office, Baker wanted to show off his knowledge of his targets and their languages.

Tribal Markings

It would be a mistake to see Mose the curator as interested only in the correspondence between mug shots and their referents, or photographs and their contents. He also gave the Security Police crucial insights into the ANC and its operations—even if these insights came cloaked in the language of race and ethnology. In August 1974, he gave a detailed description of a key ANC operative named Mongameli Johnson Tshali (who went by the *noms de guerre* Mjojo Mxwaku and Lennox Lagu). After giving a breakdown of Tshali's work for the ANC between 1966 and 1971, Mose added the following physical description: "Subject is of light complexion, medium build and bears the physical characteristics of a Bushman. His peculiarities are very broad shoulders and large buttocks."[36] When Mose is asked again two years later to identify Tshali, now based in the Mozambican capital Maputo and going by the name Lennox Lagu, Mose says: "Should a member of the ANC be based in Maputo and is referred to by the name of Lennox I am only able to conclude that such person is probably identical to . . . Tshali. . . . His photograph appears on page 170 of the official photograph album of terrorists and trainee terrorists."[37] Mose makes no reference to Tshali's looks. But Baker does in his evaluation of Mose's information. Baker writes: "Subject's outstanding feature is his Hottentot-Bushman physique and facial features although he is a member of the Ngqika clan and the Nqaphayi clan of the Xhosa ethnic group." What began as a trivial observation by Mose had, by the time it flowed from Baker's typewriter two years later, turned into statements of fact about Tshali's ethnic background. In a report about another ANC insurgent named Do Mahlasela, Mose gives the following description: The subject is light-brown in complexion, speaks in a low, sharp tone, is 5′6″ and well-built. Then he adds: "Facial appearance: striking tribal markings on face which are peculiar to the Bhaca tribe. Marks most peculiar."[38] It is tempting to ask what intelligence value, if any, the Security Police would have derived from Mose's description of Tshali's large buttocks or Mahlasela's facial markings. But it would be to miss the point of Mose's reports to ask that question. As Barbara Miller says, triteness is the very stuff of intelligence documents.[39] This does not mean that the apparently trivial information fed to the security agencies is in fact trivial. As Miller says, "The seemingly harmless pieces of information . . . were like fragments of a mosaic and often only became meaningful when combined with information from other informers."[40] Notice, for instance, how Mose's physical description of Tshali assumes a different meaning when Baker plays it back. But these were not just random observations about ethnicity, phenotype, and race.

When Mose gave his descriptions of Tshali and Mahlasela, South Africa was in the process of setting up its first Bantustan.[41] As part of an attempt to cut black people down to demographic size, the apartheid government sought to assign every black person in South Africa to an ethnic group and an ethnic homeland. On July 22, 1976—two months before South Africa declared the Transkei its first homeland—Mose submitted a list of ANC members eligible to claim Transkeian citizenship. He gave forty-four names, including those of ANC president Oliver Tambo, Chris Hani, and Thabo Mbeki. "To the best of my knowledge and belief," he attested, "the following ANC members abroad and known to me will be able to claim Transkei citizenship."[42] For good measure, Mose appended a short list showing which of the forty-four had not received military training. It is not clear if the Security Police acted on this information and, if so, how. But in January 1985, President P. W. Botha offered to release Nelson Mandela, then twenty-three years into his life sentence on Robben Island, if Mandela would renounce violence, agree to retire from politics, and settle in the Transkei. Mandela rejected the offer.[43]

The Security Police's interest in ethnicity went beyond the set of ethnic boxes in which the insurgents supposedly all fit. It extended to the very composition of the ANC itself. In January 1974, Mose reported on divisions within the ANC.[44] The five-page report is the only one in Mose's file to have received a B1 evaluation, indicating that the Security Police deemed its source (Mose) "usually reliable" and its contents "confirmed by other independent and reliable sources." This report gives us insight into what the Security Police considered valuable intelligence and how they processed that information. More than that, it lets us see the world as the Security Police saw it. Mose began: "There is no absolute unity within the ranks of the ANC. This state of affairs is obvious and can be clearly seen in the character and manner of the various ethnical groups and tribes involved." Attributing this to history and to "leadership mongering," he continued:

> The two groups or factions that are distinctly involved in this type of friction are the Zulus and Xhosas. Both the Sothos and the Tswanas are divided in opinion on which faction to support but the majority are in favor of the Zulus. This became clear in the ANC transit camp . . . in Tanzania and also in Zambia during 1968. Even the leadership divided into cliques that constituted people who were speaking the same vernacular. However, there were always the individuals who "played" neutral.[45]

Mose cited a memorandum, written in Lusaka in 1968 by Chris Hani and six other members of the ANC's military wing, that criticized the leadership of the ANC.[46] "On account of this document being drafted by mostly Xhosa-speaking members, all the Zulus and a vast majority of others took exception and bloodshed was nigh." He went on: "In regard to the leadership, the main complaint is by the Zulus who regard themselves superior to all other races and feel that as they are members of a superior nation, they object to and cannot be led by their inferiors." He then gave a breakdown, by name, of the two main factions. He called the Xhosa group (with eleven members in the leadership) "faction A," and called the Zulu bloc (with seven members in the leadership) "faction B.", This left five ANC leaders (J. B. Marks, Moses Kotane, Thomas Nkobi, Joe Modise, and Duma Nokwe) in a "neutral" camp. Mose said that, while faction A controlled the organization, faction B, led by Moses Mabhida, "enjoys the support of the treasury, which is an important factor." Mose went on to detail how the ANC sought to paper over these divisions by electing a three-person presidential council made up of Tambo, Mabhida, and Marks at a special conference held in the Tanzanian town of Morogoro in 1969.[47] But the real insight into the apartheid worldview comes from Baker's analysis of Mose's report. Baker wrote: "That is just how the Bantu are. So long as they can keep their tribal identity, they will never stand together and the Zulus will dominate everyone."[48]

Referring to one of the leaders identified with the Zulu faction, Baker concluded, "It is clear that [he] will cause trouble again and that the ANC rank and file will fight again." The point here is not to suggest that Mose made up the ethnic differences, or to deny that the ANC was riven with tribal differences. The point is that the Security Police and the apartheid state sought to naturalize these differences and divisions in ways that rendered black South Africans nonpolitical subjects. By turning them into nonpolitical subjects, the apartheid state sought to make blacks (especially Africans) bearers of customs—not rights.[49] As such, blacks could not bid for political power, meaning they could not demand political equality.[50] For bureaucrats like Baker, tribalism was as natural as ethnic differences were immutable. That is why these bureaucrats had a hard time with the concept of nonracialism and the idea that South Africa could become a nonracial democracy.

To them, this was nothing more than utopian nonsense that, if not stopped, risked serving as a Trojan horse for communism. That is why the Security Police worried constantly about Indian and white communists allegedly leading contented African tribals astray. The Security Police also fretted over Africans forging unity as black political subjects. They made it their business to know the ethnicity of each African insurgent and, where possible, to use that to foment division within the ANC and other liberation groups. In a 1974 report titled

"ANC Trained Terrorists: Ethnic Groups," Mose gave the police an estimated breakdown of trained ANC members by ethnicity.[51] According to Mose, there were 284 trained members in total at the time. Of these, 140 were Sotho (composed of Pedi, Sotho, and Tswana) and 135 belonged to the Nguni group (made up of Hlubi, Ndebele, Pondo, Xhosa, and Zulu); the rest included four Shangaan, one Venda, two Indian, one Colored, and one white. On its own, this categorization did not amount to much. Coupled with apartheid assumptions about ethnicity and race, however, it assumed significance way beyond what those concepts could do on their own. This is apparent in the analysis that accompanies Mose's report. Mose noted that Oliver Tambo, the ANC president, belonged to the Pondo tribe but that only one of his "tribesmen" was a trained terrorist.[52] Tambo himself, a devout Anglican, had not received any training but, Mose noted, he enjoyed the support of the Xhosa tribe. Mose identified Moses Mabhida, the most senior Zulu-speaking leader of the ANC at the time, as Tambo's rival and described Mabhida's Zulu group as being much stronger than the Xhosa. Mose was essentially playing on the colonial and imperial stereotype of the Zulu as a martial race. The stereotype came out of clashes, starting in the late eighteenth century, between the Zulu kingdom and British imperial forces.[53]

The Albino Terrorist

In January 1976, poet Breyten Breytenbach, a year into a nine-year prison sentence for terrorism, wrote two reports on the ANC for the Security Police.[54] The first was a short report about the Mayibuye Cultural Unit, an ANC performing group based in London.[55] He identified four members of the unit: Barry Feinberg, Ronnie Kasrils, John

Matshikiza, and Billy Nanan. In his assessment of Breytenbach's information, Mose confirmed only the identity of Ronnie Kasrils, saying his mug shot appeared on page 33 of the Terrorist Album. In his commentary, Baker said that Barry Feinberg and Billy Nanan were "subjects of file," meaning the Security Police had files on them. Referring to Feinberg, Baker called him "another Jew like Ronnie Kasrils" on a fundraising mission and propaganda campaign for the ANC.[56] The conflation of Feinberg's and Kasrils's Jewishness with fundraising was no accident. Baker's casual anti-Semitism was common in the Security Police. As was the case with Afrikaner nationalists in general, the Security Police believed that Jews were, paradoxically, capitalists and communists at the same time.[57] Breytenbach's second report offered a seven-page assessment of the ANC in exile. Breytenbach began his report thus: "My information is based on conversations I had over the years" with a number of ANC leaders, including Tambo.[58] Breytenbach said there were moves to force Tambo to relinquish his position in favor of a collective leadership. "It is obvious that the South African Communist Party has gobbled up the ANC—the parasite has eaten up the host—and it depends on their evaluation of the tactics to be followed (and perhaps on those devouring tactics themselves; an inbuilt law of any Communist Party is that it must gain control in any coalition) whether this takeover will become publicly apparent." Commenting on Jonny Makhathini, a friend and French-speaking ANC diplomat active in North Africa and France, Breytenbach wrote:

> He is secretive, but careless and certainly no good at clandestine activity. Since he tries to do everything at the same time, nothing gets prepared properly and consequently few results are obtained. He is unreliable, late for appointments, gets lost, forgets things, and doesn't "follow through. . . ." He is badly informed about

South Africa. Although he claims to know the Zulu-character very well—considering them a querulous lot easily regimented for battle, even on the wrong side!—he is careful to avoid giving the impression of being with a Zulu clan within the ANC. He has the true African's distrust of the white man though he personally gets along easily with them, and is easily influenced by them.[59]

Thus was apartheid intelligence made—through talk of querulous Zulus and true Africans. Asked to comment on Breytenbach's report, Mose said: "Having read this report, I can conclude that the man who has written it has full information on what is actually happening within the ranks of the ANC." For his part, Baker added:

Breyten Breytenbach (source) repents for acting against his land of birth, South Africa, and in my humble opinion is honest in his endeavor to cooperate with the Security Police in order to compensate for his transgressions. However, bearing in mind underground ANC activities in South Africa, only time will tell whether he has fully cooperated and not withheld illuminatory data.

Breytenbach's remorse and cooperation with the Security Police—if that is indeed what produced the two reports—do not seem to have won him any favors. He served his full nine-year sentence and, upon his release in 1982, left for France.[60] As for Mose, we have no record of his involvement with the Terrorist Album after 1976. But he served the Security Police for the next fourteen years until, as Baker put it in his obituary, he was called away for "higher service." By then, the most important part of his work with the album was done. He had spent the first five years of his time with the Security Police curating the album. He had filled it with detail, put names to faces, and made it a living object. How that object lived on is the subject of the next chapter.

FOUR

Perusals

ON OCTOBER 3, 1975, Kompol, the Security Police headquarters in Pretoria, sent a confidential circular titled "Emigration: Trainee Terrorists" to its divisional commanders around the country.[1] The police had discovered that young "Bantu men" were being recruited to leave South Africa via Botswana, Mozambique, and Swaziland for military training farther north. Kompol ordered the Northern Transvaal Division (responsible for the border with Rhodesia), Eastern Transvaal (Swaziland and Mozambique), Western Transvaal (Botswana), and Natal (Mozambique) to pay attention to their border regions and to look out especially for groups of young black men leaving South Africa, "legally or otherwise." Two weeks later, a Constable Van Vuuren from the Security Police in Matatiele, in the Eastern Cape and on the border with Lesotho, acted on the orders from Kompol. He announced that a local "Bantu schoolteacher" named Cosmos Aloys Sechaba Setsubi had disappeared.[2] Setsubi, the constable discovered, had told his father on August 2, 1975, that he was visiting the coastal city of Durban and would return two days later. At the same time, however, he had also sent a letter to his wife, Yvonne Setsubi, saying he was in Johannesburg looking for a job. Van Vuuren noted that Setsubi's letter to his wife did not have a return address. The constable proceeded to give Setsubi's details, including his age (twenty-eight) and a physical description: "5'5", brown complexion, well-built, wears a long beard, missing two bottom front teeth." Van Vuuren remarked on a few more aspects of Setsubi's disappearance: Despite telling his wife that he was looking for a job in Johannesburg, Setsubi had not resigned his teaching post in Matatiele; the wife had destroyed the letter from her husband shortly after receiving it; and Setsubi was a graduate of the University of Fort Hare, a hotbed of student activism at the time.

"The suspicion," Van Vuuren concluded, "is that subject has left the country. As far as we can tell, he does not possess a passport. The investigation continues." Thus begins one of the most extensive paper trails we have connected to the Terrorist Album.[3] The trail covers the years 1975 to 1991 and shows that the Security Police were using the album as late as September 1991—almost two years after the unbanning of the ANC and the release of Nelson Mandela from prison. This timeline shows the extent to which the album had outgrown its original purpose—namely, to keep track of individuals who had left South Africa without government permission. Considering that the unbanning of the ANC and other groupings had included the decriminalization of flight to exile, the album should have been obsolete by 1990. It was not. The paper trail behind Setsubi's name shows how a cast of characters, with the Security Police in the director's seat, went about tracking Setsubi across different stages around the world: from Angola, Lesotho, and Mozambique, to Tanzania, the Soviet Union, and Zambia—and back to South Africa. In their pursuit of Setsubi over fifteen years, these trackers went after phantoms and rumors: Was that him in Zambia at the execution of an ANC member suspected of being a police spy in December 1979? Was that him sneaking across the border in December 1982 to visit his parents for Christmas? Was he the man who had died in Swaziland in 1984? Among Setsubi's pursuers was a cousin working for the Security Police; among the many agents and informers on his trail were United Nations (UN) and state bureaucrats in Lesotho on the payroll of the South African Security Police. But these were not the only players enacting this drama on different stages across the world. Also involved were Setsubi's former comrades—captured ANC insurgents who, more than anyone apart from the Security Police, made the album a constant presence, as both actor and prop, in this fifteen-year pursuit of Setsubi.

The hunt for Setsubi was one of the most public dramas ever scripted by the Security Police—even if every text connected to this drama came with the words *confidential* and *secret*.[4] Here was a political hunt, involving scores of secret agents, conducted in public but in secret. The Security Police made a point of letting everyone connected to Setsubi (from his parents and siblings to his ANC comrades) know that they were looking for him, but they insisted on cloaking their hunt in secrecy. This paradoxical use of secrecy should not surprise us. As Luise White reminds us, far from being instruments of concealment, secrets are ways of making information known.[5] The Security Police wanted it known that they were after Setsubi. They wanted it known that they had mobilized an army of informers and secret agents to track Setsubi down. But they did not want it known who those agents and informers were.

If Chapter 3 offered insight into the production of the album from the point of view of one of its key curators, this chapter shifts the angle of vision to reveal the end result of that curation, to show us what the product of that exercise looked like. More than that, this chapter traces how documents pertaining to individuals subjected to the album moved from police desk to police desk, from division to division, and up and down the chain of command. We do not get Setsubi's point of view. Based as it is on police reports, this chapter offers the reader only a limited perspective. But this does not mean that it cannot look before and beyond the album. Although the chapter follows the chronology laid down by the Security Police in Setsubi's police file, it has the weakness characteristic of all historians—that they are by definition always late.

Historians arrive at the scene long after the event has passed.[6] But it is precisely this tardiness that makes it possible for the historian to understand the context or process behind an event better than the historical agents themselves might have done. By retracing the steps followed by some of the documents and reports that make up Setsubi's file, we are able to see, for example, how informer reports moved from the mouths of informers to the informers' police handlers, and from there to various divisions of the Security Police, passing through a number of desks and offices as they did so. By retracing the movements of the reports in Setsubi's file, we are able to show how Security Police apparatchiks were not the only ones harnessed to the apparatus of the state.[7] So were the countless agents and informers who made the work of the Security Police possible. By following the routes that Setsubi's file took in its fifteen-year odyssey through the apartheid security apparatus, we can notice the ways in which, for some of the trackers, the hunt for Setsubi was personal. More than that, we can map the transnational network that cast its net over Setsubi and show the different actors holding ever so tenuously to each corner of the net as they sought to trap Setsubi—as he moved constantly in some of the key sites of the Cold War. If the police file is to be believed, Setsubi seems to have taken to his status as a political fugitive like a fish to water. He moved furtively from place to place, always ahead of his pursuers. If Gladstone Mose conducted his curatorial work behind a desk at Kompol—perusing the album from cover to cover, reading insurgent publications for intelligence tidbits—the actors who went after Setsubi composed the album on the move. They scripted Setsubi's profile as he and they moved from place to place and across borders. They did not find him, but their search yielded a substantial police file whose content allows us to see how that search was conducted.

From Suspicion to Surveillance

On November 7, 1975, an unnamed police source gave his handlers the following information:

> I am reliably informed that the Maluti (Sotho) section under the leadership of Chief J. D. Moshesh and Chief N. Sibi have sent four boys to central Africa to train as terrorists. One of these boys is Sechaba Setsubi, whose father is principal of Haderberg Junior Secondary School. The intention is that these boys must train others as an underground army at Maluti to fight against the Transkei after independence. They (Maluti Sotho) have not given up the idea of pulling the Maluti area out of the Transkei. This underground army is meant to be one of a number of methods of fighting for their freedom. The Maluti Sothos are very vicious and wicked.

When the source gave this report, the Transkei was about a year away from becoming South Africa's first homeland. Founded on the fiction that South Africa was a multinational state or, to use apartheid-speak, a country of plural affairs, homelands were meant to serve as ethnic enclaves allowing each nation (defined by apartheid planners as a homogeneous ethnic group with a singular culture and language) to govern itself as it saw fit. In truth, homelands sought to nullify black South Africans as a political group, thereby obviating the need for political equality. To do that, the apartheid government peddled the fiction that, by granting homelands independence or self-governing status, it was merely recognizing facts on the ground. But, as the source's report shows, the Transkei (the most territorially contiguous of the homelands) was no ethnic monolith. Setsubi, for example, was ethnically Sotho but equally at home in both Sotho and Xhosa. In the Eastern Cape, as in most parts of Africa, ethnic identity was negotiated—not fixed. How one identified depended on various factors, some of them material but many not. Sharing borders with Lesotho to its northwest and Zulu-speaking areas to its north, the Transkei was a multiethnic territory with overlapping identities. The homeland policy threatened to freeze these identities. Not surprisingly, there was considerable discontent among the non-Xhosas when the apartheid government earmarked the Transkei for South Africa's first Xhosa homeland (there would be two in the end). They understood that the establishment of the Transkei as a Xhosa homeland would lead to the privileging of one ethnic identity over others in the region. The police source understood this. "I have every reason to believe this story and I would suggest that investigation be conducted on this immediately," the source said. "I know the Sothos would stop at nothing if they have decided on this."

The Security Police were certainly aware of the adverse implications of the homeland policy for ethnically diverse regions such as the Transkei. Captain Petzer of the Security Police in Umtata, the capital of the Transkei, put it simply: "The Basotho residents feel that their language and culture are discriminated against by the Transkei government." Petzer and the source did not once question the ethnic assumptions behind their conclusions. They took it for granted that Sothos were a monolithic group and that, as such, they all felt the same way about the Transkei. Tellingly, neither the source nor Petzer said anything about who abroad would give the fugitive young men military training. The ANC did not even merit a mention. Its vision of a unitary state founded on nonracial principles did not accord with South Africa's homeland policy. So they ignored the ANC.[8] But they worried about Setsubi and other young men leaving the country for military training abroad.

On November 10, 1975, the divisional commander of the Security Police Natal Division confirmed the initial suspicions that Setsubi had gone abroad for military training.[9] He sent a letter to his colleagues in Matatiele and Umtata asking them to open a file on Setsubi and find out as much as they could. They were also to compile a *geskiedenisverslag*—a history report—about Setsubi. To know Setsubi, the police had to tell his life story in their own words. They had to distill his biography in terms that made sense in their world of Bantus and non-whites. Constable van Vuuren, the Matatiele policeman who had stumbled upon the news of Setsubi's disappearance in the first place, duly delivered Setsubi's history report on November 18, 1975.[10] Van Vuuren's five-page report was more skeletal than historical. He had no idea what car Setsubi drove, for example, but noted that Setsubi "loves to dance."

As if to confirm what a phantom Setsubi was to the Security Police, Van Vuuren said: "Subject first came to the attention of this [the Matatiele Security Police] office when he disappeared." Far from giving the police a comprehensive account of Setsubi, Van Vuuren's report showed just how little the Security Police knew. But Van Vuuren had to give his colleagues in the Natal Division something. The Natal Division had also asked Matatiele and Umtata to provide a docket number from the Register of Charges Investigated (RCI)—ROM in Afrikaans—the monthly record of charges investigated at any police station. Once an investigation was completed and the charge office sergeant agreed that charges could be filed against a suspect, the investigation officer then added the case to the Register of Charges Accepted. By asking that Matatiele and the Transkei generate an RCI number for Setsubi, the Natal Division effectively turned Setsubi from a subject of suspicion to a subject of surveillance.

Even though the Security Police were fairly certain by November 1975 that Setsubi had left the country for military training abroad, it was not the charge against him of plotting terror that they wanted to see investigated. They were more interested in whether or not he had left the country with the permission of the state. This marked the beginning of Setsubi's life as the subject of a police file—with a biography constantly being written and rewritten by multiple authors.[11] On December 8, 1975, Major J. J. Diedericks, commanding officer of the Natal Division, informed the police commissioner that his division had opened an investigation into whether Setsubi had left the country without a valid passport.[12] "It would be appreciated," Diedericks instructed, "if a short statement could be obtained from the relevant department to prove that subject did not receive a passport." Diedericks wanted the police commissioner to ask the Department of the Interior, which was responsible for the issuance of passports, to say if Setsubi had a passport.

The police commissioner acted quickly on the request: two days after his receipt of Diedericks's letter, Lieutenant-Colonel H. W. Mc-Donald, stationed at Kompol, wrote to the secretary for Internal affairs asking for an affidavit on whether that department had issued a passport to Setsubi.[13] That same day, McDonald also wrote to the commanding officer of the South African Criminal Bureau asking for two certified copies of Setsubi's C26 card, four mug shots, and one set of fingerprints.[14] The bureau duly obliged. On January 30, 1976, Lieutenant G. van Rooyen, the officer in charge of the bureau, informed the police commissioner: "A provisional archive has been filed for this Bantu and appropriately endorsed."[15] Van Rooyen's letter included six mug shots, two C26 forms, and one set of fingerprints. On February 23, 1976, the Department of Internal Affairs announced that no passport had been issued in Setsubi's name.[16]

Fugitive Traces

The announcement by the Department of Internal Affairs confirmed Setsubi's status as a fugitive. However, the first direct mention of the Terrorist Album in connection with Setsubi does not come until two years later. On July 4, 1978, Lieutenant-Colonel G. N. Erasmus, commanding officer of the Natal Division, reported to Kompol and to his colleagues in Bloemfontein, in the Orange Free State, that Setsubi's wife had applied for political asylum in Lesotho.[17] "Subject is the wife of expatriate Cosmos," Erasmus wrote, referring them to "Setsubi (S4 / 42390), S77 in photo album." This is the first mention of Setsubi's place in the album, at 77. Erasmus's report shows the Security Police branding Setsubi with a number that not only fixes his race (S4) but also pegs him on the list of political fugitives. On October 22, 1978, captured insurgent Raymond Madonsela picked Setsubi out of the album.[18] Madonsela told his police interrogators that Setsubi was "currently in Lesotho. Also known as Charles. Received military training in Russia." In November 1978, the Security Police offered a much longer account of what Madonsela had told them about Setsubi.[19] Madonsela claimed to have received political instruction from Setsubi in Luanda, Angola, and "Madonsela also claims that [Setsubi] underwent training in Russia and is to be found in Lesotho." This was, for the Security Police, the first positive sighting of Setsubi since August 1975, when they had received information that he was in Mozambique. From early 1975 through 1978, Setsubi had moved between two continents and through at least five countries. According to Erasmus, Yvonne Setsubi had disappeared from her home in Matatiele on the night of May 8, 1978. She had resurfaced in Lesotho, where she had applied for political asylum on May 30, 1978. "We would like you to find out if [Setsubi] is in Lesotho," said Erasmus to his colleagues in Bloemfontein, Matatiele and Pretoria. "The possibility is that his wife has joined him."

To find out if Setsubi was indeed in Lesotho, the Security Police mobilized their informers and sources. A source codenamed FSS 280, whose information the Security Police graded B2 (meaning the source was "usually reliable" and their information "probably true"), reported as follows: "I have no record that such a person has applied for political asylum or being in Lesotho."[20] In his evaluation of source FSS 280, Sergeant G. T. M. Jooste of the Security Police in Ladybrand (on the border with Lesotho) made a notation: "This office is in possession of [Yvonne Setsubi's] application for political asylum in Lesotho, where she is currently. Other sources are being asked to try and identify [Setsubi]." Jooste's short report alerts us to the complicated relationship between South Africa's security agencies and United Nations bureaucracies in southern Africa. The South Africans infiltrated these agencies, especially the United Nations High Commission for Refugees, to keep track of South Africans seeking political asylum abroad.[21]

The Security Police also targeted regional airlines for infiltration. Dirk Coetzee was a policeman who defected to the ANC in 1989, after falling out with his colleagues in the Security Police. "Refugees from South Africa went to the UNHCR in Swaziland," he later recalled, referring to the United Nations High Commissioner for Refugees agency, "from where they were flown to Maputo with the Delta Airline . . . Major Nick van Rensburg [of the Security Police] required passenger lists of these refugees to keep the 'terrorist' files up to date."[22] Coetzee said the men who ran the airline were apartheid agents.[23] This was one way in which the South Africans kept track of individuals leaving the country without government permission. But South Africa's sixteen-hundred-mile boundary was so extensive that the police could not manage it all. Despite the intense police interest in them, individuals such as Yvonne Setsubi were still able to slip in and out of South Africa.

On December 18, 1978, a source codenamed NV. Z-1327 reported as follows to the Security Police: "I returned from Maseru on Friday 8th of December, 1978, after a week's investigation. It has become too diffi-cult to trace Sechaba Setsubi because he is not a known figure to all my friends, but what I can mention is that all refugees in Maseru are grouped at one place in a stand owned by one man; Motlatsi Thakale-koala, who is a communist. . . . When I was at the aerodrome on the 7th December 1978, there arrived six boys who were said to be coming from Soweto. They were sent down by Lesotho government from Qachasnek. How they came to Qachasnek nobody knows. I will try to find their names from Qachasnek airstrip." This was a written report, submitted by a source who not only had friends in Lesotho but was able to travel in and out of the country. Tellingly, the source submitted the report to the Matatiele office of the Security Police, suggesting that he or she knew Setsubi (whom he or she referred to by his home name, "Sechaba") from Matatiele. While it is not known who this source was, a few details are suggestive: This was a written report, in English, and with idiomatic expressions (like the dropping of the article before the term "Lesotho government") suggesting that the source was a reasonably well-educated person in possession of a valid passport. The timing of the source's visit to Lesotho also suggests that the source was a state functionary—possibly a teacher or other type of public servant—whose December trip would not have aroused suspicion among his or her friends in Lesotho (especially if they were fugitives). December is a big holiday month in southern Africa, when people tend to visit friends and relatives. The source might also have had a lot in common with insurgents such as Setsubi, making it possible for him or her to blend in with South African exiles or insurgents in Lesotho. Mark Orkin found, in a 1988 study of rationales for guerilla involvement among black South Africans, that the people who tended to become insurgents had a lot in common. In Orkin's summation, they were "not too poor to have expectations; educated sufficiently to be keenly disappointed by inequality in general and discrimination in particular; and therefore deeply enough involved in political effort to be massively affronted when this last recourse was summarily closed by the state in one way or another."[24] It is possible that, like Setsubi, who was a university graduate and the son of a headmaster, the source came from a background of some means, even if those means were limited by apartheid. But, for reasons known only to the source, he or she had chosen to spy for the Security Police. Why? Was it for money? Had he or she been compromised in some way and then forced to work for the Security Police? Or was the source a supporter of apartheid who needed no inducement to inform on friends?

What made the source, if he or she did share Setsubi's background, choose to work for the Security Police instead of the anti-apartheid movement? We can speculate but we cannot offer any definitive answers to the question of why some (black) South Africans chose to resist apartheid and others chose to collaborate. Neither choice was natural. We cannot even assume that the sources who informed on Setsubi had anything in common, beyond their all working for the Security

Police. For the Security Police, the only question worth asking was whether a source was reliable enough. It certainly helped to know what motivated each source to do what he or she did, but it did not matter as much as knowing that a source was in place. As Peter Gill points out, "The productivity of informers cannot be measured just in terms of their information-gathering potential. . . . the significance of informers is that their presence, or even suspicion of their presence, may be highly disruptive."[25]

On March 12, 1979, source FSS 280 (whom we first meet on December 13, 1978, informing the Security Police that there is no record in Lesotho of Setsubi applying for political asylum) and source FSS 151 sought to account for Setsubi's movements in Lesotho, in a circular synthesized into one report.[26] South African refugees, source FSS 151 wrote, "stay and work at different places in Maseru, Lesotho. Motlatsi Thakalekoala is not known to me." Source FSS 280 added, "I have no record of Motlatsi Thakalekoala being in Lesotho." Both accounts, which the Security Police graded B2, were follow-ups to information provided by source NV. Z-1327 on December 18, 1978. As Sergeant Jooste of the Security Police in Ladybrand said in his evaluation of the two accounts, "Nothing positive has come out about the refugees in Qachasnek. So far, this office knows nothing about South African refugees residing in Qachasnek, Maseru."

On their own, these two informer reports do nothing more than show how elusive Setsubi was and how little the Security Police knew, despite their much-vaunted and self-perpetuated reputation as the best in Africa.[27] Read outside of their closed circuit of confidentiality and secrecy, however, the reports are suggestive of what kinds of people informed for the Security Police. Take FSS 280. It is telling that his or her reports concern either asylum applications or the presence of people in Lesotho. This suggests that FSS 280 was a Lesotho bureaucrat or government official in a position to know who had applied for asylum and whether an individual was in the country. It would have made sense for the South Africans to target such a person for recruitment. Insurgents knew this, of course, and that is why Setsubi did not apply for asylum in Lesotho, even though that consigned him to living in the shadows and under the constant threat of deportation. His wife, Yvonne, on the other hand, applied for asylum because that made her status regular and allowed her to find a job.

On March 17, 1980, a source codenamed FSS 367 informed the Security Police in Ladybrand about the movements of Setsubi and Yvonne in Lesotho.[28] The source said that Setsubi first moved to Lesotho at the beginning of 1978 but did not apply for political asylum. Yvonne Setsubi applied for asylum in Lesotho in May 1978 and later found a teaching job at Life Secondary School in the Lesotho capital, Maseru. "During the night of December 31, 1978, and January 1, 1979, an unknown person shot Setsubi with a revolver," reported source FSS 367. "He was flown immediately to Maputo for treatment. He is currently receiving treatment at a hospital in Lusaka, Zambia. I suspect he is paralyzed to an extent. The validity of Nompumelelo Yvonne Setsubi's UN Convention Travel Document (CTD) NO. 0066 has been extended by a year." Commenting on the source's report, a Major C. L. Smith of the Security Police in Ladybrand said, "This office's other informants have not tracked Setsubi's movements in Lesotho before." Attached to this report was a UNHCR letter from Diarra Boubacar, the UNHCR representative in Lesotho, to O.T. Sefako, permanent secretary in Lesotho's Ministry of the Interior, asking that Yvonne Setsubi's UN travel document be extended and made valid for the "largest possible number of countries, including Zambia."[29] In it, Boubacar explains that "Mrs. Setsubi wishes to travel to Lusaka where her husband is undergoing therapy and rehabilitation following surgery in Maputo; and since her [UN Convention travel document] expired on April 29, 1979, it would be much appreciated if you extend its validity so as to enable her to join her husband." The UNHCR trail goes cold after this letter and we cannot know if Yvonne Setsubi was able to visit her husband in Zambia. We only know from the source that the Lesotho government extended her travel document by a year. But these unnamed sources were not the only actors to bring Setsubi closer to the police—to bring him within imaginative reach of the Security Police.

Guerilla Talk

On May 17, 1979, Sydney Skwadi Tshoma, an ANC guerilla who had been captured in the Eastern Transvaal the previous February, picked Setsubi out of the album during interrogation. According to the secret report accompanying Tshoma's positive identification, "Tshoma met Setsubi in 1976 in Moscow, where Setsubi was taking part in a military commander's course. Setsubi was in the third group of 20 [ANC members] to undergo the course. Setsubi left Moscow roughly during August 1976."[30] Tshoma was a singularly remarkable eyewitness to Setsubi's peregrinations. Tshoma had left South Africa illegally for Swaziland in July 1975. He had joined the Pan Africanist Congress, which had sent him to Benghazi, Libya, via Uganda, for military training. In February 1976, he had defected to the ANC after falling out with Pan Africanist Congress leaders.

In May 1976, the ANC had sent him for further military training in Moscow—where he had met Setsubi for the first time. Tshoma had served as a military instructor at ANC camps in Angola before being sent for military operations in South Africa. He was arrested there on February 8, 1979. Tshoma was one of many insurgents who would be used by the Security Police over the years to populate the album and associated documents with tidbits of information about Setsubi. On July 24, 1979, an ANC insurgent named James Daniel Mange also identified Setsubi in the album.[31] Mange said he had seen Setsubi in Luanda, Angola, in December 1976. Mange had left South Africa illegally for Botswana in October 1976 and had trained in Angola and the Soviet Union before being arrested by the Security Police in October 1979. As more insurgents came back into the country and the Security Police arrested many of them, Setsubi's file grew; various captured insurgents who knew him from exile told their interrogators about his whereabouts.

On January 14, 1980, the Security Police arrested Duckworth Gwaza Twalo.[32] His interrogators reported on May 7, 1980, that "He has identified [Setsubi] with the help of the photo-album." The interrogators' report added the information that "Twalo saw [Setsubi] for a while in Lesotho in 1977 / 8, but did not see him in 1979." In October 1980, Titus Maleka, arrested in February 1979, also identified Setsubi's mug shot in the album.[33] Maleka said he had also first met Setsubi in Russia in 1976 while both were undergoing military training and that, after that, he had seen him at an ANC camp in Angola in 1977. On April 7, 1981, an arrested insurgent named Mbundu told his interrogators the following about Setsubi: "In 1977 he was in Benguela [Angola]. In 1979 he was in Lilane, Zambia, where he was delivering food to the [ANC] residences. At the time, he was employed as a driver and was driving a beige Landcruiser. In 1980, he was still in Zambia, still employed in the same role."

Mbundu had been arrested in Johannesburg on October 26, 1980, while on a mission to reconnoiter fuel installations for possible sabotage.[34] On July 9, 1982, Jerry Semano Mosololi, arrested in 1981 and executed by the apartheid government in 1983 for offenses related to terrorism, also drew on the album to give the following account of Setsubi: "In March 1977, he was in Benguela, he had already received training and also possibly had attended a training course in the Soviet Union. Mosololi left him in Benguela in May 1977, he [Setsubi] was at that stage a company commissar. He has gold fillings in his top teeth and at that time had a heavy beard."[35]

On March 8, 1983, Oscar Nkosinathi Ntombela, arrested sometime in 1982, had more information to share (fig. 4.1).

On their own, these guerilla identifications amounted to nothing more than a pile of details: Setsubi is in Angola, Lesotho, Russia, Zambia; he drives a beige Landcruiser, with which he delivers food to ANC residences in Zambia; "he has gold fillings in his top teeth," says Mosololi about his encounters with Setsubi in Angola, in 1977, "and at that time had a heavy beard." Notice, however, the details in Ntombela's account of his encounters with Setsubi. In addition to the usual story about how he knows Setsubi and where he met him, Ntombela also tells the following story: "Sustained gunshot wounds after a squabble with Mbali. He was consequently sent to the G.D.R. [German Democratic Republic] for treatment. He left Maputo in company of the GDR president who had been visiting Mozambique during 1979."

```
SETSUBI, S A                                          S4/42390
MK = CHARLES NTAYI. First seen by NTOMBELA during 1977    NATAL (TS;
at Benguela in Angola. He had already undergone military
training under the ANC banner in the USSR. Next seen
during 1978 in Maseru in Lesotho. Sustained gunshot
wounds after a squabble with MBALI (M.347 - S4/34257 supra).
He was consequently sent to the GDR for treatment. He
left Maputo in company of the GDR president who had been
visiting Mocambique during 1979. CHARLES NTAYI periodically
visits his spouse in Lesotho. During 1982 he was based in
Lusaka, Zambia where he was elevated to the Revolutionary
Council. His wife is S.350 - S4/5       .
```

FIGURE 4.1 Snippet of a report by the insurgent Ntombela. Courtesy of National Archives and Records Service of South Africa.

Ntombela's story adds flesh to the account given by source FSS 367 in March 1980. Recall that the source reported on Setsubi being shot with a revolver by an unknown assailant on New Year's Eve in 1979 and being paralyzed as a result of the attack. Ntombela not only confirmed the source's information about the shooting but gave details that allowed the Security Police to get a better sense of what happened. It would appear from Ntombela's report that Setsubi's attacker, Mbali, was also a member of the ANC.

That is how the Security Police made their sources speak to captured insurgents. It was not a direct conversation, to be sure, and it likely involved torture. Nor was it an open dialogue involving captured insurgents, sources, and the police. The police's obsession with secrecy would not have allowed that. But to confirm the veracity of certain information, or to fill in details missing from their sources' reports, the police needed both captured insurgents and their sources. Thanks to source FSS 367, the Security Police knew that Setsubi had been shot. But it was only when they put the album before Ntombela that they were able to get more details about Setsubi's shooting. The album served as a spur to memory, allowing Ntombela to recall events that had happened three years before his arrest. Through the album, Ntombela was able not only to identify Setsubi but also to pick out his assailant. We know this because embedded in Ntombela's description of Setsubi are the name of his attacker and these numbers: M.347—S4 / 34257. The last number (S4 / 34257) meant that the attacker was also the subject of a police file. His mug shot was also in the album. Ntombela likely gave his interrogators information about the attacker, too. But his account of Setsubi is the most detailed we have from a captured insurgent. None of the reports that came after Ntombela's arrest matched the detail found in his account. In December 1983, nine months after Ntombela gave his statement, Vincent Nyasulu told his interrogators the following about

Setsubi's mug shot: "[Setsubi] came to Benguela [Angola] from Russia and was in Zambia by the end of 1978."[36] Collin Vikelisizwe Khumalo, kidnapped by the Security Police from a jail in Swaziland in 1984, also had very little to say about Setsubi, other than to point out where they had crossed paths (in Angola, Russia, and Zambia).[37] It is possible that Ntombela developed a better rapport with his interrogators, which is why he gave the police more detail. It is also likely that he knew Setsubi better than the others did.

The Ephemeral Target

In July 1984, an unregistered source (that is, one who had no assigned code and informed for the police only occasionally) reported that Setsubi's brother Lesibo Remigius Setsubi had traveled to Botswana in June 1984 for a funeral and then visited his parents in Matatiele afterwards. The Security Police wondered if this meant that Setsubi had died in exile. They set the source to work. The source asked Lesibo who among the Setsubis had died and Lesibo answered that his "brother, who was abroad, had died. He [Lesibo] also told the source that his brother had died during a shootout between the Swaziland Police and members of the ANC."[38] This sent the Security Police scrambling. In August 1984, an unregistered police source (likely the same person as before) reported on the death of another brother to Setsubi, Victor Tohlang Setsubi, who had been stabbed to death in April of that year.[39]

The source reported that Lesibo Remigius Setsubi had attended the funeral. But while the news about Victor's death and the funeral was certainly true, the police gave it a C3 grading, evidently considering the source to be only "fairly reliable" and the information only "possibly true." In their commentary on the source's report, the police wrote, "The information that Lesibo Setsubi went to Botswana to attend the funeral of his brother Sechaba Setsubi cannot be confirmed." This, it turned out, would not be the last time the police had to deal with false reports about Setsubi's death. In September 1984, Captain Christo Deetlefts of the Security Police in Ermelo, Eastern Transvaal, reported the following information from a source codenamed OTV.G. 93: "Source could not get confirmation that [Setsubi] has been shot dead. Mtunzi Wanner Luxomo is the only ANC member shot dead by the Swaziland Police."[40]

It would be a mistake to conclude from the above that the search for Setsubi was a haphazard venture led by disinterested policemen and sources of varying reliability. There was a personal element to the search. Family members come in and out of this story; some relatives may have been police sources. There were familial connections that exposed many individuals to the risk of exposure and arrest. On February 17, 1984, the Security Police in Northern Natal wrote to their colleagues in the Natal Division and at headquarters in Pretoria to relay information received from a source codenamed NN. G304.[41] According to NN. G304, Setsubi's sister Lilian Setsubi (a student nurse) had asked the source if she could rent the source's house for a party celebrating her successful conclusion of an exam. Lilian told the source that she would like to invite her fugitive brother in Lesotho "but did not know how to get in touch with him. However, she said that two of her brothers are members of the South African Police in Matatiele and that one of them usually helps. She allegedly told the source's wife that she had received a congratulations card from her sister-in-law [Yvonne Setsubi]." Commenting on the source's information, a policeman remarked: "It is doubtful whether S. A. Setsubi will make his appearance here—nevertheless source remains on alert. Since she did not say what her brother was helping with, the deduction is that he might act as an intermediary. It can also be that she means something else by 'help.'" Lilian Setsubi's conversation with the source and his wife posed a threat to the Setsubis and their relatives. Were there Setsubis in the police force and were they helping Setsubi evade capture? On March 7, 1984, Detective Warrant Officer (DWO) Kakole of the Security Police in Matatiele submitted a report graded A1, meaning that the source was "completely reliable" and the information "confirmed by other independent and reliable sources."[42]

The report, titled "Possible Assistance to Terrorist S.A. Setsubi and His Wife N. Y. Setsubi by Members of the Security Police in Matatiele," gave a list of Setsubi's four siblings, starting with his sister Lilian. Kakole said: "The information that Black female Lilian Setsubi's two brothers are members of the South African Police stationed at Matatiele is incorrect." It was left to Kakole's commanding officer, Lieutenant Hendrikz, to explain why this information was incorrect. Hendrikz said: "DWO Kakole, who is a member of this Branch, knows this family well. He is related to the family as follows: The grandmother of S.A. Setsubi . . . is a sister to the mother of DWO Kakole. . . . There are no other known members of the South African Police at Matatiele who are in any way related to the Setsubis." As Setsubi's cousin, Kakole had to address source NN. G304's claims about Lilian. He had to show that no member of the Setsubi family was working with insurgents. Kakole's response must have worked, because we find him in November 1987 still on his cousin's trail. In a report dated November 10, 1987, Kakole relayed information from a colleague in the Transkei Security Police, whose source had spotted Setsubi and a nephew named Motlatsi Kakole at a café in Qachasnek in Lesotho.[43] The Transkei policeman had told Kakole, "My informer is a Lesotho citizen who lives in Qachasnek. My informer claims that he knows the two men very well." Warrant Officer Kakole added that another source (this one unregistered and graded C3) had also spotted Setsubi at the café in Qachasnek. This source knew Setsubi and in fact spoke to him. The last report we have from Kakole is dated December 9, 1987, and in it he relays information from an unregistered source (graded C3) about five members of the Setsubi family crossing the border from Lesotho into the Transkei.[44] Kakole proceeds to describe the five: Setsubi's parents, Ernest and Innocentia Setsubi; Setsubi's sister, Eugenia; and Setsubi's two daughters.

Kakole said the source's information confirmed reports that Setsubi's parents had taken their grandchildren to visit their parents in Lusaka, Zambia. Kakole would not have needed the album in his pursuit of Setsubi. He knew what his cousin looked like. Setsubi was family. They knew each other. But this does not mean that, for Kakole, the search for Setsubi was necessarily personal. Understanding the personal connection, however, between Kakole and Setsubi—between the hunter and the hunted—does help us put the album in perspective. The album was not the be-all and end-all of the police hunt for insurgents; it was of limited utility. One implication is that scholars of contemporary South African history must rethink their approaches to apartheid bureaucracies and violence. Thinking of apartheid South Africa's counterinsurgency campaigns only in terms of efficiency and technocratic prowess blinds us to the complex ways in which apartheid and the struggle against it were messy affairs, in which family and race did not necessarily determine individual loyalties.

If anything, the story of Setsubi speaks of the failure of the Security Police to frame and to apprehend him. In fact, the Security Police never did catch Setsubi. He died in March 2018, aged seventy, having come back to South Africa following the unbanning of the ANC in 1990.[45] I received the file that constitutes this chapter shortly after Setsubi died— meaning that I was not able to ask him about its contents. I was not able to speak to him about what it meant to be hunted by one's own relatives. Setsubi comes to us in these pages only through the eyes of his hunters. The following chapters offer a different perspective, however, looking at the album through the eyes of some of those framed within its pages. What did it mean to have one's mug shot placed in the album and be branded a terrorist? How do individuals understand how they came to be in the Terrorist Album? Those are the questions we will take up next.

FIVE

The Petty State

"IT'S VERY NOTICEABLE to me that these are mug shots," said Paula Ensor, gazing at her own mug shot alongside others in the Terrorist Album (fig. 5.1). "I mean, look how sullen everyone looks. Even this picture of mine, I'm not smiling, and it's very unusual for me to be in a photo where I'm not smiling."[1]

Ensor had her photograph taken in 1971 for a passport application, which the government then rejected. She was twenty. This chapter draws on Ensor's declassified file from the apartheid Ministry of Justice to retrace the bureaucratic and political steps that led to her inclusion in the album—and to expose the lengths to which the apartheid government went to frame dissent. The file covers the years 1971 to 1990, a period in which Ensor was active in the anti-apartheid movement as an undergraduate student at the University of Natal, then as a postgraduate student at the University of Cape Town (UCT), as a leader of the National Union of South African Students (NUSAS), and, finally, as an exiled academic and activist in Botswana and Britain. Like thousands

328

FIGURE 5.1 Mug shot of Paula Ensor in the Terrorist Album. Courtesy of National Archives & Records Service of South Africa.

of other exiles whose portraits ended up in the album, Ensor earned her entry by leaving South Africa illegally—that is, without the passport the government refused to give her. Throughout her opposition to apartheid Ensor did not once take up arms, yet she ended up in the album—a citizen of nowhere who spent years traveling on a United Nations passport because the country of her birth would not give her one. Looking at Ensor's mug shot with her and reading her declassified file over her shoulder, we are able to get a sense of how various branches of the apartheid state—from magistrates, the Security Police and the intelligence agencies, to the Minister of Justice—worked in concert to render Ensor both stateless and a terrorist.

We are able to see the bureaucratic process that prevented Ensor from obtaining a passport and branded her a terrorist because, like authoritarian states everywhere, the apartheid state could not stop talking about itself. Like the Soviet edifice studied by Stephen Kotkin,

South Africa "produced an almost endless flow of words about what it was trying to do, why, how, and with what results."[2] This flow has been preserved in a remarkable collection of documents, the only part of the apartheid security archive that seems to have emerged intact from the "paper Auschwitz" to which apartheid-era records were subjected, especially between 1990 and 1993.[3] The collection, from which Ensor's file was drawn, belonged to the Department of Justice's Security Legislation Directorate.[4] The department established the directorate in 1982 to administer all aspects of security legislation. The directorate replaced the Internal Security Division, which was itself a replacement for an ad hoc arrangement going back to 1949 whereby various individuals in the Department of Justice handled legal matters related to state security. The directorate administered the Suppression of Communism Act, the Terrorism Act, the Internal Security Act, the Affected Organizations Act, the Unlawful Organizations Act, and the Public Safety Act. The directorate decided, by way of recommendations to the ministers of Justice and of Law and Order, whether an individual or an organization should be banned; whether a public meeting should be permitted, whether an individual should be restricted, and whether an individual should receive a passport. Because of its small size and its location within one department, the directorate kept its records in one strong room and, for some reason, ignored a 1993 government instruction to destroy classified records.

When the directorate ceased operation in 1991 it left among the records in its collection case files on about 8000 individuals. These cover the period 1949 to 1991. There are also files on organizations and publications spanning the period 1920 to 1991, as well as administrative reports, policy documents, and correspondence. The personal files and the correspondence are valuable to affected individuals and scholars because, through them, we are able to recreate official conversations and lines of reasoning between various state departments. We are able, for example, to get a sense of what the Bureau of State Security (BOSS) thought about Ensor even though we have no access to the BOSS records themselves, as they were part of the forty-four-ton archive destroyed in the early 1990s by the National Intelligence Service (the successor to BOSS).[5] Because apartheid South Africa took itself seriously as a country of laws, its bureaucracy produced an excess of paper that ultimately it could not control. There is no better illustration of this than the directorate's collection of records. While the intelligence service, the military, and the Security Police purged their archives in the 1990s, traces of what these three agencies did and thought remain in the directorate's archive. This does not mean that we can subject these traces to positivist readings, expecting them to tell us what actually happened. But by reading Ensor's file, we can do more than read it against the grain. We can read it back into its historical context, thereby avoiding the mistake of taking its distortions for granted. As Katherine Verdery reminds us, security files work by reducing complexity to simplicity and by degrading the multiple voices and meanings in a person's life to such an extent that only one interpretation of a targeted person's actions is possible: "the target's identification as an enemy."[6]

By moving back and forth between Ensor and her file, we can trouble the neat story that various government agencies told one another about how she became an enemy of the state. We can, in other words, read the file against itself. By denying the file pride of place as a source in this chapter, we can also call attention to the taint that marks it, even as we use it to get some sense of how the apartheid security apparatus worked. As this chapter will show, the file did more than mark Ensor as an enemy of the state. It also slandered her and violated her privacy—all the more to justify government's decision to place her beyond the legal and political pale. The various agencies behind the decision to deny Ensor a passport and to brand her a terrorist needed reasons to explain why a twenty-year-old should be treated in the way that Ensor was. If security files produce that which they seek to surveil—namely, the enemy of the state—then what does Ensor's file tell us about how the state rendered her an enemy? How did the state come to that decision? Let us begin with Ensor's version of events before turning to the file. The immediate cause of Ensor's inclusion in the album was her flight to exile in May 1976. Ensor explained:

> I was banned in February '73. I carried on with the activities that I had been engaged with up until that time, which had increasingly shifted away from student activism towards work in the black labor movement. Although banned, I continued to produce materials for worker education, and consulted regularly with activists who were in the process of setting up the Western Province Workers' Advice Bureau. I was married at the time to Rob Petersen, who was an advocate at the Cape Bar. We were both involved in this work, but became increasingly frustrated by the lack of political leadership in the country. The ANC and SACP had very little active presence in the country at this time, and the Black Consciousness Movement had made little if any impact on workers. It was this frustration, and a desire to find a political home, that was the major reason we left South Africa. I didn't have a passport but he did. So the idea was that I would fly in disguise to Johannesburg and he would assist me to the Botswana border and collect me on the other side.[7]

Using the Suppression of Communism Act, Justice Minister Petrus Pelser banned Ensor, together with seven other leaders of NUSAS, for five years on February 26, 1973. By the terms of the ban, Ensor had to stay within the magisterial districts of the Cape and Wynberg, meaning she could not leave Cape Town without permission. She could not be on the premises of any educational institution; she could not be in any building associated with NUSAS; she could not associate with any academic or student grouping; she could not go to any factory or harbor, and she could not visit any area defined by law as belonging to Africans, Coloreds, and Indians. She could not be in the company of more than one other person at a time. Pelser set these restrictions to expire on March 31, 1978. Ensor told me:

> The airport was outside the magisterial area. I purchased a blonde wig and I flew to Johannesburg. Rob picked me up from the airport and we drove to the border. Neither of us had any knowledge at all of the terrain in that area so we looked at a road ordnance map and found a place where the road on the South African side and the road on the Botswana side came fairly close together. It was pretty hit and miss, actually. He dropped me off on the South African side at about midnight, one o'clock in the morning, and I walked from there. It was pitch dark . . . I could not see my feet, nor could I see where I was walking. Although I had a torch, I was afraid to use it because it could draw attention to me. I struggled for hours through what I think was farmland, through patches of very long grass and thickets of acacia bush, until I reached the outskirts of Ramotswa. Things didn't quite work out as planned . . . we didn't get the positioning correct in terms of where I would end up and where we were going to meet . . . but I managed to hitch a lift . . . and he picked me up on the other end. That's how I did it.[8]

Ensor applied for refugee status in Botswana and for a British visa, which took ten weeks to arrive. She and her husband then flew to London, where they worked for the South African Congress of Trade Unions, which had moved its operations to London after the South African government crippled its local operations in December 1962 with the arrest and harassment of its leaders. It did not take the Security Police long to learn that Ensor had left. On May 13, 1976, the *Rand Daily Mail,* an anti-apartheid newspaper, trumpeted the news of Ensor's escape with a story headlined: "Pair flee South Africa 'until it changes.'" The following day, a police spokesman told the pro-apartheid newspaper *Die Burger:* "We are investigating the matter, as Mrs. Petersen [Ensor's married name at the time] has violated her restriction order."[9] This is when Ensor's mug shot is most likely to have been added to the album.

The Bureaucratic Eye

On May 19, 1976, the Security Police informed the Secretary of Justice that Ensor and her husband had indeed left South Africa. By now the police had confirmed that Ensor was not only in exile but involved in the anti-apartheid movement. On March 8, 1978, the Security Police recommended to the Secretary of Justice that restrictions barring Ensor from being quoted in the media be kept in place. The police were anticipating the formal expiry of Ensor's ban at the end March 31, 1978. The police said Ensor was engaged in exile in political and trade union activities "against the Republic of South Africa."[10] To the Security Police and the intelligence service, Ensor had moved from being a banned person to being officially an enemy of the state. The police did not want her voice in the media. They wanted to ensure that Ensor could not speak on her own terms. They feared Ensor's voice. In fact, it was precisely because she was articulate that the police moved against her in the first place. They cited her powerful voice and oratorical skills as one reason why she was denied a passport in 1971 and was banned in 1973.

Let us turn now to those contents of Ensor's file that speak actively in the voice of the state. We start with a secret memorandum drafted by BOSS on February 23, 1973, following an order by Prime Minister John Vorster that Ensor and seven other leaders of NUSAS be banned as their "activities are such that they promote the realization of the aims of communism."[11] Justice Minister Petrus Pelser banned Ensor three days after receiving the memorandum. The document, signed by BOSS's secretary of security information, covered the years 1968 to 1973 in Ensor's life. BOSS prepared it to lay the ground for the five-year banning order imposed on Ensor on February 26, 1973. The document, which claimed to be the result of an investigation, mixed the personal with the political and wove these into a rope to hang Ensor. According to the eleven-page note, Ensor first attracted the attention of the state in April 1967 when she attended a six-day seminar hosted by NUSAS in the Natal city of Pietermaritzburg.[12] Ensor matriculated from Durban Girls' High School in 1968 with six distinctions, making her one of the top three high school students in Natal. At school, she had been a prefect and house captain. She enrolled at the University of Natal in February 1969 and ran for the Students' Representative Council towards the end of that year. Her election manifesto struck a rebellious note: "I believe that it is only possible for a University to fulfil its functions if it remains unhindered and unrestrained by Government interference. I thus firmly uphold the principles of University Autonomy and Academic Freedom. I am an active member of NUSAS and firmly uphold the ideals for which it stands." The BOSS memorandum noted that Ensor attended NUSAS's forty-fifth annual congress in Cape Town from July 6 to 14, 1969. Interspersed within this timeline were details that, on their own, did not amount to much. But strung together into a narrative, they told a story intended to mark Ensor as politically and socially deviant. "According to information obtained by the Security

Police from a delicate source," the memorandum said, "Ensor spent the night of 14–15 May 1969 at the home of Colleen Crawford in Johannesburg. (Colleen Crawford is a member of the alleged Communist cell in Johannesburg.)" On February 2, 1970, another delicate source told the police that Ensor met Toppy Mtimkulu, president of the (black) Students' Representative Council at the University of Natal. On February 20, 1970, Ensor met Neville Curtis, national president of NUSAS, and the two "attended mixed parties and receptions."[13]

The memorandum reported that on March 6, 1970, Ensor visited Steve Biko, a student at the University of Natal at the time, in his room.[14] The memorandum continued: "On the evening of 8 March 1970, Ensor and a number of leftist white and non-white students attended an event at the home of Janine Schmahman. . . . Alcohol flowed freely and there was free intermingling. Ensor danced with Steve Biko and it was apparent that they were intimately involved." On August 24, 1970, Ensor "mingled freely with the non-white guests" at a multiracial event. In September 1970 Ensor and Paul Pretorius, a fellow NUSAS activist, arranged multiracial soccer and rugby matches involving students from the university's segregated campuses. The report offered the following description of Ensor:

> She is fanatical, egotistical and very dangerous. A real agitator among the non-whites. Enjoys openly defying people, for example, sitting in the streets of Stellenbosch holding hands with non-whites from the [NUSAS] seminar. She continuously propagates violence and threatens to turn violent herself. She is a bit of a nymphomaniac (man-mad) and will easily portray herself as a martyr. She is highly intelligent, a good orator and a major advocate of women's liberation, which she tries to express in her everyday life. She swears like a sailor and believes personal

incitement among non-whites is essential. She classifies herself as an instigator.

I quote this slanderous description at length to show what information BOSS, the Security Police, and the Minister of Justice used to ban Ensor. Although a committed activist, Ensor's biggest crime seems to have been her mingling with people of other races. By befriending black people, dancing with them, playing sports with them, and engaging in political activities with them, she defied apartheid in ways both simple and profound. Not only did Ensor defy apartheid in her personal life, she did the same in her political life: "At the time of the banning," she told me, "I had become involved in the incipient black labor movement, and the restrictions on my ability to enter African townships, the ban on my doing any educational or publication work, or to be with more than one person at a time, was very constraining. I did it anyway—I produced materials for workers education, and had weekly meetings with worker leaders, but it all had to be organized under the Security Police radar."[15] That made her dangerous. She did not know her place in South Africa's pigmentocracy. She refused to know it. It did not help matters that she was a feminist—a word that was, in the eyes of apartheid's security services, synonymous with communist. In fact, the police noted Ensor's attitude to race as early as 1971 in a secret letter, dated February 19, proposing that she be warned officially about her social and political activities. The commissioner of police said that "along with the fact that she devotes her attention to non-white students in particular and is herself pro-black, it is recommended that she be summonsed to appear before a magistrate . . . to be warned to refrain from engaging in activities intended to promote the achievement of one or more of the aims of communism."[16]

Ensor was twenty-two when BOSS presented its memorandum to the Justice Minister, setting in train the machinations that would lead to her banning in February 1973. Even though the file was redacted and passages scrubbed out, Ensor was able to draw a number of conclusions from it. She could tell, for example, that BOSS and the Security Police had informers in the Alan Taylor Residence, the dormitory for black students at the University of Natal where Steve Biko stayed. When I asked Ensor if she could identify the individuals who informed on her, she said, "I can tell that there must have been somebody in Alan Taylor residence who was a security policeman and [at] their parties, at the social events that I went to there, who was providing reports. But I can't pinpoint who, you can see . . . it's redacted all the way but I was able to work out some of it."[17]

> Are you able to say who some of these informers might have been?
> I knew that Eckie Eckhart was working for the Security Police.[18]
>> He confessed after I was banned, after a number of us were banned. He confessed to that. But there are others that I would not be able to identify. I haven't made a very close study, but when I got these [the reports in her file] I scrutinized them quite carefully . . .

> Were there any surprises for you when you read your file?
> One surprise was that they obviously hated me. The fact that [they claim] I'm an egotist . . . "she's a fanatic, egotistical and very dangerous—*n regte opryer*," a proper agitator, among non-blankes . . . she is openly provocative, for example . . . and holds hands with non-whites . . .

> Was that provocative in the '60s and '70s?
> . . . Something about me being a martyr, [a good orator and a major advocate] of the women's liberation movement and tries to live it out, and there's a follow-on from this, which I

was deeply offended by . . . they describe me as a nympho-maniac. The fact that I was a liberated woman, they were unable to countenance within their worldview, so I had to be a nymphomaniac. I mean there is not a shred of evidence here. Apart from one person who they keep circling around, there is no evidence whatsoever for that claim in terms of my sexual behavior and I know in terms of my own lifestyle that that certainly wasn't the case. This was written in 1971 so I was twenty. This was written to the minister to moti-vate for me to be warned that if I carried on with my activi-ties I would be banned. It says at the end, and my Afrikaans is not that good, that I am still very young, "she is undoubt-edly busy undermining, and if she carries on in her present steps there would clearly need to be action taken against her, but she is still young . . . and probably a warning will have the desired outcome." I think that's what it means.

Ensor had certainly been warned. On March 15, 1971, the secretary of justice had ordered M.E. Goodhead, the magistrate for Durban, "to administer to Miss Margaret Paula Ensor . . . a warning to refrain from engaging in activities calculated to further the achievement of any of the objects of communism."[19] The order included what must have been an early draft of the BOSS memorandum issued in February 1973 in sup-port of Ensor's ban. Goodhead summonsed Ensor to his office on March 26, 1971. He warned Ensor, accompanied by a lawyer, to refrain from taking part in activities the government considered communist. In a report sent to the Secretary of Justice after his meeting with Ensor, Goodhead said: "I had intended reading to her the full definition of 'communism' but when she informed me that since receiving my letter she had read both section 10 [of the Suppression of Communism Act] and the definition of 'communism,' I did not read the definition to her but drew her attention to the wideness of the definition."[20] Goodhead went on to say that he found Ensor an impressive and intelligent young woman. "There was nothing to suggest hostility or aggressiveness on her part and she gave the impression of being genuine and sincere when she said that she was at a loss to know what activities of hers were in question." Ensor was not the only one confused about what aspect of her work with the avowedly liberal NUSAS might qualify as communist. Francis Stock, the vice-chancellor and principal of the University of Natal, wrote to the minister of justice on March 31, 1971, to express his concern about the warning issued to Ensor. Stock said the university had found no evidence to support claims that Ensor had been engaged in communist activities on campus. Stock said that, while Ensor was active in NUSAS, her conduct was above "reproach and could not be interpreted in any way as subversive."[21] Stock went on: "I am, however, particularly concerned that as the chief administrator of this University I should be unaware of behavior so prejudicial to good order as to necessitate a warning and the threat of banning. I have no personal powers of investigation, but if I am to maintain order in the University it is imperative that I should be aware of all potential threats to disrupt it." Stock asked that the Minister give reasons for the warning to Ensor and to say if the warning concerned activities on or off campus. Stock was effectively calling the government's bluff.

He wanted the minister of justice to say what evidence he had for his claim that Ensor was a communist. The gambit failed. In a letter dated May 28, 1971, O. A. Meyer, the head of ministerial services in the Ministry of Justice, said, "I wish to inform you that the Minister acted upon reliable information about Miss Ensor's activities when he caused the warning to be issued. Some of this information is of a personal nature. Quite apart from security reasons the Minister considers that it will be wrong for him to go scandal-mongering to university principals about their students, to employers about their workers, to parents about their children and to bishops about their flocks. To assist you in your task to maintain order in the University . . . the Minister would suggest that you arrange a consultation with the Head of the Security Police about methods used by communist agents to infiltrate students organizations and to influence young susceptible minds."[22] In one move, Meyer patronizingly dismissed Stock while casting aspersions on Ensor. These aspersions—whose revelation would amount to "scandal-mongering," Meyer said—became the lens through which the apartheid state viewed Ensor. The state cast these slurs on Ensor every chance it got. For example, as a prelude to banning Ensor and the other NUSAS leaders in February 1973, the government set up a commission of inquiry, chaired by member of parliament Alwyn Schlebusch, in 1972 to look into the activities of NUSAS, the University Christian Movement, the Christian Institute, and the South African Institute of Race Relations. Called the Schlebusch Commission, the inquiry examined the activities, organization, and international funding of these four groups. The idea was to curtail their activities by starving them of overseas funding. Ensor was among the NUSAS representatives who appeared before the commission.

Like other agencies of the state, the commission sought to brand Ensor as both politically and sexually deviant. Ensor knew from the questions to which she was subjected by the commission—not to mention the denial of her passport application in 1971—that the state had her in its sights. In her words:

> I know from the interview that I had with the Schlebusch commission what some of their concerns were. . . . They referred to activities that I was involved in in my first three weeks of university. In the Security Police [records] subsequent to this [her file],

they say that the first time they noticed me was at a seminar at Redacres in April of 1969. But it is clear from these files that I was noticed earlier than this. In my first few weeks at university in 1969 I participated in the freshers' reception, two weeks of orientation. As part of this the organizers staged a debate on the topic that living in sin was preferable to marriage. I'd been at university for, like, two weeks and I was asked to argue that living in sin was preferable to marriage. They [the Security Police] could remember that. The Schlebusch commission questioned me about this. They asked me about the debate.[23] I think that's where the nymphomaniac [slur] comes from.

Here is Ensor being asked by the commission about her friendship with Steve Biko.

> COMMISSION: Miss Ensor, to what extent were you influenced in your views by people within SASO [South African Students' Organization]? I will start off with a man by the name of Steve Biko. I think that is how you pronounce his name.
> ENSOR: Yes.
>
> COMMISSION: Do you have a particular contact with him?
> ENSOR: I know him quite well, yes.
>
> COMMISSION: How well do you know him?
> ENSOR: He's a very good friend of mine.
>
> COMMISSION: And you see him often?
> ENSOR: I used to see him quite often. I don't see him anymore.
>
> COMMISSION: At the time when SASO was in its, when it was emerging?
> ENSOR: SASO was emerging when I was still at school.

COMMISSION: Yes, but when it was becoming strong, when it dissociated itself from NUSAS, when it broke away?

ENSOR: I first met Steve Biko in about August / September of 1969 and I really only got to know him the following year, the beginning of the following year. He had an influence on my thinking in the sense that he, you know, articulated certain viewpoints that were held by Black students. And I was made to realize that this type of thinking was a reality and that white students had to respond to it in some sort of way.

COMMISSION: So you would say that he influenced you to a very, he influenced you extensively?

ENSOR: He influenced me in the sense that he challenged many of my assumptions.

COMMISSION: Miss Ensor, tell me, has Steve Biko been your boyfriend?

ENSOR: No.

COMMISSION: Are you sure of that?

ENSOR: I am very, very close to him. I am very close to him and I am very, very fond of him. I think at one time there might have been a feeling—there was a feeling on my part that I would like to get closer to him, but I mean, it would have been politically unwise and he is married and I don't think he wanted it particularly.

The Police Client

Within five years, Ensor moved from being one of the brightest high school students in South Africa to being a banned person. The government secretly added her name to the "passport restriction list" in September 1970, rejected her application for a passport in January 1971, summonsed her to a magistrate's office for an official warning in March 1971, and, finally, banned her for five years in February 1973. In the three years between her banning and escape from South Africa, Ensor lived like a prisoner, locked within a magisterial district and barred from going anywhere near a university campus. There is nothing in Ensor's file to suggest that the government used the banning order to get rid of her; they merely threatened to act against her should she continue undermining apartheid. The government believed that the banning order would serve as a deterrent and bar Ensor from continued involvement in the student and labor movement. She continued her activism. Still, the order was so restrictive that it is a surprise that Ensor put up with it for three years before resolving to go into exile. It is possible that the security establishment saw exile as a useful way to get rid of political opponents—individuals the state saw as nuisances but could not be bothered to prosecute. But making life for banned individuals so suffocating that they had no choice but to leave the country only swelled the ranks of the anti-apartheid movement, leading to yet another entry in the album. In trying to manage opposition to apartheid, the state made its own enemies. One reason for this was structural: the petty and the grand went together in apartheid. That is, there was a fine line between crime and political opposition, and the state saw to it that people crossed that line all the time. Put another way, the police criminalized political opposition while neglecting real crimes in the country, especially in the black areas. This led to what some scholars described as the criminalization of politics and the politicization of crime. However, even though apartheid's security agencies drove Ensor to exile, we should not accord them too much power. As Ensor told me, "A more compelling factor was the search for a fresh political program and leadership, given the absence at the time of an active ANC and SACP presence on the ground in South Africa."[24]

On April 2, 1973, about a month after her banning, Ensor asked the chief magistrate of Cape Town for an exemption to the legal provision barring her from attending university. Ensor, who had obtained a BA with honors in Economics at UCT in 1972, wanted to pursue a Master's in Economics at the same institution. Ensor told the magistrate that she planned to pursue a "socio-economic study of the position of women in the labor market, with particular reference to the garment industry." Sheila van der Horst, a world-renowned labor economist, had agreed to supervise the thesis. Ensor said, "Professor van der Horst has agreed to supervise my thesis off campus so the pursuance of my studies in itself will not necessitate my presence on campus. I must stress the importance of my being able to register at UCT, for no other university in South Africa is known to be able to provide the staff facilities to give me the necessary specialized assistance (i.e. in the field of labor economics.)"[25]

Ensor wanted two exemptions from her banning order. The first was an exemption from the rule prohibiting her, as a banned person, from publishing. That would be required, after all, of her thesis. The second was an exemption from the rule preventing her from entering any library—and here she was willing to accept a limited exemption that would allow her only limited hours in the library. Sir Richard Luyt, the vice-chancellor and principal of UCT, supported Ensor's application. Luyt said the university would consider whatever arrangements the Security Police thought necessary to grant Ensor access to the library.[26] The police, however, rejected Ensor's application. In a confidential letter dated May 16, 1973, the commissioner of police declared that granting Ensor access to the library would undermine the ban placed on her. The commissioner added that, while it was not clear if Ensor needed police permission to write her thesis, the police were opposed to it.[27] This decision must not have been communicated to Ensor because, two months after her initial request, she sent another note to the chief magistrate asking for a response to her April letter. "I wish to make it clear that for the last three months I have been unemployed," Ensor wrote, "and have made no concerted attempt to find employment as I have been awaiting some response to my request to study. I have been maintaining myself on money given to me by my father for study purposes, but there is a limit to what extent I may continue to use this money while not engaged in study. Money will be made available to me by UCT as soon as I am able to register."[28] Finally, on July 23, 1973, the Department of Justice rejected Ensor's application. The department cited the police's opposition to Ensor's application. The police advised that, while they did not believe that Ensor would resume her NUSAS activities if allowed on campus, they would not be able to monitor her at all times: "The object of her restriction will to a great extent be defeated if she is allowed on the campus for any reason whatever."[29]

The police also said that Ensor did not require access to the University of Cape Town's libraries, as they could source whatever books she needed from other institutions. But the nub of the police's opposition to Ensor's bid was ideological. According to the police: "Miss Ensor was prior to her restriction the Secretary General of NUSWEL [the welfare arm of NUSAS] and played an active part in the activities of the Wages Commission of NUSAS amongst the Non-Europeans. It comes as no surprise that she now chooses a subject for her thesis in which she could set the seal on her political views. A refusal now may not cause as much criticism as a refusal to publish her thesis after completion."[30] So rather than deal with her thesis later, the police killed it before it was even born.[31] Ensor was not deterred, however.

On November 13, 1973, she applied for another exemption to visit the university's libraries. She informed the chief magistrate: "I have registered with London University to do a BA Hons, which decision I took after I was refused permission to continue with my Masters in Economics. However, I am having considerable difficulty finding adequate reading material. The scope of the City Library is limited . . . as is that of the State Library, which is not a lending library."[32] Ensor wanted permission to use the Jagger library at the University of Cape Town. This request, too, went up the bureaucratic chain, including to BOSS, the Minister of Justice, and the police. The police had no objection to Ensor using the Jagger library between 9:00 AM and 10:30 AM on Saturdays. BOSS also had no objection, provided Ensor used the library between 4:00 PM and 5:00 PM on Saturdays. (It fell to the police to tell the much-vaunted BOSS that the library was open only from 8:30 AM to noon on Saturdays.)

On December 20, 1973, the secretary for justice decided, based on the support of BOSS and the police, to approve Ensor's request. During the correspondence, BOSS referred to Ensor as a "police client," making it sound as if she were a consumer armed with choices in these transactions about her life and future.[33] Of course, what BOSS was trying to communicate was that the police bore primary responsibility for Ensor, meaning that BOSS would support whatever decision the police made regarding her access to the library. In a letter dated December 5, 1973, BOSS sent its verdict: "As Ensor is a police client and, according to you, the police have no objection to her making use of the facilities for one hour per day, the Bureau would not object to such a concession either.".[34] Thus were human lives traded, with victims of apartheid authoritarianism turned into clients in a market place of rights and privileges that could be offered or taken at will.

This was not the only way in which the government sought to control Ensor's life. Because Ensor was restricted to the Cape and Wynberg magisterial districts, she had to apply for permission each time she wanted to travel. On July 8, 1974, Ensor asked the chief magistrate of Cape Town for permission to travel to Durban, Natal, for her wedding to Robert Petersen. The magistrate agreed, on the condition that Ensor must stay at her parents' house in Durban. The magistrate lifted the absolute restriction on Ensor's being in a group, but allowed it "only for the purpose of making preparations and arrangements in connection with your wedding and the celebrations therewith."[35] The magistrate added, "the forward journey must be undertaken by air on flight SA 608 S.A. Airways which departs from Cape Town on 28.7.1974 at 3.30 PM and the return journey by air on flight SA 607 which departs at 10.40 AM from Durban and arriving at Cape Town at 1.20 PM on 4.8.1974."

Keep in mind that this was a magistrate writing—not a travel agent. When Ensor sought permission on November 18, 1974, to visit her mother in Durban, the magistrate not only told her where to stay in the city but which flights to catch.[36] On November 4, 1975, Ensor asked the chief magistrate for permission to visit her family in Durban. The magistrate agreed that Ensor could visit her family from December 12, 1975 to January 5, 1976, provided she traveled by a train that departed Cape Town at 6 PM on December 19 and left Durban at 4 PM on January 5, 1976.[37] Ensor had to report her arrival and departure at the Woodstock Police Station in Cape Town, and do the same at the Umbilo Police Station in Durban. Such was the life of a banned person. Is it any wonder, then, that Ensor chose to leave South Africa? With the state going on the offensive in the 1970s against organizations such as NUSAS and making it difficult for them to accept overseas funding, it is likely that the state would have renewed Ensor's ban when it expired in 1978.

This chapter has focused on the quotidian operations of apartheid repression, showing how, as Ivan Evans has observed, apartheid amounted to rule by administration.[38] As the story of Ensor's exile and appearance in the album shows, when it came to the administration of apartheid, the devil was truly in the detail. How else to explain a government whose security agencies moonlighted as academic assessors? Or a government that turned its magistrates into travel agents? How else to talk about seemingly omnipotent security agencies that referred to their victims as clients—but did not have a clue about the opening hours of one of the country's top university libraries? But it would be a mistake to limit our focus only to the pedestrianism and the detail. Behind that vapidity lurked an evil that knew no bounds and respected no norms. As we reflect on how the security agencies hounded Ensor out of South Africa, we must also think of the fate that befell her closest friends, including Steve Biko and Jeanette (Curtis) Schoon. The Security Police killed Biko in detention in September 1977 and blew up Schoon and her daughter Katryn in 1984. They also drove thousands of people into exile, branding them terrorists when all that these individuals wanted was to be free. The brutality and the bureaucracy that defined apartheid are worth recalling because they help us explode the apocalyptic myth that the struggle for South Africa was between east and west, and between the forces of God and the godless Soviets and their local dupes. Reading Ensor's file at some historic remove from when it was first put together, we cannot help but realize that her biggest political crime was not her fight for justice and equality but the fact that she sought to live as if apartheid did not exist.[39] Otherwise, why would a secret state agent concern him or herself about whose black hands Ensor was holding in public, which black man she was dancing with, and whom she was visiting? This is not to diminish the important activist work that Ensor did, but to show how the combination of that work and Ensor's public defiance made her an enemy of the state. She had to be silenced. She had to be branded.

SIX

The Embarrassed State

ON THE FACE OF IT, Eric Abraham ended up in the Terrorist Album because he left South Africa in 1977 without government permission. That, after all, was the album's official intention: to keep track of individuals who had fled the country illegally. In truth, however, the government branded Abraham a terrorist because he embarrassed the government—at least three times. In 1973, he unmasked an apartheid agent targeting the anti-apartheid movement in Britain. In 1974, he exposed a plot to recruit him to spy on fellow student activists at the University of Cape Town.[1] When South Africa invaded Angola in 1975, Abraham documented the torture that followed. He was not yet twenty-one when he performed such feats; security officials were left with the task of explaining how it was that such a young man could humiliate the (self-described) best police force and military in Africa. To be sure, the exposés did not, by themselves, lead automatically to Abraham's inclusion in the album. But, viewed in the light of his activism and journalism, they provided grounds for

Abraham's punishment. As the apartheid operative Craig Williamson told me, Abraham was "one of the white activists who was a nuisance."[2] The exposés gave the Security Police reason to frame him as a national security threat. In November 1976, the secretary of justice issued a secret memorandum laying the legal and political groundwork for the house arrest that would drive Abraham to a fifteen-year exile. "Abraham's continued encroachment on internal security," it declared, "has now reached a high watermark."[3] As in the previous chapter, I draw here on Abraham's declassified file from the Directorate of Security Legislation to retrace the bureaucratic steps that led to his branding as a terrorist. The file allows us to see the lengths to which branches of the apartheid state went in their attempts, first, to recruit Abraham to their side and, when that failed, to punish him.

In reading Abraham's file, the reader must contend with the confidence of those who wrote it. Convinced of the correctness of their political project and imbued with a religious faith in its permanence, the

FIGURE 6.1 Mug shot of Eric Abraham in the Terrorist Album. Courtesy of National Archives & Records Service of South Africa.

apartheid bureaucrats who composed Abraham's file did not see the need to dissemble in their confidential correspondence. The Security Police considered Abraham to be a special threat because, remarkably for a person of his age, he had international connections; he was a conduit allowing victims of apartheid to share their experience with the world. A talented journalist, Abraham wrote and broadcast for, among others, the BBC African and World Service, the *Guardian, Oslo Dagbladet,* and *AFRICA* magazine. In 1972, Abraham was a first-year Sociology student serving on the Students' Representative Council (SRC) of the University of Cape Town. In that capacity, he hosted a lunch for Jeremy Thorpe, the leader of the British Liberal Party, during the latter's visit to South Africa.[4] It was a connection that came in handy when Abraham moved to Britain in October 1972 for health and political reasons, and Thorpe helped him find a job at Amnesty International. "That's how I ended up at Amnesty running their first global anti-torture campaign and conference. While [I was] at Amnesty, my student activist friends Paula Ensor, Neville and Jeanette Curtis, and Chris Wood were banned and I wrote up their case reports to have them declared Amnesty Prisoners of Conscience."[5] These links made Abraham part of an international network that could, through appeals to conscience, embarrass South Africa. In 1975, following his return to South Africa and the resumption of his studies at the University of Cape Town, Abraham founded the Southern African News Agency (SANA), which focused on black politics and human rights abuses in Namibia and in South Africa. Abraham also established a photographic agency, SANAPIC, which licensed photos to the international media. This drew the immediate attention of the government, which expelled Margaret Valentim, a British citizen and SANA's correspondent in Namibia, and detained and tortured Thenjiwe Mtintso, SANA's reporter for the Eastern Cape. Mtintso, who is also in the album, eventually fled South

Africa for exile in 1978. Recalling the government's ire toward him, Abraham said:

> I was a special case because of my profile abroad, having worked for Amnesty International . . . [and] with Martin Ennals [Secretary General of Amnesty International from 1968 to 1980] and Amnesty Chairman Sean MacBride, former Foreign Minister of Ireland, and then United Nations High Commissioner for Namibia. I had many contacts in the foreign media, NGOs, and other international organizations and some governments. This was a time when the apartheid regime was still concerned about its image abroad and my connections acted as a kind of protection for me. This was coupled with my friendship and continued association with people like Winnie Mandela, Helen Joseph, Jeanette Curtis, and Neville Curtis, amongst others.

As the secretary of justice conceded in the memorandum mentioned above, there was "insufficient evidence for his arrest." But the government wanted Abraham dealt with.[6] This official frankness saves us from having to read Abraham's file against the grain. We do not need to look for meaning hidden between the lines, given the file's status as a secret document. This does not mean, however, that we can treat the file as if it were a repository of the truth. Abraham had to be punished because he had become a security risk, and he had become a security risk because he revealed basic truths about apartheid in the international press. As we shall see below, however, behind that cruel logic lay a pettiness that was no less nasty because it came from offices of the state. Abraham did not have to lie to embarrass South Africa. His police tormentors knew this, but they could not let him get away with it. So they hounded him, harassed him, placed him under house arrest, and, when it suited their purposes, planned his getaway to the last detail—all so they could use his escape as cover for Craig Williamson, a valuable Security Police agent within the domestic white left that the police wanted to deploy against South African exiles.

As Abraham recalled, "In addition to providing some black politicians with access to the international media, since most resident foreign correspondents feared being expelled by talking to them, it was probably my reportage on Namibia, where in 1975 / 6 the border war was hotting up, that got to them most."[7] Abraham helped the *Guardian* expose the widespread use of torture by the South African Defense Force in Namibia, and reported on a major political trial, as well as labor disputes in that country, in 1976. When a South African policeman attacked Abraham while he was taking pictures of policemen assaulting a group of Namibian demonstrators, Abraham sued both the policeman and Jimmy Kruger, the Minister of Justice and Police. This upset Kruger. So the Security Police plotted to get rid of Abraham. They let him flee South Africa so that they could get Williamson, already suspected by the white left of being an apartheid agent, out of South Africa, and put him to work spying on the anti-apartheid movement in Europe and parts of Africa.[8]

The Security Police dearly wanted to insert Williamson into the International University Exchange Fund (IUEF), a Geneva-based but Swedish-supported relief agency dedicated to the welfare of victims of political repression in Latin America and southern Africa.[9] Having positioned Williamson at the fund, they hoped to use him to infiltrate the London-based International Defense and Aid Fund, a key source of funding for South African activists and exiles. To cement Williamson's cover as a victim of apartheid, the Security Police also placed his mug shot in the album. Later, in 1979, Arthur McGiven, an apartheid security agent fleeing persecution by his colleagues for being gay, would expose Williamson in the British media as an apartheid spy—and

Williamson and his police masters would retaliate for this setback by killing Ruth First in Mozambique in 1982 and Jeanette Curtis and her daughter Katryn (at age six) in Angola in 1984.[10] But before proceeding to the details of the story as it is told by Abraham, it is instructive to ask: How did the Security Police themselves tell the story? What narrative arc and timeline did they construct in their branding of Abraham as a terrorist?[11]

The Official Timeline

To trouble the police narrative about how Abraham became a terrorist, let us weave into that account details from Abraham that the police left out of their file. According to the Security Police memorandum cited above, Abraham first came "under suspicion" in 1972 when he was arrested during a demonstration in Cape Town organized by the National Union of South African Students (NUSAS) "to promote equal rights for all people."[12] The police say he paid an admission-of-guilt fine of R20 after the police charged him with obstructing their work. He was eighteen years old. But this account of how Abraham first came to the attention of the police is inaccurate. When Abraham was seventeen and a student at the South African College High School in Cape Town, he became chairman of National Youth Action, a nonracial union of high school students fighting for political equality. Members of the union had frequent encounters with the Security Police, such as in December 1971, when the union's inaugural conference at the University of Cape Town drew representatives of thirty schools in the Western Cape.[13] NUSAS president Neville Curtis addressed the conference. Abraham told me how the Security Police came to take an interest in him :

> My father [George Abraham]—a Hungarian refugee who left
> Hungary in the mid-late 1930s because of antisemitism, who be-
> came a highly-regarded engineer who helped to build Sasol [a
> state-owned petrochemical company]—became worried about his
> position given my nonracial school activism, and volunteered to
> the Security Police / BOSS to keep an eye on me. We were visited
> by a certain Captain Nic Basson posing as a friend of my father.
> He was Afrikaans and not unlike certain people at Sasol. I thought
> at the time it seemed strange. It was only later on that I discov-
> ered that my father regularly went through my desk and passed
> over copies of documents relating to the National Youth Action.
> This and his threats for me to stop my activism prompted me to
> leave home in early 1972. I have had very little contact with my
> father or mother or family since.[14]

Abraham enrolled at the University of Cape Town early in 1972 and
attended his first protest on June 2, 1972. The demonstration, on the
steps of St. George's Cathedral in the city, was held to demand free
education for all. The police broke up the rally violently and, as students fled into the church, followed them inside and assaulted them
with batons. "It took months before I could see a uniformed policeman
without shaking involuntarily," Abraham recalled.[15] With that June
protest, the Security Police developed what would prove to be an en-
during interest in Abraham and other young white activists. It had
not been long since the Security Police had crushed the largely white
student-led African Resistance Movement, an insurgent group whose
members planned acts of violence against the state.[16] The police worried that this new activism might be a resurrection of the insurgent
group they had smashed in the 1960s. "They feared a repeat of the ARM
and demanded to meet me on two occasions and, on the advice of my

fellow activists, I met them. They said if I wanted to leave the country I would only be allowed out if I agreed to spy for them. I said of course not."[17] That is when Abraham decided to leave South Africa. According to the Security Police, on September 17, 1972, Abraham said the following to a person who turned out to be a police source: "I believe in one man one vote . . . I personally think that there is nothing I can do at the present moment that can change the affairs in this country and that's why I'm going away."[18] A few weeks later, Abraham moved to Britain. On March 14, 1973, Abraham took part in a rally outside the South African Embassy in London in support of Greek-Australian Alex Moumbaris and Irishman Sean Hosey, international volunteers for the ANC recently found guilty of terrorism by the Pretoria High Court following their capture in South Africa.[19] During the demonstration, the police said, Abraham "pointed to a former member of the force to those present and identified him as a member of our Security Police."[20]

Abraham gave this account: "I was there with the Amnesty researcher on South Africa and had a small camera with me so I took [the agent's] picture and gave it to . . . *The Guardian*. A front page exposé followed and questions were raised in the British Parliament."[21] The unmasked spy, fearing deportation from Britain, fled back to his embarrassed masters in South Africa. The memorandum is silent on the details, but Michael Morris was the police agent in question.[22] Republican Intelligence, South Africa's state intelligence agency founded in the previous decade following the advice of the British government, had recruited Morris in 1963.[23] His mission was to spy on the Liberal Party, the only legal political party in South Africa with membership open to all races. (This would soon change. In 1968, the government passed the Prohibition of Political Interference Act, a law aimed at destroying the Liberal Party by making it illegal for any political organization to have members of different races.) In 1966, Republican Intelligence posted Morris to the University of Cape Town to spy on NUSAS and other student groupings opposed to apartheid. In 1973, the successor agency to Republican Intelligence—the Bureau of State Security (BOSS), established in August 1968—sent Morris to London to spy on South Africa's growing exile community, as well as on Britain's fast-growing anti-apartheid movement. Morris's international spying career came to an abrupt end, however, after Abraham, who had known about Morris spying on student activists in Cape Town, spotted him at that March 1973 demonstration in London and exposed him to the world.[24] While a humiliated Morris returned to Cape Town to head a government-funded Terrorism Research Center, Abraham came back to South Africa to resume his studies at the University of Cape Town.[25] Martin Ennals, the secretary general of Amnesty International, who was friends with Swedish premier Olof Palme and IUEF director Lars-Gunnar Eriksson, helped secure a scholarship from the fund for Abraham. According to the police memorandum, on the day of his return to South Africa, Abraham "reported to a source that he intended to keep his head down (play things cool) in order to mislead the authorities with regard to his activities."[26] Abraham recalls how he then met Williamson:

> On [my] arrival at Jan Smuts Airport in Johannesburg, Jeanette Curtis picked me up and took me to her labor union office to collect something. It was here that I met Craig Williamson for the first time. To me he looked like an Afrikaner policeman and I was taken aback by his feigned familiarity, which jarred with me. It was only Jeanette and Lars Gunnar Eriksson's bona fides about Williamson that persuaded me to talk to him, which I did only two or three times between 1973 and 1976. I was told he was Lars-Gunnar's undercover representative in SA and had Lars Gunnar's full trust and confidence.[27]

The police memorandum does not mention this but, shortly after Abraham's return from Britain, the Security Police tried to recruit him to spy on fellow activists at the University of Cape Town. An officer of the Security Police / BOSS named Basson invited Abraham to a meeting.[28] Abraham, sensing that this was yet another attempt at recruitment, accepted the invitation but asked that he and Basson meet in the central Cape Town park, the Company's Garden, just footsteps from Parliament and St. George's Cathedral. Unbeknownst to Abraham, Basson brought along a police photographer who hid behind a hedge to document the meeting, hoping perhaps to use the photographs later to blackmail Abraham (fig. 6.2). At the same time, however, unbeknownst to Basson and his photographer, Abraham brought along his own photographer, his NUSAS comrade Gerhard Maré, to capture the meeting.[29] Maré, who often took pictures at NUSAS events, stumbled upon the police photographer as they both hid behind the same shrub and aimed their lenses at Abraham and Basson, sitting in the distance. Meanwhile, as Abraham told me later, "I also had a tape recorder in my briefcase with which I recorded the meeting."[30] While Basson and the police photographer decamped to their offices after the meeting, Abraham and Maré gave the story, complete with Maré's photographs and transcript of the meeting, to the *Sunday Tribune*. The paper splashed the story of Abraham's failed recruitment on its pages, causing the Security Police and BOSS acute embarrassment.[31] Abraham fled to Botswana briefly when the story broke and waited for the storm to die down before returning to Cape Town.

Abraham was a marked man after this episode, and police informants began focusing on his activities and utterances. In April 1974, he was recorded dismissing claims that South Africa was a victim of the Cold War and asserting that South Africans were "killing fellow South Africans on the national border" because of apartheid. "Moscow

FIGURE 6.2 News account of Eric Abraham and Nic Basson meeting, April 30, 1974. Courtesy of *Sunday Tribune*.

and Peking could not be blamed for it."[32] In September 1974, he issued a pamphlet denouncing South Africa's illegal occupation of Namibia. If Abraham's humiliation of the security agencies was bad in their eyes, however, his journalism in favor of human rights and the humane treatment of detainees and political prisoners was worse. "I specifically focused on interviewing Black politicians like Winnie Mandela and Namibian black activists and supporters of SWAPO," Abraham said, referring to the South West African People's Organization. He wanted "to help provide them with an opportunity to be heard abroad. Namibia was a special case given the widespread use of torture by the

South African Defense Force and the South African Police."[33] In September 1975, Abraham, who supported himself by working as a stringer for the BBC and some European newspapers, informed Amnesty International and the IUEF of the arrests of Gordon Young and Horst Kleinschmidt, both of them white activists accused of helping poet Breyten Breytenbach avoid arrest.[34]

The police memorandum documented Abraham's extensive travels throughout the region as he reported on Mozambique's independence celebrations in June 1975, took overseas visitors on fact-finding trips around Cape Town and other parts of the region, and collected photographs that could be used by the international media and anti-apartheid organizations. Among the photographs in Abraham's possession, the police said, were "photos of Robben Island and of shanty town houses taken from an aircraft."[35] Abraham also traveled to Northern Namibia. Because this was a military-controlled zone as a result of South Africa's invasion of Angola in 1975, Abraham made it only as far as Oshakati, whence he reported on the consequences of the conflict between South African troops and SWAPO insurgents. As the police reported in their memorandum, Abraham collected information from families of SWAPO prisoners in need of financial aid, and reported on torture cases and South Africa's military sorties into Angola. The memorandum did not dispute the substance of Abraham's journalism. Its purpose was merely to show what Abraham was up to, including taking pictures of on-duty policemen. The police also took note of Abraham's attempts to raise money abroad to expand his agency and to support self-help programs for young blacks in Johannesburg.

The memorandum recorded the withdrawal of Abraham's passport by the minister of home affairs in November 1975. This was to prevent Abraham from raising funds abroad for SANA. Out of spite, the Security Police informed Abraham that his passport had been withdrawn only as he was about to board a plane bound for Europe. The police did not arrest Abraham because, as they well knew, he had not broken any laws. Abraham later said he thought his white skin had saved him: "Doubtless, had I been black I would not be alive."[36] Long before the mid-1970s, the Security Police had acquired a taste for subjecting white activists to beatings, solitary confinements, and other tortures. But they had yet to develop their lust for extrajudicial killing; that started in 1977 with the assassination of academic Rick Turner.[37] Abraham also thought it might be a factor that his father, George Abraham, was a lieutenant-commander in the South African Navy:

> Perhaps my reputation abroad as a member of the international press community and among human rights NGOs might have helped. My father was a commander in the navy who was very active in the border war—transporting specialists to sabotage oil refineries in Angola and infiltrating special forces to take out SWAPO guerilla camps and Cuban support there. I remember the only time he visited me under house-arrest—only he or my mother separately were allowed to visit in terms of the house arrest order. A uniformed policeman was manning my telephone to intercept the death threats so the three of us were in this cramped studio. It was tense. My father said: "If I was them I'd also want to kill you." Perhaps this was for the benefit of the bugging device to indicate to the authorities he was on-side but I asked him to leave immediately.[38]

Winnie Mandela

It is true that George Abraham sold his son out to the Security Police, but the police would likely have gone after Abraham even without the father's help. Abraham had embarrassed them repeatedly and they wanted to stop him. One of the realities of apartheid—that the application of the law depended on the whim of its security agencies—was here on full display. Most likely, however, Abraham's interviews with Winnie Mandela in December 1975 and March 1976 tipped the Security Police over the edge.[39] Winnie Madikizela, an activist in her own right, had married Nelson Mandela in 1958. She was left to raise their two daughters by herself, however, when Nelson was sentenced to five years in jail in November 1962 for leaving South Africa without a passport and, subsequently, sentenced to life in prison for treason. In 1962, the government invoked the Suppression of Communism Act to ban her from public life. The police arrested her that same year for allegedly violating her banning order—and the arrests would only continue, in 1967, 1969, 1970, 1971, 1972, 1973, 1974, 1975, and 1976.[40] Between 1969 and 1970 she spent seventeen months in solitary confinement as a detainee under the Terrorism Act.

After that detention spell, the state charged her and twenty-one others under the Suppression of Communism Act. Those charges were withdrawn in February 1970, but instead of letting her and the others go, the state immediately detained them again, and Winnie was returned to solitary confinement. It was not until September 1970 that the police freed the twenty-two. Again, however, the state promptly charged them, this time under the Terrorism Act, and was able to win a court conviction—only to see the accused acquitted on appeal. At this point, instead of letting Winnie alone, the police "banned" her for five years, meaning that she could not attend any gathering with more than two people or be quoted in the media. Abraham's subsequent interviews with Winnie shed light on her resilience and offered a rare public account by Winnie of the toll police torture had taken on her.[41]

The text of a speech that Winnie delivered in October 1975, during a temporary lull in her banning, accompanied the interview published in December 1975. Winnie spoke at length about the physical and psychological costs of torture. If the 1975 speech and interview were remarkable for the honesty with which she spoke about her detention, harassment, torture, and imprisonment, her 1976 interview stood out for its defiant tone. If the Security Police assumed that thirteen years of torture had broken her, they must have been disappointed. This must have provided yet another reason to despise Abraham. The Winnie who spoke to Abraham in December 1975 was astute and humble—not the arrogant, intolerant firebrand who would emerge in the 1980s. Nothing brings out Winnie's humility better than her reflections on her torture and numerous detentions:

> Detention means that midnight knock when all about you is quiet. It means those blinding torches shone simultaneously through every window of your house before the door is kicked open. It means the exclusive right the Security Branch have to read each and every letter in the house, no matter how personal it might be. . . . Ultimately, it means your seizure at dawn, dragged away from little children screaming and clinging to your skirt, imploring the white man dragging mummy to leave her alone. . . . It means the haunting memories of those screams of the loved ones, the beginning of that horror story told many a time and that has become common knowledge, yet the actual experience remains petrifying.[42]

She went on to detail her confinement in a "single cell with the light burning twenty-four hours so that I lost track of time and was unable to tell whether it was day or night." She spoke about the unbearable "frightful emptiness of those hours of solitude" in solitary confinement, with the detainee deprived of both choice in her life and control over her fate: "All this is in preparation for the inevitable Hell—interrogation.

It is meant to crush your individuality completely, to change you into a docile being from whom no resistance can arise, to terrorize you, to intimidate you into silence." Winnie was free when she gave the speech, meaning she was not subject to any banning order. Still, it was brave of Abraham to publish it, considering that government censors were on the prowl.[43] Indeed, in January 1976, they banned that month's edition of the SANA newsletter for publishing pictures of a shantytown in Cape Town, and reports of "alleged emergency situations" in the country. Abraham was not deterred. He published these interviews and distributed them around the world, giving Winnie and fellow activists a lifeline to the outside world. Winnie understood this. As she pointed out in the interview, she knew that, for the struggle against apartheid to succeed, it had to be made an international cause.

Abraham's interviews with Mandela, not to mention his continued exposés of South African excesses in Namibia, drew a harsh response from the Security Police. In November 1976, with the support of BOSS, they demanded that he be banned, put under house arrest, for five years. "Abraham aims mainly to publish distorted and provocative information," the police said, "and provide this for the Republic's enemies."[44] The Justice Department, also considering his reports about South African troops in Namibia to be dangerous, labeled him a security risk. Both the Justice Department and the police wanted a ban that would prevent Abraham from engaging in journalism and restrict him from traveling around the country and to Namibia. The police also wanted Abraham excluded from the campus of the University of Cape Town, where he was in the final year of his BA in Sociology and Psychology.

The police said his banning would be "less effective unless he is prohibited from accessing the premises" of the university. The police suggested that, to be allowed to take his final examinations, Abraham should have to apply to the chief magistrate of Cape Town for a temporary exemption from his ban. "Fortunately, my final exams happened days before I was banned and house-arrested," Abraham recalled. "I graduated but wasn't allowed to attend the graduation ceremony. My degree was delivered to me under house arrest without the messenger being allowed to set foot in my studio in John Street, Mowbray," outside Cape Town.[45] Jimmy Kruger, the minister of justice, duly delivered Abraham's banning order on November 23, 1976. Calling Abraham's actions a danger to public order, Kruger banned Abraham from attending any public gatherings and engaging in journalism until November 30, 1981. The ban restricted Abraham to his flat in Mowbray. He could not leave his apartment on weekends (or public holidays) and could only do so from 6 AM to 6 PM on weekdays. Only his parents and a doctor vetted by the police could visit him. A Captain P. J. J. Fourie and a Major N. J. W. Basson served the banning order in person on Abraham on November 29, 1976. He was twenty-two. Thus began the odyssey that would lead Abraham to exile and into the album. On December 2, 1976, about eight days after the government placed Abraham under house arrest, he instructed a Cape Town law firm to petition the chief magistrate of Cape Town for permission to move house. Describing the dwelling to which Abraham was confined by his house arrest order, the lawyers wrote that "the house is particularly small and has no garden."[46] The lawyers also asked that the order be amended to allow him to attend church on Sundays. The police rejected Abraham's request to move house but said he could attend church between 9 AM and noon on Sundays, "although before his restriction he never attended a church service and had no church connection."[47]

On December 9, 1976, Abraham opened a case of harassment against the police, saying that unidentified individuals were making his life a living hell. Anonymous harassers ordered a consignment of alcohol to be delivered to his flat, without Abraham's knowledge; they had flowers and a card congratulating him on his banning order conveyed to his apartment; they sent a hearse allegedly to collect his corpse from the apartment; and they repeatedly made phone calls threatening to kill Abraham.[48] Someone sawed halfway through the brake cable of Abraham's VW Beetle.[49] It is highly likely that the Security Police and their right-wing associates were behind all this—out of spite. Abraham hired a private security guard to protect him from a band of white right-wingers led by a man named David Beelders, self-declared head of Scorpio, a group that would in 1977 claim responsibility for the assassination of academic and anti-apartheid activist Richard Turner.[50] "This group had claimed responsibility for firing gunshots at and petrol bombing activists' houses," Abraham later recalled. "I slept in the bath since my studio had two large windows onto the street and I was very vulnerable."[51]

Having confiscated his passport in November 1975 and denied him an exit permit in December 1976, the Security Police were wagering that constant harassment would break Abraham. In December 1976, Abraham was admitted to Groote Schuur Hospital after taking tranquilizers and other pills. The police called it an attempted suicide; the liberal media said Abraham had taken the medication for his ulcer.[52] Abraham gave me his explanation: "My exit visa had just been refused. I had reason to believe through my lawyers that charges were about to be brought against me under the wide-ranging internal security laws. I was on tranquilizers and anti-ulcer medication and must have passed out after I telephoned a friend who called the police who alerted the Security Police who broke down my door and I was taken under police guard to Groote Schuur hospital." On December 7, 1976, a member of the UN Secretariat in New York gave a member of South Africa's Permanent Mission a copy of a telegram that Abraham had sent, via Amnesty International, to UN General Secretary Kurt Wald-heim: "My life has been threatened by right wing fanatics on at least seven occasions in the past 24 hours. Last threat stated I am to be killed tonight by a right wing group called 'Scorpio.' I appeal to you to inter-vene with Prime Minister Vorster for me to be allowed to leave South Africa. And also take note of the victimization of a large number of black journalists currently taking place in this country."[53] On Jan-uary 6, 1977, a few days after Abraham fled South Africa, Hermann A. Hanekom, South Africa's permanent representative to the UN in New York, asked his bosses in Pretoria for "information we can utilize in private, or in public, to expose Abraham for what he is, should he make his appearance at the United Nations."[54] Hanekom worried that Abraham, having escaped from South Africa only the day before, would appear at the UN.

"Bearing in mind the attention 'refugees' from South Africa enjoy overseas, especially since June 1976, plus the fact that 'Abraham's plight' has already been brought to the attention of the United Nations by Am-nesty International," Hanekom said, he wanted whatever dirt his col-leagues, especially the Security Police, could dish up on Abraham. The police obliged. In a secret letter dated January 31, 1977, the police de-nounced SANA as a one-man show devoted to "publicizing the precar-ious position of South African restricted persons and the accused in ideological trials. They are shown as victims of a cruel regime that de-votes its authoritative bodies to crushing all opposition." The police accused Abraham of using his agency to give voice to communists and said his reports were "full of allegations and accusations against the authorities without any attempt to support them with proof." The police also suggested that Abraham was delusional for thinking that he was "prey to a police vendetta against him." The police went on: "Abraham has an unstable personality and on various occasions attempted suicide, by using excessive pills. In addition, he has a tendency towards alcoholism and has on occasion received psychiatric treatment."

Hanekom did not get to use this information, as Abraham did not appear before the United Nations. But it is important to notice in the police missive the mix of the personal and the political. It was not enough for the police to comment adversely on Abraham's journalism; they also felt the need to slander him. They had to do it in a way that connected Abraham's critical journalism to his mental health. The police damaged Abraham's reputation for no greater reason than that they could.

To understand the motivations of state functionaries and the authoritarian bureaucracies they served, it is always important to pay attention to the ideologies and motivations animating their actions. In the South African context, this means taking seriously their anti-communism. If we limit our focus to the ideological, however, and assume that this anti-communism was simply in the service of a greater existential struggle for survival by whites in apartheid South Africa, we risk misunderstanding the actions of the police and underestimating their cynical use of power. When it comes to understanding the police, the devil truly is in the detail. We know, for example, that Johann Coetzee, the policeman whose name was attached to the above response, knew more than he let on to his colleagues in the South African foreign service about Abraham's escape from South Africa. In fact, he planned it. Coetzee had recruited Craig Williamson to the Security Police in 1971 to spy on the white left at the University of Witwatersrand in Johannesburg. Williamson, private school–educated and the son of a businessman, had distinguished himself at St. John's College, an Anglican school in the north of Johannesburg, by his virulent anti-black racism. He joined the South African Police in 1968, and by 1971 was a sergeant in the uniformed branch. Coetzee had studied Williamson's middle-class background and come to believe that Williamson, with his pronounced racist attitudes, could be persuaded to use his English-speaking background to target the white left. Williamson did not need much convincing.

By February 1972, he was a first-year student at the University of Witwatersrand, with his sights set on NUSAS. By 1974, Williamson was an elected member of the NUSAS executive, responsible for finance. This was a strategic position as Coetzee wanted to use Williamson to disrupt the flow of money, especially from the IUEF, coming into South Africa to support victims of political repression. Williamson's position in the NUSAS executive also placed him at the center of communications between NUSAS, prohibited since 1974 from receiving funding from abroad, and individuals such as Abraham, who might approach the IUEF for financial support or help getting out of South Africa. Lacking a passport and having had his request for an exit permit turned down, Abraham asked IUEF head Lars-Gunnar Eriksson, through an intermediary, to help him get out of South Africa. Eriksson, a former trade unionist and student leader in Sweden, asked Williamson to help Abraham, unaware that Williamson was an apartheid spy. Eriksson was close to Prime Minister Olof Palme of Sweden, who ensured that his government's financial contribution to anti-apartheid causes was the most generous and significant at that time. Eriksson, impressed by Williamson's bookkeeping skills and efficiency, had made Williamson his point man in South Africa, especially on matters requiring his fund's assistance. Williamson duly approached Abraham and offered to help get him out. As Abraham explained in 2017, "Williamson clearly got me out in order to increase his credibility with the Swedes." Williamson and his police bosses arranged a "suitably theatrical departure" to make the escape look legitimate. Williamson told Abraham that a telegram from someone named Paul with the words "courage and strength" would be his signal that the escape was on. Abraham recalled, "If I received this, I was to leave my studio immediately after 6 AM on January 2, taking nothing with me and to wait along the road leading to Rhodes Memorial on Table Mountain which was within my magisterial district. I would be picked up by an accomplice."[55] The accomplice took Abraham to a barber and then to the airport in Cape Town, from where he flew to Johannesburg. From there, Williamson and accomplices drove Abraham to a spot near the Botswana border.

> Williamson and I set off into the bush. . . . Before starting out he said we could not talk on the journey because sound carried and this was a military-patrolled zone since it was the main route the Soweto kids caught up in the 1976 uprising used to leave the country. . . . We walked for several more hours and arrived at the SA border marked by a not very formidable barbed-wire fence which we scrambled over. Crossed a short no-man's land and then over the also not formidable Botswana border fence just as the sun rose.[56]

After crossing into Botswana, the two men announced their presence to the local police and requested refugee status. Williamson also confirmed their escape to the South African press, resulting in a *Rand Daily Mail* headline on January 6, 1977: "Two in dash across the border."[57] The story in the *Rand Daily Mail,* one of the few that publicized the escape, quoted Williamson at length. He claimed that the minister of the interior had taken his passport and that he had decided to flee as he was due for a year-long conscription into the military (compulsory since 1967 for all white males over sixteen). Williamson told the *Rand Daily Mail* that he and Abraham had decided to leave South Africa independently. "It was a coincidence that we arrived at the same time."[58] Williamson said the British government had promised Abraham travel documents to allow him to proceed to Britain while a number of media houses had offered him jobs. As for Williamson, "All I can do is hope and pray for change rapid and radical enough to allow me to return to my homeland."[59] While it would be more than fifteen years before Abraham was able to return to South Africa, Williamson would be back in South Africa within two years of his dramatic departure. In December 1979, Arthur McGiven, a member of BOSS and, like Williamson, a former university spy, defected to Britain after his colleagues began hounding him for being gay.[60] McGiven exposed the workings of BOSS, including Williamson's shenanigans, in the British media. Thus ended Williamson's double life. Asked to recall his reaction to the unmasking of Williamson, Abraham said, "There was an element of me that was not surprised. He looked like a Security Branch man."[61] When Abraham went into exile, he resolved to start a new life and not "to live like many refugees with their heads in South Africa and bodies in the UK."[62] He took a job with BBC TV's premier current affairs show, *Panorama*. But his mug shot remained in the album. Indeed, his was the first face that captured insurgents would see upon opening the album. It was Williamson, in fact, who first alerted me to Abraham and his story. As Williamson and I were going through my digital copy of the album in August 2016, he casually pointed to Abraham's photograph: "I know him. I helped him go into exile."[63] Behind Williamson's casualness, however, lay cunning and violence that claimed lives. Abraham did not simply stumble into the album. The police dragged him there. They pulled him into the album because they had given themselves the power to brand and maim. They might have explained their actions in terms of reason of state. But those actions bespoke a violence that was as personal as it was petty.

SEVEN

Comrade Rashid

ABOOBAKER ISMAIL WAS one of the most wanted men in South Africa. Yet, for more than a decade, the Security Police did not know what he looked like. They knew he was Indian and was born on Christmas Day.[1] They knew he commanded ANC units responsible for some of the organization's most spectacular military operations. But they had no mug shot of the man who went by the nom de guerre Rashid Patel. When police interrogators asked captured insurgents and informers to identify Ismail in surveillance photographs and in the Terrorist Album, they routinely identified Barry Gilder, a tall white man of Jewish descent, as Rashid. The Security Police opened a file in Gilder's name and put every scrap of information they had about Rashid in it, thereby confounding apartheid's logic of racial separation.

Eugene Fourie, the officer whose C2 unit maintained the album, said the police "knew he was an Indian, but we opened a white file because everyone said he is Barry Gilder. He had an S1 file but we knew he was an Indian."[2] Recall that, in Security Police parlance, S1 referred to white

FIGURE 7.1 Mug shot of Barry Gilder,
incorrectly labeled as Rashid's. Courtesy of
National Archives & Records Service of South
Africa.

security suspects, S2 to Indians, S3 to Coloreds, and S4 to Africans. In
a world where every person was supposed to know definitively his own
race and that of others, the police could not dismiss eyewitness descriptions of Rashid as white, even though the police themselves knew
him to be Indian. Every South African had to belong to a racial category. Race was central to the ideological conception of apartheid and
to the manner in which the police confronted political subversion. The
police even divided their work along racial lines, with some officers assigned to the "white desk," others to the "Indian desk," and so on. The
police slotted Ismail into a "white file" because they were not prepared
to admit that their system was fallible. They were not ready to con-
cede that, when it came to their enemy, they did not know as much as
they pretended to know.

Because the Security Police saw their work as being about the maintenance of apartheid's racial boundaries, they took a special interest in
Coloreds, Indians, and whites involved in the struggle against apartheid. They were especially interested in non-Africans who underwent military training abroad. So they set their agents and captured

insurgents to work on this. In November 1974, for example, ANC defector Gladstone Mose gave his Security Police masters a report entitled "Indians: Military training."[3] It identifies two people of interest:

> During 1966, whilst in the ANC camp in Khongwa, Tanzania, two South African Indians were also there. It was common cause that these Indians had already undergone military training in Czechoslovakia either in 1964 or 1965. They were known by the names Omar and Amin. These were the only Indians known of who underwent military training abroad and in 1966 both deserted the ranks of the ANC and went to Nairobi. . . . Omar is identical to Omar Moosa Bhamje. . . . His photograph appears on page 1 of Annexure 3 to the Terrorist Album. Amin is identical to Aminoddin Kajee. . . . His picture appears on page 2 of Annexure 3 to the Terrorist Album.[4]

Mose followed this up with another report on December 4, 1974, about an Indian insurgent named Moosa Moolla. He described his encounters with Moolla in the Soviet Union, Tanzania, and Zambia. "He is the only Indian that I actually witnessed undergoing military training," Mose said.[5] Mose set great store by giving his masters accurate information. But he was not above pandering to their prejudices. Going through a set of photographs taken at an ANC rally in Tanzania, Mose identified Moolla as the "sly-looking Indian sporting a goatee."[6]

The Security Police needed the kind of information that Mose could provide. But there was a limit to what even he could know. While they knew that Ismail—Comrade Rashid—was Indian, they did not have an identikit that could prove his race. The fact that they marked him white raises an important question about the status of the album as a historical source. How are we to understand it as an object in itself given that information was embedded within its covers and its accompanying documentary material that its compilers, the police, knew not to trust? To ask this question is not to wonder whether we can trust the album as a source. Rather, it is to probe the efficacy of the album as a device for the framing of political dissidence. The police knew there was a Rashid and that he commanded the ANC's special operations unit.[7] They knew that, according to apartheid's own system of racial classification, this Rashid was Indian. Without a photograph, however, they could not confirm their own knowledge. They could not frame Rashid. So they went along with assertions that he was white. As the police well knew, it was a problem that the name Rashid Patel was an alias. Another problem was that, unlike most of his fellow exiles and insurgents, Ismail left South Africa legally—that is, with a valid passport. If the purpose of the album was to keep track of individuals who left South Africa illegally, the album could not always monitor in real time those individuals who left the country with valid papers. Even though the Department of Indian Affairs had given Ismail a passport and, as will be discussed below, he had previously come to the attention of the Security Police because of his activism, the police missed him because they were focusing on the wrong places for exit points. They were looking for suspects to jump over fences when they could fly out. Like most other sections of the apartheid bureaucracy, the Security Police assumed that no one would leave South Africa willingly for exile.

They took it for granted that only the socially and politically deviant would do so, running through the bush, like Paula Ensor, and jumping over barbed wire fences, like Eric Abraham, to escape. So they were blindsided when—in respectable middle-class fashion—Ismail flew out of Jan Smuts Airport on his way to becoming one of the most effective insurgents against apartheid. They could certainly imagine him. They just could not picture him. That blind spot undermined the instrumental worth of the album, leaving Ismail free to haunt its contents, with his presence all over its pages while his likeness itself was absent. Police reports and court transcripts are full of mentions of Rashid yet the man himself is absent from the album. So how did Aboobaker Ismail become Rashid, and how did Rashid become the ghost that spooked the police for fifteen years? To chart these transformations in Ismail's life is to track the effect that apartheid had on ordinary South Africans, and to show how apartheid radicalized the average South African. The story begins in his own words:

> My name is Aboobaker Ismail. I'm also known as Rashid. I was born on 25 December 1954 in Johannesburg. My father and grandmother are both of Indian origin. My father was born in India, he came to South Africa when he was about six years old in about 1933. My mother was born in South Africa. My grandfather had come from India some years prior to that, I don't know exactly when. I'm the fourth of six children. I grew up in Johannesburg. The family basically was not very well off. My grandfather, when they came to South Africa, were tailors and farmers, came from Gujarat, India, and when they came into South Africa they didn't have very much of any resources. Initially, my father and my uncle, from the stories that we've been told when we were kids, well he only went to school until Standard Four. My mother had never been to school. They worked in clothing businesses after leaving school and that is where they learnt about retail trade, that is my father and my uncle, and later in life they then started a business in the retail business and my family basically lived on a retail shop that dealt with men's clothing.[8]

Ismail grew up in Vrededorp, a racially-mixed and historically working-class suburb of Johannesburg with a long tradition of political and trade-union activism. Ismail, whose maternal relatives owned a convenience store and grocery shop in Vrededorp, attended primary school in the suburb. His father, while not politically active, was a regular at political rallies in the neighboring suburb of Fordsburg, where the Transvaal Indian Congress was strong. The family discussed politics, too, Ismail recalled: "We'd talk a bit about Gandhi but primarily we spoke about South Africa, about the oppression, about what was going on in the country." In May 1961, South Africa declared itself a republic, severing ties with the British Commonwealth and fulfilling a long-held political ambition of Afrikaner nationalism and republicanism. This was a racially exclusive republicanism, with its promise of egalitarianism limited only to white men and, since May 1930, white women. Afrikaner nationalists insisted that there should be no equality between black and white in matters of church and state. Ismail recalled how he first learned about the declaration of the Republic of South Africa:

> We were going to school in those days and at school they had given all the children flags, a republic medallion and also sweets as part of the celebrations. When we came back from school that evening, usually, my father used to talk to the kids and we showed him what we had been given at school and he called all the children around and said to all of us, well, he talked to us about apartheid and what it represented and then he took the medallions, the flags and the sweets and threw them into the fire. He said: "That is what is going to happen to apartheid in the future."[9]

Ironically, the declaration of the South African Republic brought with it the first official acknowledgment by Afrikaner nationalists that Indians were indeed South African citizens. Having swept into office in the 1948 elections on the promise to keep the African in his place and send the Indian back to India, Afrikaner nationalists did an about-turn in 1961 and started treating Indians like citizens, albeit without a fraction of the rights enjoyed by white citizens. While Africans were promised homelands, Coloreds and Indians were given their "own affairs" departments, with government setting up the Department of Indian Affairs in 1961. The department was responsible for a number of portfolios, including education and "Indian" passports. In 1962, the government declared Vrededorp a white area, meaning that individuals and families classified as non-white had to leave. In 1964, the Security Police killed local activist Suliman Babla Saloojee, the fourth political detainee to die in police detention in South Africa in the 1960s. Saloojee's death led to demonstrations outside the police station in Fordsburg, where Ismail attended madrassa. "Even now when I go past [the Fordsburg Police Station] I can recall that day very clearly," said Ismail. "There were lots of people demonstrating outside there and some of the people suggested that we join the crowd and demonstrate outside the police station. We knew what was going on at the time." He was ten years old. In 1972, Ismail's final year of high school, the Security Police killed schoolteacher and underground ANC operative Ahmed Timol.

The police claimed that Timol had committed suicide. Ismail attended Timol's funeral, another formative event in his political development.[10] By then, the Ismails were well-off enough to send Ismail to university in 1972. "My father or my family would have wanted me to become a doctor but at that time only about six Indian students were accepted into Medical School and I was not amongst those six. I had decided to go to study at the University of Durban-Westville and I went and studied for a BSc degree with majors in physiology and microbiology. I was at Durban-Westville from 1972 to 1974." The University of Durban-Westville was yet another apartheid institution, established in 1961 for the exclusive education of Indians. Ismail had become active in the anti-apartheid movement in high school but he became more involved at university, joining up with a group of activists that included Yunus Mohamed and Pravin Gordhan, who would go on to play leading roles in the domestic and underground opposition to apartheid in the 1970s, 1980s, and 1990s. Upon graduation in 1974, Ismail returned to Johannesburg and joined the Human Rights Committee, a small activist group. As he recollected, "it was possibly the only political group in the Transvaal area at the time that continued to do a lot of political work." The committee produced propaganda material, which Ismail distributed through a Johannesburg record shop owned by his brother. In 1975, Ismail found work at a chemical-manufacturing firm called Elite Chemicals, "something which served me well also in my later years in the liberation forces." But the turning point in Ismail's life came December 10, 1974, when the Security Police arrested him. Ismail was walking back to his brother's shop when policemen in plain clothes stopped him:

So this chap says to me, "What's your name?" So I looked at him. He was tall. I said, "Why do you want to know my name?" So the chap says, "Hey, he's a hardegat." It means you're one of those difficult chaps. So I said, "Well, who are you? What do you want?" He said, "Oh, OK," and drove me off to John Vorster Square [police station] where they took me up to the 10th floor, beat me up, pushed me to the window and said, "Ja, you coolies like to jump, why don't you go and jump like Timol? Go and jump." And he was pushing me. He beat me up quite badly. I was bleeding from my ear. I think he cracked a few ribs and things and that day, 10 December 1974, was the day which to me was a critical turning point in my life. My earlier years of political work, political discussions and things, often with friends and political activists, we often talked about and said we would go for armed struggle. That day I didn't go to the meeting. We were supposed to have an

Human Rights Committee meeting. I wanted to be on my own, and I sat back and I thought this through and I thought either I'm going to be cowed by what was happening or I was going to continue with the armed struggle. I made up my mind that day because, often, we said we'd go when the time is right. So that day I made up my mind I would not be cowed. I would go forward.[11]

It would be two years, however, before Ismail finally left South Africa. When high school students in Soweto went out on strike in June 1976, starting a wave of nationwide protests that marked the beginning of the end for the apartheid state, the Security Police came looking for Ismail as part of a national crackdown against activists.

That day, as Soweto burned, I made up my mind that I had to leave the country. So a day or two later I went to my father and I told him that I wanted to leave the country. I said to him that I wanted to go and study and that there were possibilities, if I went to London, the ANC would assist in getting me to university. But the intention was, clearly, I wanted to go for military training because to me the time had come. I had made the determination on 10 December 1974. I decided very quickly thereafter. I said to my father, "Well, it looks like there's a lot of political turmoil. I should leave." They assisted in getting me organized. I had a passport at that time and I left the country. As it happened, I left on my passport.[12]

Ismail flew to Heathrow but British immigration officials deported him to Belgium after he told them naively that he was planning to attend a meeting of the Irish Republican Army. He obtained political asylum in Belgium, which also offered him a refugee passport. In January 1978, Ismail began military training in East Germany. He took part in a six-month Infantry Commander's course and at the end was among ten trainees selected for an advanced course in military engineering, and for explosives and sabotage training. In 1979, he became an instructor in military engineering and explosives at an ANC camp in Angola called Funda, which served as a "finishing school" for insurgents about to be sent into South Africa for operations. That same year, the ANC set up a special operations unit whose sole mission was to attack strategic targets such as military bases, oil refineries, and nuclear plants. In June 1980, members of the unit attacked two state-owned energy companies, National Petroleum Refiners of South Africa (NATREF) and Sasol, and in August 1981, they fired rockets at Pretoria's Voortrekkerhoogte military base, South Africa's largest military complex. In May 1983, the unit set off a car bomb outside the offices of the South African Air Force in Pretoria, killing nineteen people.

Suspect Identification

These actions brought Ismail to the attention of the Security Police—but they knew him as Rashid and had no idea what he looked like. The South African security establishment wanted Ismail dead, but were not clear on whom they were seeking. Captured insurgents kept talking about receiving orders from Comrade Rashid, but then pointing to Barry Gilder when asked to identify Rashid in the album. Meanwhile, Ismail continued sending specially-trained insurgents into South Africa. In March 1983, the Security Police captured Lungile Magxwalisa, a member of Ismail's unit, near Lesotho. Magxwalisa, who left South Africa illegally in November 1977 for military training abroad, gave a two-hundred-page statement about his activities between November 1977 and March 1983. Included in it were thirty-three pages of detail about his dealings and meetings with Rashid in Angola, Lesotho, Mozambique, Swaziland, and Zambia.[13] These were wide-ranging interactions during which Rashid gave Magxwalisa his orders, went over maps and attack plans with him, and offered him money for sustenance. Here, for example, is Magxwalisa's account of a meeting he and fellow members of his unit had with Rashid in October 1982: "Rashid told us that it would be our task to sabotage the train bridge over the Umfolozi River with explosives."[14] On March 21, 1982, Rashid gave Magxwalisa R40 and promised to give him more money the following day. Yet when it came time for Magxwalisa to point out Rashid in the album, Magxwalisa picked out Gilder. Glory Sedibe, captured in August 1986 by the Security Police, identified Barry Gilder incorrectly as a member of the ANC's special operations unit. "Rashid was commissar of the unit," Sedibe said. "He moved back-and-forth between Swaziland and Mozambique and had an affair with the wife of [another colleague]."[15] On the face of it, Sedibe knew that Gilder and Rashid were two different people.

The mention of the affair is confusing, however, as it is not clear which man—Gilder or Ismail—Sedibe was accusing of the affair. As Gilder jokingly put it to me: "As a result of this misidentification, I was carrying both my own sins and the sins of Rashid on my shoulders, which probably increased the regime's desire to get hold of me or eliminate me."[16] At the time, it was no joke. Craig Williamson claimed that he saved Gilder from assassination by the Security Police. The two men knew each other from when Williamson spied on the white left on the campus of the University of Witwatersrand. They also served together on the NUSAS executive (fig. 7.2). Gilder suspected but did not know for sure about Williamson's spying. Here is Williamson's account:

> Barry Gilder is, in fact, lucky he's alive because he was identified
> as Rashid and I consistently said in TREWITS and those places,

I said, "this is not Rashid, this is Barry Gilder."[17] And they wanted to kill him because they wanted to kill Rashid. And I said, "you are going to kill the wrong guy. That's not him." You see, that is from the album photograph. It's only because I completely, from Security Branch Intelligence, I said—in fact, I got irritated—"I know the guy. I sat with him in NUSAS. I met him in London. I watched him in London." . . . I said, "that's Barry Gilder, it's not Rashid." I think they were quite pissed off with me and if I'd said, "Yes, that's Rashid," they would have taken him out—and it would have been a lot easier to take out Barry than Rashid, because they knew where he was. He was moving. It wasn't Rashid that they were watching. It was Barry. It's a good example for you of the failure of the album. They went on. They were completely convinced and, as I said, it even got to the stage where it irritated me, because they kept on questioning.[18]

When I put Williamson's claim to Gilder, however, he responded: "This is not the first time Williamson has claimed that he saved my life. I got a call . . . sometime in 1990, I think, telling me that Williamson [was claiming to have] saved my life. If, indeed, Williamson had correctly identified the photo of me as not being Rashid, why were they still mistaking me for Rashid into the 1990s?"[19] Why indeed did the mistaken identity persist? Eugene Fourie said, "You know, every second person identified Barry Gilder as Rashid."[20] This was the source of the police confusion. Although the Security Police branded Ismail white even though they knew he was Indian, they still had to contend with the implications of that mistake for their manhunt.

How do you look for an Indian suspect when your information is telling you to look for a white suspect? How, if you are Eugene Fourie, do you convince yourself to trust your album and the bodies that the album sought to document when you know that those bodies are

FIGURE 7.2 Group portrait of NUSAS executive including Barry Gilder—and spy Craig Williamson, in a dark shirt at left. By permission of Gerhard Maré.

miscast? When I asked Fourie about this in July 2016, focusing specifically on the case of Ismail and Barry Gilder, he offered a reply:

> They must have looked alike. I've never seen them in person. They must have looked alike, and then they [the captured insurgents] would identify him and, being honest and not trying to lie or anything, they would say that [Barry Gilder was Rashid]. They don't know that the person I'm showing is Barry Gilder. They know him as Rashid. I know he's Barry Gilder because his photo comes from Johannesburg and from his Barry Gilder file. You, on that side, the name is not written on the photo. And I know, I can see here, it's Barry Gilder, but they would identify him as Rashid.[21]

Are you referring to a photograph with information on the back?
I can read all the information there.

Can the suspect see you read the information?
No, I'm holding the photo like this. He's looking at the photo but
he can't see what I'm reading.

**What about his facial expressions? Can you see how he is re-
acting to your question about the photograph?**
When he starts talking, then I put the photo down. He's already
identified him, and then I've already read everything.

**Were you ever given any psychological training, to see if the sus-
pect was lying?**
No, never.

**Was there a time when you felt that you could read the sus-
pects' facial expressions?**
With your experience later on, you know when a person is lying
or not lying. It's just through experience.

Fourie said it was only sometime between 1990 and 1991 that the Security Police finally identified Ismail. The discovery was made possible
by the political opening created in part by new apartheid leader F. W.
De Klerk. On February 2, 1990, De Klerk unbanned the ANC and a host
of other anti-apartheid organizations; nine days later he released Nelson
Mandela from prison. On May 4, 1990, De Klerk's cabinet met with an
ANC delegation led by Mandela to set the ground rules for a negotiated
end to apartheid. The parties set up a working group to look into the
normalization of political activity, the release of political prisoners, and
the return of exiles. The parties agreed to consider the decriminalization of a range of offenses, including those involving leaving South
Africa illegally and belonging to banned groups. To make it possible for

the ANC and other formerly banned organizations to return to South Africa to resume normal political activity, De Klerk's government granted immunity for political offenses. To return to the country without prosecution, exiles—especially those involved in the insurgency against apartheid—had to apply for indemnity. Ismail applied so he could return to South Africa to participate in the negotiations. That is how the Security Police were able finally to match Aboobaker Ismail to Rashid, as Fourie recalled:

> That is when we first identified Rashid. We only found out later that we had a file on Rashid [all along]. We didn't know his real name, so what happened is that, on Barry Gilder's identification . . . if somebody said "this is Barry Gilder," then we wrote the information that person gives out. But if he says "it's Rashid," then we wrote on Barry Gilder's identification as if it is Rashid. So all the info about Barry Gilder and Rashid went into one file, was under one person until . . . later. . . . We knew he came from Johannesburg, we knew he was born on Christmas Day, and then—when they left Zambia, before they left Zambia, they used to send in their latest photo, color photos, and the application form to come back to South Africa, and then we received this because the ANC sent it to us. When we received it, I used to go through them and see if there are people that we know. And I saw this photo of an Indian man, and he was born on Christmas Day, and I went to Brigadier Martin Naude and I told him, "Here's Rashid," and then we only knew what his real name was.[22]

How were you able to get his file?

> Then we entered the computers to see if we had a file on this man, that name—Aboobaker Ismail. . . . We looked on the computer systems [to see] if we had a file under that name

and we saw that at Head Office and in Johannesburg we had a file on Aboobaker Ismail, but with very little information in. So what they would have done, if the files were not destroyed, was to put all that information into a file.

So that is how the Security Police came to identify Ismail as Rashid. Recall that, in Fourie's opinion, the mistake came not from the police's own systems but from Africans' inability to identify Indian and white people. Because African insurgents could not tell their Indian and white comrades apart, Fourie believed, they fed their Security Police interrogators wrong information. And because Fourie and his colleagues could not admit the fallibility of their devices, they went along with information even when they knew it to be wrong. We could regard this as yet another illustration of apartheid's well-documented pragmatism. Far more profitable, however, would be to see this as the weakness it was. Despite claims to the contrary, the apartheid state and the various bits of its apparatus could not master race. The apartheid state could certainly create whatever fantasies it desired. But it could not forge those racial fantasies out of nothing; it had to fashion them out of the dross it was given, even when that was recognized to be nothing more than waste. To be sure, Fourie and his colleagues were not alone in this world of racial make-believe. They were not the only ones to doubt the ability of Africans to identify Indians. Here, for example, is lawyer Kessie Naidu in May 1988 cross-examining Oscar Linda Moni, an ANC insurgent who had defected under duress to the Security Police.[23] At issue was whether Moni could indeed identify Ebrahim Ebrahim, a senior ANC member of Indian descent who was on trial for treason. Moni claimed in his evidence to have met Ebrahim in an ANC office in Angola sometime between 1982 and 1983. Ebrahim, represented by Naidu, disputed this, saying he was not in Angola during that time. To be fair, Naidu was trying to save his client from the gallows and he had to do that by discrediting the evidence of state witnesses such as Moni.

> NAIDU: Is it perhaps possible that you are mistaking him with somebody else, some other Indian person that you saw?
>
> MONI: The Indian people I knew at Angola as either members of the ANC or people who had access to the ANC offices were not even more than two or three.

> NAIDU: So who was the other one or two Indian people that you knew during that period in Angola?
>
> MONI: There was a young man who used to be called Rashid of the Specials Ops, this is the Special Operations Department.

> NAIDU: Who else?
>
> MONI: Patel. I do not remember any other Indians, except for Brazzo, who is Peter. We received training together with him in the GDR [German Democratic Republic] . . .

> NAIDU: Was he an Indian person or a black person, Peter Brazzo?
>
> MONI: Yes. He was an Indian . . .

> NAIDU: Now is Peter and Peter Brazzo the same person?
>
> MONI: Well, I have made it clear that Peter Brazzo is one and the same person. There was a Patel, a black person, there was an Indian Patel who was at Luanda.

> NAIDU: Just forget about the black Patel for a moment. Let us talk about the Indian Patel.

The Other Indian

Besides Rashid, Peter Patel was the other Indian that Moni identified. Unlike Rashid, however, Peter Patel was in the album. Like Rashid,

Peter Patel was also an alias, as was the more commonly used name, Brazzo. His real name is Rayman Lalla and, while he is also of Indian descent, he comes from Durban (fig. 7.3). Whereas Rashid is of Muslim background, Lalla is of Hindu upbringing.

I asked Lalla in September 2017 to talk to me about his mug shot, and his response is intriguing:

> That picture was taken when we were arrested by the Swazis. And we were taken, I was taken, to Mbabane police station and—I think it's 1984, and at that stage a lot of comrades got arrested. I was, I was trying to think, where was I? I had left TZ's [fellow insurgent Thami Zulu's] place at the garage. TZ was staying at a garage in Mbabane, at the filling station. His flat was upstairs. I went to the flat and we had a conversation and then I left. . . . So as I was walking, Shiba, the policeman, and two other cars came up and I began to run. And I think a local chap saw the police running and he

4036

FIGURE 7.3 Mug shot of Ray Lalla in the Terrorist Album. Courtesy of National Archives & Records Service of South Africa.

tripped me. . . . So from there I was taken to Mbabane Police Station and I was under the name of Ratilal Pradeep.[24]

What did your papers say?

I didn't have papers, but I just said, "I'm Ratilal Pradeep". . . . I was beaten up quite badly . . . for running away. So I was taken there, booked in as Ratilal Pradeep, and then, in the middle of the night, Shiba came with his vehicle with two other guys. They put a hood over my head and they drove me to a place. Later on, with a little bit of knowing Swaziland, I found out—but at the first day, because of the distance that I traveled, I thought I was being taken to the border [to be handed over to the South African Security Police]. There was a hood on my head. . . . I remember going into a place. . . . I remember that clearly, and I was put in a chair with the hood still on, the handcuffs and the leg irons still on. And I was being interrogated from time to time. I was hit on the head. With the hood still on, they were questioning me. And I realized that there could have been a case of mistaken identity. Because they were questioning me about things that it was quite clear they didn't know what structure I was working in and they used the term and the reference "white C."[25]

Is it possible that a witness had identified Lalla as Rashid? Lalla said that, even though he could not see his Swazi interrogators because of his hood, he suspected that they were relaying his answers to someone else because of the time it took the interrogators to pose follow-up questions. To Lalla, it was clear that the Swazis and the South African agents directing his arrest behind the scenes had no idea whom they had arrested or how key he was to the underground operations of the ANC: "They did not know who I was. I was in the leadership of the

Natal Command, which had conducted various operations inside South Africa, making Durban the most bombed city in the country. But they did not know who I was. When they did not have their album, they did not know who they were dealing with." Lalla thought his mug shot had been taken in the Mbabane Police Station shortly after his arrest and then fed to the South African Security Police. This was quite common. Regional intelligence and police agencies kept tabs on South African exiles and shared information with their South African counterparts. South African agents are also known to have penetrated United Nations relief agencies in southern Africa and to have used these agencies to collect information on South Africans who applied for political asylum or refugee status. As Eugene Fourie told me, "That is where Botswana and Swaziland helped us a lot. A big group [of South African exiles] would come and apply for asylum and then we would get all those photos and application forms. That helped us a lot and then we had to rely on the [police] divisions, their informers, to tell them who left the country."[26]

Asked if he was able to work out why the Swazis arrested him, Lalla said, "They were just looking for stuff. People, identity, names, the normal things that we would say—'No, I don't know. I met somebody and I'm looking for the refugee center'—that kind of thing." Unlike his ANC comrades, however, Lalla did not apply for asylum or refugee status in Swaziland, and therefore lived in a twilight zone of constant police harassment and potential deportation. The Swazi police, especially, were notorious for "selling" arrested ANC exiles to the South African security services. Lalla described one tactic for eluding them:

> I basically doctored all my IDs. So what would happen is that I would use a Mozambican ID or I would use another ID. But these were rudimentary IDs. We would steam the photograph off

somebody's ID and put your own photograph, and then take a coin and just smash it with ink on the photo so it looks a little bit blurred. But later on, the ANC got more professional.[27]

Lalla joined the ANC underground in the 1970s. He had a passport and used it to move in and out of the country. He had to go into exile, however, after the South African military attacked an ANC facility in Matola, Mozambique, in January 1981 and found information that threatened to expose him. Lalla said, "I was working in the urban command at that stage and I was based internally. So when they raided Matola there was a whole chain of events that took place that forced me to leave. But I didn't leave like in—I was still legal. Systems were not so coordinated at the time. So I had to come back and close some gaps for the command because virtually the whole command in Matola was killed."[28] Lalla suspected that it was not until the mug shot taken by the Swazi police in 1984 that the South Africans finally had a "face to a name."

Because even during the period prior to that, we could reapply for passports, get someone to apply for your old passport from inside the country. You understand what I mean? It was expired and what have you. The issue here is that maybe we never went home, we never saw the people. . . . There was a lot of gaps in the system to move and maneuver. I just think it is a good starting point they [the Security Police] had for themselves, and it may have led to their limited success. But I think their main success was the laws that they had at their disposal just to capture and interrogate anybody. Even the issue of assassination and what have you, they would just shoot somebody. And in those countries—those countries never had good security to be able to manage, and that's why you found these things happening.[29]

Lalla's last legitimate passport was issued in 1981, and it was valid for a few years. But he was able to recycle it:

> The bottom line over here is that you had the Department of Home Affairs. It wasn't called Home Affairs, it was called Indian Affairs. You know all those things. There were lots of ways to get around the system, right? And part of my operational process was also to—we needed vehicles, we needed infrastructure. You know what I mean? So, you can only do it through legitimate means. Sometimes, some of these things, nobody put it together. I found out [after the end of apartheid, when Lalla joined the police as a senior leader] that it wasn't their technical ability to be able to identify us. I found [it was through] informants, impimpis, askaris, through word of mouth. I could be wrong. When I look at even some of the setbacks of some of the other cases, as well—it was my reading of the situation.[30]

Lalla operated between Mozambique, Swaziland, and Zambia. In 1990, he returned illegally to South Africa as part of a mission dubbed Operation Vula.[31] The operation sought to place senior insurgents within South Africa to take advantage of the political ferment that had engulfed South Africa since the late 1970s and had increased in intensity as the apartheid state lost its ability to impose order. The Security Police arrested Lalla a few months after his return. He spent a few months in detention, but was released when the apartheid state decided not to prosecute those involved in the mission. I asked him in September 2017 what memories came to mind when I showed him a copy of his mug shot. Lalla replied:

> When I look at this? I just think of isolation. The picture reminds me of, you know, there was a stage when we were detained and

we never knew whether anybody knew—or I never knew whether anybody knew—that I was detained . . . when I was arrested on the border. So, one of the habits that I had in prison or in every cell that I was in, I always wrote my three-four names in the cell because I thought I was going to be—you know what I mean? Because nobody—it was all one-on-one and we [were] gone.[32]

In hopes that a detained comrade might be put in the same cell, Lalla scribbled his *noms de guerre* on the wall: Peter Patel, Brazzo, Ratilal Pradeep. The names came without a picture. But Lalla hoped that someone might be able to connect that string of aliases to him and in some way help him live on. As things turned out, Lalla did not need to be memorialized through false names. He made it into a democratic South Africa, in whose relative safety he is able to look at his mug shot and remember a world long gone.

EIGHT

The Family Bible

ON DECEMBER 21, 1987, a security policeman gave Chris Giffard, an ANC operative arrested in Cape Town five days earlier, a copy of the Terrorist Album and ordered him to point out the individuals whose mug shots he recognized. Giffard, held in solitary confinement with nothing to read except a family Bible he had snatched from his parents' house as he was being led away in handcuffs, spent hours in his cell poring over the album. By the next morning, when the police reclaimed the album, Giffard had counted 5,350 mug shots (125 of which belonged to whites), and identified six individuals.[1] These included Damian de Lange, a high school friend who had joined the ANC in exile, and Tony Yengeni, an ANC military commander with whom Giffard had worked in the anti-apartheid underground in Cape Town. "I gave them three names for Tony and said I wasn't sure. I identified one white guy who I had worked with in Zimbabwe, whose real name and whereabouts I didn't know. There were some other known figures who I could identify, but no one I had worked with, so I didn't mind doing it."[2] Giffard himself was not in the album because, although he had been a member of the ANC underground since 1983, he had not spent time in exile. "My role had been running a propaganda unit. . . . Intelligence transmission for the Cape Town network, other support like helping people cross the border, and coordinating and running cells of ANC activists working in legal organizations like the United Democratic Front, the End Conscription Campaign, NUSAS."[3] The police had already smashed Giffard's network when they arrested him. They knew he was unlikely to know much, if anything, about the movement and location of armed insurgents still free. So they did not make the album the centerpiece of Giffard's interrogation during his first three months in jail. They were lax with it. They let Giffard keep it in his cell for a night, giving him something other than a Bible to look at.

In January 1988, the police drove Giffard to Piet Retief, a small town on the border with Swaziland, for an *in loco* investigation.[4] Piet Retief, about a thousand miles from Cape Town, was a key transit point for ANC insurgents moving in and out of South Africa. Giffard had been on the border in Piet Retief in September 1987 to fetch Lumka Yengeni, an ANC comrade code-named Shirley, and drive her to Cape Town, where she was to join a network led by her partner, Tony Yengeni. Tony Yengeni had returned to South Africa in 1986, after ten years in exile, to lead the ANC's military operations in the Western Cape. The Yengenis were arrested, however, in late 1987. So Lumka Yengeni came along on that January road trip, but in a separate car. The police did not want to mix detainees—even suspected terrorists—across the color line. The police needed Giffard to point out where he had picked up Lumka Yengeni and wanted Yengeni to say which route she had taken from Swaziland to rendezvous with Giffard. The inspection took a few days, during which time Giffard and Lumka Yengeni were detained at the Piet Retief Police Station. When the two arrived at the police station, they found Phumla Williams, a fellow ANC operative who had been detained at the station since her arrest in June 1987. To prevent Giffard and Yengeni from communicating with each other, the police put them in separate cells on either side of Williams. Thus it was that Giffard found himself flanked by two women who, unlike him, were in the album. Despite the police's intention to separate them, Giffard and Yengeni found a way to communicate with one another by using Williams as a go-between. "We emptied the water from our toilets and used the sewage pipe as a telephone system. She acted as an intermediary between me and Lumka," said Giffard, recalling details missing from a secret diary he kept during his incarceration, writing in his Bible. (It was a Jerusalem Bible edition with many blank pages and wide margins.)[5] So how did Yengeni and Williams come to be in the album?

Yengeni's and Williams's mug shots were among the 5,350 that Giffard tallied in December 1987. But it is doubtful that he would have recognized them. In February 2016, when I showed Williams a copy of her mug shot that Giffard would have seen in the album, she was adamant at first that it was not hers. So was her sister. It took five months for Williams to come around to the possibility that perhaps that was her identikit.[6] There was a simple reason that Yengeni and Williams were not among the six people Giffard identified. Their mug shots were old, taken when each was a young woman, not yet twenty. Giffard had not known them at that age, and the quality of the mug shots was such that the images could not be trusted to render their subjects faithfully. This, as we shall discover in Chapter 10, was one of the key weaknesses of the album: its inability to keep pace with its subjects as they grew up, aged, and changed appearance. The mug shots were static. They froze individuals in time, leaving the Security Police to rely on photographs often more than two decades old for identification and apprehension. So while Giffard could identify Yengeni the person, having traveled a thousand miles to Cape Town with her in September 1987, he could not do the same with her mug shot. The body and the image were not the same thing. As for Williams, he could identify neither her nor her mug shot, as he had not known of her existence before he was placed in a cell next to hers for about a week. In fact, during their time in the Piet Retief cells, Giffard and Williams did not meet once. They spoke every day through their makeshift telephone system but they could not have said what the other looked like. They could not have picked each other out of a police line-up. But the police did not care. Giffard and Yengeni were part of one investigation, and Williams was the subject of another. As far as the police were concerned, they had their terrorists and all they had to do was build criminal cases that would stand up in court.

Yengeni (born in 1957) and Williams (born in 1960) came of age politically in the time of the 1976 student uprisings—the first sustained protest against apartheid since the 1960s.[7] Still in high school, they joined thousands of other black students in rejecting the state's demand that classes in all-black state schools be taught not in local languages but only in Afrikaans. They were part of an entire generation raised in the environment of the black consciousness movement.[8] Like so many others, Yengeni and Williams were inspired by the movement's calls for black pride and self-help. And when the apartheid state responded to the uprisings with a wave of repression, killing hundreds and driving thousands into exile, they were also among those who left the country and sought political and military training abroad.[9] While the majority of the students who fled to exile after June 1976 were men, there were also many women. These were not abstract activists who left South Africa to swell the ranks of the revolutionary movement but individuals, and each had a story about how he or she came to be in exile. If the album has much value as a historical source, it is because it allows us to look at each mug shot and, by investigating that image, find the specific account of how this or that person fled into exile and, by doing so, came to be in the album. Of course, for the Security Police, Yengeni and Williams were S4s—African terrorists who were in the album precisely because they had left South Africa without the permission of the state. If we are to do justice to the history the mug shots reflect, however, we must take seriously the stories that each mug shot can tell about a particular period in the history of contemporary South Africa. By weaving together oral history and traces of the apartheid security archive, we are able to make the album say more than its compilers intended.[10] Even more importantly, we are able to see the complex ways in which African women negotiated their place and role in the ANC underground and in the struggle against apartheid.

Photographic Affinities?

In August 2016, I emailed Williams a copy of the mug shot that the album and accompanying index said was hers (fig. 8.1). The photograph shows an oval-faced young woman with bright eyes and a neatly-combed afro. Williams responded:

> If you had just sent this photo and asked me to identify [it], I would have genuinely told you I do not know [who this is]. I have absolutely no idea where was this taken and also not sure if indeed it's me. I honestly am not sure this is me. I do know they photographed me when I was arrested but my hair was uncombed and my folks had not even been allowed to send me the toiletry. So it can't be that one. Maybe if I got the clearer quality I might be able to assist.[11]

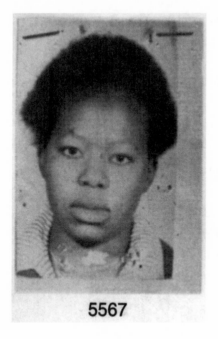

5567

FIGURE 8.1 Mug shot of Phumla
Williams in the Terrorist Album.
Courtesy of National Archives & Records
Service of South Africa.

A few minutes later, Williams sent me another email: "This is definitely
not me. I also sent it to my sister. She is also adamant it's not me in this
photo."[12] Three days later, I emailed Williams a better scan of the mug
shot. She wrote back:

> This quality seems to be telling a different story. It just might be
> me. But I have no idea where it was taken. That's why I'm so con-
> fused. I don't even recall myself with that hairstyle. In exile I gen-
> erally was in plaits. So surely it was taken whilst I was in the
> country and possibly young. I will also print and show it to my
> other relatives [to see] if they recall this picture. The other ques-
> tion is how it could have ended with the police (I assume it is from
> the police archive).[13]

Twelve days later, Williams sent me the following email:

> I had a relook and the print was clearer. It does appear to be me
> but my sister is still not convinced. The only challenge now [is] I
> have no clue where and when it was taken. It may well be my first
> Home Affairs ID photo. I just don't recall it.[14]

In January 2017, almost six months after Williams and I started emailing
each other about her mug shot, she wrote me:

> I managed to check again the photo you sent me against my ID
> photo. On closer look . . . I realize this [the police mug shot] was
> my second ID before that one, given the clothing and the hair,
> but certainly the facial features seem to be mine.[15]

This was one of the most illuminating exchanges with a person framed
by the police as a terrorist. The exchange raised a number of questions about the usefulness of the album—its tactical worth, if you
will—as a branding instrument. When Williams and I spoke about
her mug shot, we shared a relationship marked by mutual respect. I
was not a policeman torturing her for information; she was not a detainee whose very survival depended on the information that she
could provide. There was neither urgency nor pressure to our exchange.
Yet there we were over six months, going back and forth over whether
that was indeed her mug shot. How much more difficult, then, must
this have been for detainees under pressure to make the mug shots
speak?

How menacing must the encounter with the album have been for
insurgents from exile who had certainly encountered more people

in it than Giffard had? My exchange with Williams raised another question: Was the album a talisman employed by the police to show the reach of their power? The police insisted that the album was useful and that it allowed them to keep track of their enemies. But how true was that, when Giffard could only identify six out of 5,350 mug shots, and when it took Williams almost six months to identify her own identikit? I am aware of the changed context and of the fact that many of the people I interviewed for this book had never seen their mug shots, and that some had not seen these images in more than thirty years. But the very insistence by the police that the album and its index recorded South Africans who had fled the country for exile raises all of these questions. Let us turn for answers to two biographical accounts by Williams—the first given in front of a magistrate to the Security Police on June 30, 1987, about her 1978 flight to exile, and the second included in a September 2014 interview of Williams by the Government Communications and Information Service.[16] The two accounts must, of necessity, be treated differently. The first one must be taken with a grain of salt as Williams wrote it under duress; the second one was necessarily written with the benefit of hindsight and long after the end of apartheid. The first account, dictated to a white apartheid magistrate by a woman who had been detained and subjected to torture, was a five-page report that sought to explain how Williams ended up in the ANC in exile. Understood by the magistrate to be a confession, the statement was essentially a document intended to incriminate Williams in political crime.[17] The magistrate wanted Williams to explain what the Security Police and the government they represented considered to be her political deviance. Williams had to tell the magistrate and her captors how she came to exist outside of the law—apartheid law.

A Coerced Biography

My name is Phumla Mirriam Williams. I was born on the 1st of July 1960. . . . I went as far as Standard 8 in Musi High School, Pimville. I left the country in 1978 February, together with my boyfriend. . . . He stayed in Evaton, though I never knew his home address. He . . . together with myself and a gentleman . . . met at the Park Station, board[ed] a train to Breyten. It left with us in the evening and arrived at about 9:00 in the morning. From Breyten we walked until we got to the fence [on the border with Swaziland]. We crossed the fence illegally at about 4:00 in the afternoon. On the other side, we were met by a certain guy in a green Peugeot. From there he drove us to a house which we later knew to be [the] "White House," i.e. ANC house in Manzini.[18]

Williams spent two weeks, with about fifteen other ANC recruits, at the house before crossing illegally into Mozambique. ANC scouts took Williams and her fellow recruits to a house in Matola, a suburb outside the capital Maputo.

Here a proper debriefing of us was done. We were called individually and asked our names, addresses, family backgrounds. [I] was asked whether I wanted to join the military wing of the ANC or to go to school. I then told him I wanted to go to school. Reasons being that I left [South Africa] with my boyfriend with the agreement that we were going to school. I was then told if I go to school I will never be in a position to go back home. The only field that would give me an opportunity of going back home is when I join the military wing of the ANC. (I therefore agreed to join the military wing of the ANC but) further stressing my interest to further my studies. They agreed that I will get a chance of furthering my studies. From here they then prepared us to leave for Angola. That was after two weeks. We then left, being a group of about 20, [for] Lusaka en route to Angola. We arrived on a Saturday evening. We were to stay overnight then proceed the next day. Unfortunately, on the next day we couldn't proceed since one of the girls was sick. So they decided that all the girls should remain. We (girls) then stayed for a week. The girls included (Nellie, Dora Modimulo, Emily Makgabo, Mary, myself). When we proceeded to Angola we were minus Nellie since it was discovered she was pregnant.[19]

The ANC sent Williams to a military camp in Quibaxe in the north of Angola. There she received physical training and political education. Williams spent a month in Quibaxe before moving to Novo Catengue, the biggest military ANC camp, situated in the south of Angola. She spent four months at the camp undergoing firearms training and learning topography.

Thereafter, a group of about 18 of us went to Luanda. We were told that we were going for further political training. A group of 20 (6 girls and 14 men) went to Russia. There we were taught political economy, philosophy, international revolution and the history of the Soviet Union's Communist Party. The course lasted approximately one year. We then went back to Luanda. I stayed there for five months. I waited for orders. I was then sent to Maputo.[20]

In 1980, Williams joined the ANC's political machinery:

My duty was to gather information from newspapers and then to compile reports over the happenings in South Africa. This information was handed over to the higher structure by me. . . . We worked there until 1983. In 1983 I was sent to Swaziland. In 1984 I worked with 3 persons. . . . We worked together for about five months and then I was summoned again by the political committee. From approximately June 1984 I did nothing until December 1984. In the beginning of 1985 a new committee was put together. . . . We had to do the political work for the Transvaal. . . . In March 1985 I realized that I was pregnant. I was then removed until December 1985 when the child was born.[21]

Williams resumed her work with the ANC in May 1986, interviewing recruits and giving them instructions. Between June and July 1986, the ANC ordered Williams to return to South Africa for underground political work. "My duty was to do propaganda service in Soweto" Williams said. She returned to South Africa in November 1986, and stayed with a sister, with an aunt, and at hotels.

During this time, I contacted my people in Swaziland approximately 3 times. . . . I had not begun to work yet. I had problems with accommodation. My money was finished and they [the ANC] did not again send me money. The time I was in South Africa I did nothing. I actually wanted to study further. That is all. I am not completely certain about the dates. Specific dates were never arranged for when receiving money.[22]

A group of askaris kidnapped Williams on June 29, 1987, as she alighted from a taxi outside the Baragwanath Hospital in Soweto. Leading the arrest was Glory Sedibe, a senior ANC operative codenamed Comrade September who had been kidnapped from a jail in Swaziland in August 1986 and then turned by the Security Police. Williams and Sedibe had worked together in Mozambique and Swaziland. The police also tried to turn Williams, she recalled, using Sedibe and his Mozambican wife: "She was the one who was brought to tell me 'the boers are not as bad as we have been made to believe in the ANC,' those were her words in heavily-accented English, as she was Portuguese. Unfortunately, she got a rude awaken[ing] to discover I was not as easy as she was made to believe."[23] When Giffard and Yengeni joined Williams in the detention cells in Piet Retief in January 1988, the police were still trying to turn Williams. They eventually charged her with terrorism. Williams's ordeal at the hands of the Security Police ended when apartheid collapsed in the early 1990s and the state began the long process of setting political prisoners free.

Auto(biography)

Williams's second account—her 2014 autobiography—tells a different story. This is not the story of innocence recounted to a white magistrate and the Security Police. Neither is it a tale of a young woman following her boyfriend to exile. Instead, Williams's free account tells of her poor upbringing as the child of a single mother, a live-in domestic servant who barely saw her own children but spent her time looking after white children the same age as her own.[24] As Williams said, "Even though I could not conceptualize the differences [between herself and the white children that her mother looked after], I knew that they had shoes and I did not." By the time she was a high school student, Williams said, "I knew that the system was wrong. I knew that something had to change. It wasn't a problem for me to get involved. It felt natural." She resolved to leave the country for military training abroad after seeing the police violence that greeted the 1976 student uprisings. "I left the country with my Mom's blessing. I didn't like leaving my Mom," said Williams. But she felt she had no choice. That is how she ended up in the album.[25]

When Williams told the second story—a narrative that centered on her mother's exploitation at the hands of a white family—apartheid had been dead (at least in the statute books) for twenty years. Williams spoke as a citizen of a democratic South Africa and a civil servant in a government founded on the will of the majority. That second account took us past the mug shot and to a world in which Williams could look back with some satisfaction on her family's life of struggle. As Williams explained in the second account, she went into exile with her mother's blessings. Far from being a young woman following a boyfriend into worlds unknown, Williams went into exile because she desired freedom. Her mother also desired freedom and for her children to grow up in a world freed from apartheid. That Williams's departure led her into the album was something she could not control. The Security Police could frame her however they wanted; they could not alter her resolve to fight for freedom. That is how people like Williams make their mug shots speak anew; that is how they open these frozen images to new interpretations and meanings. While her mug shot sought to freeze her in one moment, Williams grew in exile. She became a trained guerilla and political operator, a mother, a student, and an insurgent. She traveled the world and became a fuller person, one whose links to her family remained strong, despite her fugitive status and the counterinsurgents constantly on the prowl for her and for people like her. So when she finally agreed that it was her mug shot in the album, she could recall a world filled with both pain and possibility.

Lumka / Be Careful

"You know my body, my structure of the body, it assisted me. I was a very tiny somebody at that stage. You can see I look innocent even if

I have dirty dreads . . . when you look at me you wouldn't look at someone who would incite people to leave school," said Lumka Yengeni in 2017 as she looked at her mug shot (fig. 8.2).[26] Unlike Williams, Yengeni knew when her photograph was taken: sometime after her first arrest in late 1977.

On September 25, 1977, Yengeni was among the twenty thousand mourners who attended the funeral of Steve Biko, tortured to death by the police on September 12. Yengeni, already a student activist in the Eastern Cape, managed to attend the funeral despite a massive police hunt for her. "They checked all over looking for me. They did not find me and I managed to go to Steve Biko's funeral as well, by the way. I was there." But Yengeni's luck ran out a few weeks after the funeral. The police arrested her as she was walking past a fire station in East London on her way to see her mother, a domestic worker in Quigney, a white suburb of East London. Her mother had arranged for Yengeni

3032

FIGURE 8.2 Mug shot of Lumka Yengeni in the Terrorist Album. Courtesy of National Archives & Records Service of South Africa.

to lie low with relatives in a rural area nearby. Unbeknownst to Yengeni, the fire station housed a secret Security Police office.

> Just before I crossed the robots, and I was on my own—it was in the morning, about ten o'clock in the morning—in front of me, I saw cars. And I knew. I saw Ngcoko [a local policeman with a reputation for brutality]. . . . Ngcoko was not Special Branch. He was very notorious. . . . I was not arrested by the Special Branch. I was arrested by Ngcoko.[27]

Ngcoko and his fellow detectives were angry when they finally caught up with Yengeni, who had been running rings around them, because they had imagined her larger than life. "Really, they thought they would see a woman of substance," said Yengeni, who was not yet eighteen at the time. Ngcoko handed Yengeni over to the Security Police, who took her to a police station in Cambridge, another suburb of East London.

> And then when I got to Cambridge, I was put—you know, that was my first experience of arrest, that was my first—put in a cell . . . and they just locked me in. It's so dirty, you don't know where to sit. Toilets, blankets, grey, dirty. It stinks. The toilet is, like, blocked. . . . I was severely beaten in that thing because they wanted names of people. They wanted people who were behind all this. I did not agree. . . . One thing with me, I don't know how I have done it, throughout my detentions—that was the first. That was the most cruel. Maybe it's because we went there knowing that there are two things: either you sell out, either you sell out or you die. If you don't sell out you are going to die. So we were so militant to the extent that [we thought] "let me be killed than sell other people." I was beaten until I was bleeding.[28]

The police detained Yengeni for three months, during which time she was subjected to merciless beatings.

> You know, I was in a ring. You were put in a ring. If you are kicked by this one, you will be kicked by this one, you will fall on the other. You are literally in the ring . . . they *moered* [hit] me. I was bruised. Anybody [who] could have seen me, would not [have recognized me]. I think I was seen and people say "No, we think it's her." They could not recognize me. . . . I was hit. I think that's when I went to hospital. I was literally bleeding and I bled for some time—something that I didn't understand.[29]

The police photographed Yengeni sometime during the early part of her incarceration. Yengeni tried to work out the timing as she studied the mug shot I showed her:

> I don't think they gave you the photographs that they take on the spot. If they give you the photograph that they take on the spot, I'm not going to be like this. This one is after days, when you are there, you don't know what to do, your hair is—you sit there. When you come back beaten up, you tie your hair and it's—but I had nothing to change [into]. The things that are here [in the photograph] are things that I was arrested with. That polo-neck I still remember. I had a beige polo-neck. So I have not appeared in court—because once you are still in Section 6, once you—or it will be the first day you appeared in court after detention. Because that's where your family will see you for the first time, and, after that, when you are in a trial, you'll get things, food . . . [30]

When I asked Yengeni if she had seen the photograph before I showed it to her in September 2017, she believed she had:

I've seen this photograph somewhere. I don't remember [where]. I thought of it but I couldn't remember. But what I do remember is that this photograph—I was in detention, as I said, that day—I remember what is in my head. Because most of the time you can't call, you have no cord, you have nothing. So you just tie your hair. I don't know, but it's not a photograph that I have. If this photograph I have seen, I've seen it in the police file. I don't have this photograph.[31]

At the end of her three months in detention, Yengeni was charged with public violence. This was in connection with the unrest that followed Biko's funeral. Protesters burned down government property, including beer halls and police vehicles. In 1978, the Grahamstown Supreme Court found Yengeni guilty of public violence and sentenced her to four years in prison, two of which were suspended. Yengeni began serving her sentence at Rooi Hel (Red Hell), a notorious prison in Port Elizabeth.[32] When prisoners there marked the second anniversary of the 1976 student uprisings with protest songs, prison warders attacked them. "You know, they have those bells," Yengeni recalled. "They blow that whistle and, remember, that corner is a corner with terrorists. We were flying all over the place." To break the women's protests, the prison authorities separated them and moved them to different prisons around the country. Yengeni served the last year of her two-year sentence in Pretoria. When Yengeni was released in 1980, she threw herself back into activist work. She worked with student organizations and trade unions in East London. She was detained for a weekend sometime between June and July 1980. By then, Yengeni had been recruited to the ANC underground in East London. The ANC feared that, were Yengeni to be subjected to torture again, she might compromise its underground network in the area. So the organization ordered her to go into exile. She knew this was because "really, I was deeply involved. I was sort of a security risk. Because if I would be arrested and maybe made—beaten to an extent of, I would really—but then, I was ready. My whole mind and everything was there. So it was a nice thing, as well. So when they [the ANC] came, I didn't have to think. Everything was arranged. Someone took me." Despite Yengeni's single-minded resolve to go into exile for the sake of her comrades, her decision to leave was still wrenching. In fact, Yengeni cried in September 2017 when she told me the story of her departure.

> You know, I had promised my mother that I would go back to school and study so that I can change the [family's] economic conditions. I'm the eldest and my Mom was there. She supported me throughout, not a single prison, when I was on trial. . . . When I came back [from prison] my mother was everywhere I was, giving support. My mother is a single parent. I'm the eldest at home. I was one who was advanced then because, at that stage, when you are doing JC [Junior Certificate], Form Three, you were closer to [finishing school]. And then my siblings were young, still in primary [school]. So I came back [from jail] and promised [to help the family]. But she gave the support throughout. . . . So when I came back [from prison], I look at my mother. I look at my family. I look at my conditions. I said then, "I'm going to leave them and I'm not going to fulfill this promise." That's what makes me to break down. And now that I'm back and I'd promised that I would go back to school, she had that hope. And she was not fine. She was already suffering from heart problems, sugar diabetes, high blood pressure, and all that. So and when I look at the situation I say, "I'm going to leave my mother like this again, there's no contribution that I will do." Unfortunately, I opted for the nation because liberating South Africa would have longer-lasting appeals even [for]

those . . . generations[s] that would come [after], even from a family. If I was going to work, I was going to still work under the same [apartheid] conditions. I wanted to be a part and not a spectator in the freedom and liberation that was taking place.[33]

If Yengeni had honored her promise to her mother to stay and look for a job, her prospects would have been bleak. She had not finished high school, had spent two years in jail—meaning she had a criminal record—and came from a family of modest means. By the late seventies, moreover, the South African economy was faltering after reaching highs in the 1960s that had made it second only to Japan in terms of growth. With South Africa beginning its long slide into chronic mass unemployment, Yengeni would have struggled to find a decent job. She did her calculations and reasoned that she would be better off working as a full-time revolutionary than a domestic servant cleaning after East London's white families. "I saw other people dying. I heard people dying. I wanted, I was determined that I want to be among those who will bring freedom in South Africa, whether with my blood. Nobody ever thought that we would see freedom in our lifetime. You would never [have] thought that. We lived in an era that it's either you sell out or you die. That was the slogan." There was more, however, than the sight and sound of people dying at the hands of the police behind Yengeni's decision to go into exile. There was also the humiliation to which her mother was subjected by some of her white employers. One family in particular demanded of Yengeni's mother that she and her children undergo regular medical check-ups, so concerned were they that the black family might spread infectious diseases. This insistence on regular check-ups was not out of concern for Yengeni's family's well-being; these were employers who would not even let Yengeni and her siblings visit their mother while she was working in their homes.

So those ones were really fascist. . . . Those ones, they were worried. We would go there when we are going to be taken for X-rays
and many other check-ups so that my mother does not bring them
disease when she goes and visits. So that was the only reason that we
would regularly go for check-ups. And we were not allowed to visit.[34]

For Yengeni, as she considered leaving South Africa to take up arms
against apartheid, such humiliations made the decision personal. She
understood enough politically to know that the struggle against apartheid was not against whites per se; but she knew enough personally to
understand that fighting apartheid meant fighting the complicity of ordinary whites who propped up apartheid with their attitudes, behav-
iors, and moral vacuity. The night before she left for exile in late 1980,
Yengeni and her siblings sang hymns. Their mother was away at work.

I sat there that night. I was singing with them. We are Anglicans
and my, we were singing a number of songs, but like church. I was
happy, making them happy. We cooked that night and my younger
sister, all of them, were there: my younger sister, my younger
brother, all my siblings. I cooked, happy, gave them money. . . . I
made them so happy. I never said a damn that tomorrow morning
I'm leaving. But, looking at them, it was difficult to sleep because
it's like "Guys, I'm going to war. I might come back, I might not
come back, but sorry that I can't assist to change your economic
conditions." I had a big cry, but I left.[35]

The following morning, an ANC operative who was to lead Yengeni
to exile fetched her from home. They took a bus to the East London
train station and, from there, boarded a train for Johannesburg. Yengeni and her colleague spent a few days in Soweto before boarding a
taxi bound for the border with Lesotho. To get to Lesotho, they had to

cross the Caledon River but not knowing the best place to cross, they approached a local family for help. Yengeni told the story of how she and her companion, pretending to be husband and wife, sought help:

> We want this family to go with us, to cross with us the river, because that's where they go. It's a rural place. They get water there. They wash clothes there. And we can't—both of us, we can't even speak. He was just straight:. "We can't [cross]. So, as husband and wife, we are going to Lesotho because we have a problem. We can't have children and we have been told that there is someone, a *sangoma* [traditional healer] there that can make us to have children."[36]

They found a family willing to take them across. That was in late 1980. Yengeni spent some time in Lesotho, working in the ANC underground.

> I stayed in Lesotho for some time. It was OK, working with people who are coming from this side [South Africa]. Political education, political education in the ANC, was there. You know, everybody knew why he was there and everything now changed. We went there to go and fight back. We wanted nothing else but arms and we were told, "No, you can't shoot when you don't know why you are going to shoot. The enemy is not the white person." The ANC started there [with the political lesson] first. You'll come there and, you know, they'll persuade you to go to school. But with many of us they did not succeed because we were still very angry. And we thought that there'd be very few people that would want to go and face the situation. So I was not among those. I did not want to go to school.[37]

In 1982, Yengeni went to Bulgaria for a short course on trade unionism. In 1984, she moved to the Soviet Union for a two-year course at the

Institute of Social Sciences, also known as the Lenin Party School, in Moscow. When Yengeni completed her training at the Lenin school, the ANC sent her to South Africa through Swaziland. That is how she came to meet Giffard for the first time. Yengeni had been away from South Africa for seven years. Only one sister had been able to visit Yengeni in exile in Lesotho, shortly after her return from Bulgaria in 1982. Yengeni had a child in Lesotho in 1984. "So then, the child had to be smuggled inside the country because it was—there were too [many] raids and attacks around everywhere. Botswana, Swaziland, you know. And when I came back, I had the child. In fact, when I left for the Soviet Union, my child was six months but was already smuggled inside the country."[38]

The Security Police arrested Yengeni shortly after her infiltration into South Africa in September 1987. The police had intercepted members of her unit and, through torture, worked their way to Tony Yengeni. His arrest and torture led to Lumka Yengeni's capture. (In fact, Tony Yengeni's truth commission confrontation with the policeman who tortured him is one of the most vivid memories that came out of the commission.) Asked if the police used the album during her torture, Yengeni answered:

> There were so many albums. That album, you get it first day, you get it—OK, the first day, they would be dealing with you, but you'll get it in the first week. Those albums are many. And at times you will see that they are forcing you to [identify people] and they will expect that you know this person and you don't know this person. You know, and you know the album. I don't even remember people that I have seen.[39]

Yengeni was subjected to such harrowing torture that when she and Giffard arrived in Piet Retief in January 1988, she tried to kill herself.

When the police demanded to know which route Yengeni used to enter South Africa, Yengeni kept pointing out wrong places as she did not want the police to intercept other ANC operatives using the same infiltration route. So the police tortured her. During their time in Piet Retief, Giffard and Yengeni would go out at separate times, and the police used one to corroborate the evidence of the other. Often, Yengeni would come back in tears. Tellingly, the police did not subject Giffard to physical torture—although, to be sure, there was psychological torture. They chose to ignore his political commitment to the ANC and to view him instead as a harmless dupe. But it was a different story with Yengeni. Hence, her suicide attempt. Giffard, Yengeni, and eleven others were charged with treason (after more than a year awaiting trial) in 1989. The state switched the treason charge to terrorism but then dropped the case shortly before President F. W. De Klerk unbanned the ANC and released Nelson Mandela from prison in February 1990. Thus, Giffard, Yengeni, and their colleagues earned their freedom. But that freedom came at great cost as some, like Tony Yengeni, had a difficult time coming to terms with the after-effects of their torture—as the truth commission demonstrated.

I interviewed Lumka Yengeni in September 2017, and asked her what came to mind as I showed her the album and a copy of her mug shot. Her head seemed to fill with questions::

It definitely took me back. But I think the first thing that was in my mind—I've been trying to remember where I was. Where did I see that photo? Because I've seen the photo. As I said, I don't *have* the photo, but where was I then, at which stage of my detention? I did not miss that I was in detention. I was in detention. That's what was in my head. I really—I really still want to know. If you got this thing from the police, the album, you know, you're there.

Before you are panel-beaten, they do take photographs. Where are the other photographs?[40]

Where indeed are the other photographs? Should we accept as a given that the other photographs were fed to incinerators? Should we take former apartheid operatives at their word when they claim they destroyed the apartheid security archive to save the future? Yengeni's questions challenge those claims. Even though my questions, not to mention the mug shot, compelled Yengeni to peel back layers of personal and political pain and to talk about matters she had not discussed in four decades, she did not shy away from asking about the gaping hole at the center of South Africa's official archive. How can individuals like Yengeni process their pain when gaps exist in the official records of what was done to them in the name of a criminal state? Is it fair to rely on the memories and the pain imprinted on the bodies of individuals such as Yengeni and Williams for the task of archival recuperation? How much collective pain can an individual bear before she collapses under all that psychic weight? For Yengeni, seeing a copy of her mug shot did not bring about knowledge. Knowing did not lead to closure. In the place of knowledge, she had questions: At what stage of my detention was this photograph taken? How much pain had I endured by the time this image was taken? Of what state of mind does this photograph speak? If Yengeni is still grappling with these questions, so is South Africa.

NINE

The Dompas

BEHIND LUNGILE WISEMAN Magxwalisa's mug shot lies a mother's anguish.[1] Taken in 1970, when Magxwalisa was fifteen, the photograph shows a boy in school uniform looking intently into the camera, unsure whether to smile (fig. 9.1). It was for Magxwalisa's pass book, the identity document colloquially called the *dompas*—Afrikaans for "stupid pass." Every black adult had to carry one in apartheid South Africa.[2] Magxwalisa sat for his dompas picture at a labor bureau in the coastal city of Port Elizabeth. The bureau was part of a network of government-run offices tasked with the mobilization and management of cheap black labor in South Africa. "I really don't know why my mother wanted me to have an ID, because I was still at school. . . . Maybe she was trying to protect me," Magxwalisa told me in 2017.[3] Indeed she was.

Nellie Magxwalisa took her son, the youngest of her six children, to the bureau not because she wanted to prepare him for the labor market, but because of her anxieties about what might happen to him should the police mistake him for an adult. Magxwalisa's beard had started

2005

FIGURE 9.1 Mug shot of Lungile
Magxwalisa in the Terrorist Album.
Courtesy of National Archives & Records
Service of South Africa.

coming in and his mother worried that he might get caught in one of
the regular police raids targeting Africans without dompases. So she
insisted, as soon as she saw whiskers on his chin, that he apply for a
dompas. Nellie Magxwalisa wanted to shield her youngest son from the
depredations of the pass laws, a set of rules that criminalized millions of
Africans over the course of the twentieth century. Because Magxwalisa
was a minor, his mother had to accompany him. "I went to the Labor
Office with her two days in succession," he recalled. Always packed
with people, and marked by bureaucratic brutality and sometimes physical violence, labor bureaus required the utmost patience from their
patrons, who had no choice but to spend days waiting in line to obtain
the documents necessary to survive in apartheid South Africa.

Ironically, Magxwalisa's picture—taken to save him from the laws
of apartheid—ended up in the Security Police album, branding him a
terrorist. In fact, because most of the people in the album were African

(and male), dompas photographs made up the majority of the mug shots. Each time the Security Police went after an African suspected of fleeing into exile, they began their search in the vast database built up during the implementation of the pass laws. So ubiquitous was the pass book and so consequential was its effect on individual lives that, more than three decades after the apartheid government abolished it in 1986, people could still remember how old they were, where they were, and how government officials treated them when they applied for their passes. Such memories can help us establish the provenance of each mug shot taken from a pass book. The images themselves cannot tell us anything, however, about the emotional and personal investment that went into their creation.

One cannot decipher a mother's anxiety simply by looking at Magxwalisa's photograph. It is only by talking to him, asking him to remember when and why he posed for the image, that we can go beyond the mug shot's two dimensions and indexicality. Doing so means posing a number of questions: How might asking Magxwalisa and Stanley Manong, another exile whose identikit I consider below, about the so-called Terrorist Album shape the way we feel its effect? How might looking at the album through their experience and eyes affect the way we apprehend not just its materiality but its meaning, as well? For behind each mug shot was an individual who inhabited a world of feelings—not just objects and laws. By taking Magxwalisa and Manong out of their police framing, this chapter examines how two African families responded to the complex ways in which branches of the apartheid bureaucracy worked in tandem to make African bodies legible and easy to discipline. The pass book was central to that exercise in legibility and discipline.

Also known during the twentieth century as influx control, pass laws went back to the first century of European rule in southern

Africa.[4] The Dutch, who established a victualing station in the Cape in 1652, introduced pass laws in 1760 to regulate the movement of slaves. A slave could not move about without a pass showing that he or she had the permission of his or her master to do so. The idea was to curb desertion by limiting the ability of an enslaved person to move freely. But, from the very beginning, Europeans demanded contradictory outcomes from the laws. On the one hand, they wanted pass laws to exclude Africans from so-called white areas. On the other hand, they wanted the laws to include Africans in white areas in sufficient numbers to cover labor needs. These clashing needs led, especially during the first half of the twentieth century, to a pragmatic legislative approach by government and fluid administrative practices geared to ensure a steady supply of labor.[5] As the rapid industrialization of South Africa early in the twentieth century led to an increase in the country's urban population, however, with millions of Africans moving from rural to urban areas, the government had trouble balancing the two needs that shaped the pass laws. It struggled to respond to a radical white left intent on monopolizing skilled industrial work for whites, and to Afrikaner nationalists concerned about the "poor white problem." In the 1920s, for example, government demoted black workers or expelled them from the workforce, most notably in the railways, and replaced them with poor whites. It also tried to limit their presence in urban areas.[6] But the thrust of pass laws in the first half of the twentieth century remained inclusionary, aimed at drawing Africans into the labor market. This changed after Afrikaner nationalists won the 1948 elections promising to introduce apartheid to keep Africans out of urban areas.

Afrikaner nationalist rule ushered in a heightened emphasis on the more exclusionary objective of the pass laws.[7] Starting with the Population Registration Act of 1950, the nationalist government sought to classify every South African according to distinct racial categories, developed arbitrarily by the state. In 1951, government introduced the Bantu Authorities Act, designed to retribalize Africans by beefing up and in some cases inventing the powers of traditional authorities. In 1952, government introduced the Abolition of Passes and Coordination of Documents Act. This law, which might as well have been called the "Hubris Act of 1952," aimed to standardize the pass laws by consolidating the stack of identity documents that Africans had to carry into one "book of life"—meaning one pass book.

In 1959, parliament passed the Promotion of Bantu Self-Government Act. The act took the Bantu Authorities Act of 1959 to its logical exclusion by turning so-called tribal areas into homelands and then transforming these *bantustans* into sovereign nation-states. This was, said Steve Biko, the biggest fraud ever perpetrated by the white man in South Africa.[8] The 1959 act not only created new nation-states, it also deprived Africans of rights to citizenship in white South Africa. Both the 1951 and 1959 acts found full expression in the Bantu Homelands Citizenship Act of 1970, which effectively denationalized millions of Africans by assigning them to tribes and, based on that allocation, declaring each a citizen of whatever bantustan the government deemed appropriate. A person need never have set foot in a place for her to become a citizen of that homeland. As one apartheid cabinet minister put it, these laws were designed to ensure that there would not be "one Black man with South African citizenship."[9] These were not simply political ambitions brought to life by resourceful bureaucrats, but real schemes that moved millions of people—not just on paper but in real life, too.

The pass laws were key to the implementation of these acts of hubris. The apartheid state believed it could move millions of people like pieces on a chessboard after decreeing that a given place was either black or white. But the pass laws not only reconfigured the geography of South Africa; they criminalized millions of Africans. Between 1916 and 1984, for example, the state arrested and prosecuted more than seventeen million Africans for offenses related to pass laws.[10] Magxwalisa's and Manong's mothers feared that their children might wind up in jail if they did not have passes. They worried about what might happen to their children were they to be arrested for pass offenses and deported to "their" bantustans. So they saw to it that their children obtained passes as soon as they could.[11] The threats of arrest and deportation were real. Between 1960 and 1986, the government subjected more than three and a half million people to removals, expelling them from white areas to homelands.[12] Again, an expelled or "endorsed" person, to use the word preferred by the government, did not require any connection to a bantustan to be dumped there. If the state decided that a person was Xhosa, then he or she would be dumped or told to move to one of the two Xhosa homelands, Ciskei or Transkei. Although a nuisance, the pass book did offer its bearer some protections. For one, it meant that the bearer could stay in an urban area without molestation, especially if the bearer and his or her family had a permit authorizing them to be in an urban area. Second, a pass book allowed its bearer to look for a job without worrying about getting picked up by the police. But this could be flimsy protection. Stories abound of people who wound up in jail because they forgot to transfer their passes from one jacket to another. There are also stories of police officers and other state functionaries abusing their pass-checking power to harass people, regardless of whether they carried passes or not. Some cities and towns even had policemen whose sole job was to run after individuals who did not have passes. To get a sense of what the pass meant, here is Soweto poet Mtutuzeli Matshoba recounting a story of being at the mercy of these pass policemen:

It is almost magical how powerful those pass laws were. A black-jack [a municipal police officer responsible for the enforcement of pass laws] walks in to see your pass, he takes it, puts it in his pocket, and you must follow him. He gathers a few people like this. One cop followed by 12 people. He is on his bicycle, the 12 are jogging to keep up with him. He stops to see this and that one, to drink and to visit, and the 12 wait for him outside. Then he gets on his bicycle again, and the 12 jog again to keep up with him. He has your pass book in his pocket, and you are nothing without it. You cannot be without your pass book. You must follow him.[13]

Matshoba is describing a fate that befell millions of Africans. In the two-man play *Sizwe Banzi is Dead,* by Athol Fugard, John Kani, and Winston Ntshona, which premiered in 1972, the main character is a rural migrant who, unable to find a job in Port Elizabeth, seizes the opportunity to steal the pass book of a dead man whose body he stumbles upon outside a shebeen. In the poem "City Johannesburg," poet Mongane Wally Serote paints a picture of a man frantically searching his pockets "For my pass, my life / . . . . My hand like a starved snake rears my pockets / For my thin, ever lean wallet / While my stomach groans a friendly smile to hunger." (Not surprisingly, Serote is also in the album, having fled to exile to escape apartheid censorship.)[14] While Africans dismissed the pass book as a dompas, they could not ignore it or do without it. They needed one to move around.

Without a pass book, they could not be. They could not exist. Magxwalisa's and Manong's mothers knew this. What they did not know was that, by helping their boys to get their pass books, they were also making it possible for the Security Police to brand them *terrorists*. Nellie Magxwalisa and Emily Manong sought to protect their children from apartheid by seeing to it that their children worked, however superficially, within its laws. That meant helping a child obtain the much-despised dompas as soon as he needed it. A dompas, however, was a double-edged sword. Not only did it condemn its holder officially to a life of inferiority, it also made it easy for the state to designate dissidents as terrorists.

For the Security Police, the two men's entry into the album was straightforward enough. Each left South Africa without government permission, Manong in December 1976 and Magxwalisa in November 1977. For the two men, however, their journeys into exile were complicated affairs bound up with the fate of their mothers. Both were already in exile when their mothers died, meaning the men could not attend the funerals. For each man, the story of exile became the story of the mother left behind. Magxwalisa's mother died in 1980, three years after her son's departure for exile. Manong's mother died in December 1985, the victim of an arson attack that Manong blamed on the apartheid state—and on himself for unintentionally endangering her life by going into exile. Having failed to get Emily Manong to testify in a 1977 political trial against the man it accused of taking her son into exile, the state decided to punish her by turning her small community against her. Manong describes how in a memoir he wrote after his return from exile in 1992:

> My mother was burnt to death by local people from Victoria West during the disturbances of 1985. She was killed because of the allegations of "collaborator" that were leveled against Enoch, one of my elder brothers. The majority of those who were involved in her death were all known to me. They were either my blood relatives, close friends with whom I grew up or people who were ordinary acquaintances. As Victoria West is a small town of not more than four thousand inhabitants, of which a thousand were Africans, residents of the town knew one another very well.[15]

Manong had other reasons to feel guilty about the death of his mother, a single parent. As a refugee, he had arranged financial support for his mother through the International Defense and Aid Fund (IDAF), a London-based organization dedicated to supporting exiles, political detainees and prisoners, and refugees, and to maintaining their families. Banned in South Africa in 1966, the organization used volunteers, who were mostly ordinary British citizens, to channel money to people like Manong's mother in South Africa. The Security Police knew this but, unable to prove it, they could not stop Manong's mother from getting the money. It would not have gone unnoticed, in a community as small and as tight-knit as Victoria West, that Emily Manong had a comfortable income; the IDAF stipend of R500 a month was well above the average monthly salary earned by Africans in the town. And it certainly did not help that the person Manong relied on to keep in touch with his mother while he was in exile was, in fact, a apartheid double agent named Joe Mamasela.[16] When Manong wrote letters to his mother and asked Mamasela to mail them from inside South Africa, Mamasela agreed—then simply handed them to his Security Police handlers.

The police would visit his mother often, asking about his whereabouts. She, unaware that the police already knew more than she did, pretended not to have any idea where her son was and promised to let them know as soon as she found out. "In the end the Security Police decided to get rid of her and as a decoy use some agents within the community and assisted by some of my close relatives in killing her."[17]

"This Was My Dompas Picture"

Manong and Magxwalisa both had their dompas photographs taken in the year 1970, as sixteen-year-olds, and in the same region (Eastern

Cape). They were 151 miles apart, with Manong in the inland town of Cradock and Magxwalisa on the coast in Port Elizabeth.

Manong shared with me what he remembered about the image (fig. 9.2) and the day it was taken:

> What they used to do, the Special Branch, when you left the country, when they are compiling [the album] . . . was to go to the archives in Pretoria. If you had a dompas before you left, your pass book, so they go to the archive. They got this from the archives. And the first time when I [saw my mug shot in the album] . . . I was not sure, but I saw the collar of my sweater—not sweater, let me say my golf shirt. When I saw it I said, "No, no, definitely that is the dompas one, when I was sixteen." It [the golf shirt] is lime in color. The material those days, it was the in thing, it was crimplene . . . it was stretchy. . . . But that was the in-thing those days . . . that is the shirt I was wearing when I took my photo at Cradock in 1970.[18]

Manong went to Cradock, about 217 miles from his hometown of Victoria West, because his hometown, a sheep-farming region, did not have a high school for Africans. Tamie Victor Yose, the school principal in Victoria West, had found places for Manong and a few of his classmates in the Bantu Secondary School in Cradock. Yose had also persuaded Emily Manong to allow both her son, the eighth of her nine children, and his cousin Lindiwe to move to Cradock for high school. While whites in apartheid South Africa were guaranteed free education by law, Africans had to pay for their schooling. Emily Manong was reluctant to let her son go because that would have strained her family's resources even further. "I fully understood the reason why my mother was reluctant to send us to high school," Manong said. "As a domestic worker, she was only earning about R7 a month."[19] It was only in Feb-

1781

FIGURE 9.2 Mug shot of Stanley Manong in the Terrorist Album. Courtesy of National Archives & Records Service of South Africa.

ruary 1968, three weeks after classes had already started, that Manong and his cousin were able to travel to their new school, as they had to wait for his mother to get paid at the end of February.

Cradock gave Manong more than a regular education. It also taught him about South African history and the area's rich history of resistance to white rule. James Calata, a canon in the Anglican Church and secretary-general of the ANC from 1936 to 1949, was a prominent resident of the town.[20] Matthew Goniwe, a schoolteacher later assassinated by a Security Police death squad, in 1985, taught Manong science and mathematics.[21] Manong applied for his dompas in 1970 because he was about to sit for the Junior Certificate (JC), a national test that every high school student had to take. Manong had caddied for white golfers in Victoria West (there were no golfing facilities for blacks in the town) to help his mother make ends meet. He picked up the fashion sense there that had led to his lime-colored golf shirt. "Because I was going to take my dompas photograph, I had to get my best clothing on."[22]

Manong could not remember what else he wore that day. But he remembered the attitude of the Bantu Affairs Commissioner, the state official in charge of taking Manong's application:

> The Bantu Affairs Commissioner was scolding me. He was reluctant. He was saying, "You are sixteen. Why do you hurry to take your dompas now? You are required by law when you are eighteen, not sixteen." I said, "No, but I am writing my external, my JC examination." You know, those days, Grade Ten was an external examination. So I wanted my reference number, dompas number, to be written on my certificate. This is what I said to him. No, he was reluctant. "You need to go back and come back after two years." But I said "I'm not staying in Cradock, I'm staying somewhere else." That is what I remember about it. But he finally decided, "let me take the photo."[23]

Was the Bantu Affairs Commissioner black or white?
He was black.

Was the dompas issued on the spot?
No, we had to wait. Like the ID now, it must go to Pretoria, the forms, then after—I can't remember. How long was it, two months? I can't remember. Then they said, "Come after two, three months and check if it is around." They wouldn't phone you. There were no phones in the townships. There was no way.

Where was the dompas when you went into exile in December 1976?

I was having it, with my travel document, which was a travel document / passport somehow. It was a travel document. It
was not really a passport. It only enabled you to go to Botswana, Lesotho, Swaziland—that's all. No other place. That
is why it was a travel document.

By the time Manong fled to exile, he was on the Security Police's
wanted list. The police had found out that Manong, who completed
high school in 1972 and was a civil engineering student at a technical
college for blacks in the Transvaal, was active in the ANC underground.
The police discovered Manong's connection to the ANC during a
swoop on student activists after the 1976 high school uprisings. A detained activist told the police that Manong had introduced her to the
ANC.

So now, anything with the ANC—you know what was happening. They would tolerate [you] if you were a BPC [Black
People's Convention] activist or SASO [South African Students'
Organization]. But not ANC, because the ANC was involved in
armed struggle. They knew that SASO, BPC—these are just
students. But ANC means you are involved in supporting armed
struggle. So anybody who is a member underground, or sympa-
thizer, they dealt with you. They kill you, you know. So me, I
knew I was in trouble.[24]

Seeking help, Manong approached Joe Mati, an ANC veteran who
had spent ten years on Robben Island for sabotage. Mati was a recruiter
for the ANC and ran a pipeline that took recruits to exile. They discussed the idea of having Manong use Mati's travel documents. But
Manong refused, fearing they would lead him straight into police
hands. Manong, Mati, and a third ANC operative left South Africa on

December 18, 1976, driving 640 miles from the Eastern Cape to the Pongola border post with Swaziland:

> [Joe Mati] had to go and communicate with the Swaziland ANC. He would live underground, go to Swaziland and come back, skip the fence. So I left with him. So the driver—what the driver used to do, he would drop us off just before the border gate . . . he would cross and go through the border with his travel document and pick us up on the other side. So on this day, he dropped us about three kilometers from the border. As we alighted from the car in broad daylight, lunchtime, apparently the police at the border spotted us, you see. They came. . . . Man, just before we skipped the fence, I heard the old man [Mati] say to me, "Ey, take off your pants, take off your pants." By that time he was naked already, he was sitting [squatting]. The policeman [came] screeching. . . . I'd taken off my pants, pretending as if I was relieving myself. The poor policeman said, "Hey you kaffirs, what are you doing there?" The old man said, "We are just relieving ourselves, my boss." He said, "okay." He left. That time, ooh, I was, I was stone dead [from fright].[25]

Manong crossed successfully into Swaziland and from there to Mozambique, and on to Angola, where he received military training. He worked for the ANC in Zambia and was then deployed to Botswana. I asked him when he first came to know about the album.

> When we were in exile, they told us, "No, the police have compiled an album. Everybody who is arrested, those who were arrested before they skip, they say when they're arrested the police will take out an album and ask them questions: Whom do they know who has left, the name and so on." That was when they were compiling this album, but I do not know about the details. But I knew about it.[26]

In fact, an ANC operative who had been captured by the Security Police in 1977 and turned into a double agent, told the ANC about the album after the ANC caught him. Manong explained:

> Now it is him . . . who came out and told us about this album. When he was being interrogated . . . [he said] that the police, they've got an album with the numbers of each and every person who has left the country, and he was made to identify all the people whom he met in the [ANC] camps. They say, "Right, whom did you meet again?" "So and so." "This person, do you know him?" "No, I don't." "This one?" "Yes, yes, I know her." "What is her name?" "What is her MK name or his MK name?" So this is how they were verifying, and if someone else is also arrested, they would come and say, "verify. . . ." So, many people, even if they were not arrested—they were compiling this album from captured people.[27]

Thinking of Mother

Lungile Magxwalisa was among the captured insurgents the police questioned to keep the album up to date. As Magxwalisa said in a statement he gave to the Security Police after his capture near Lesotho in July 1983, he left South Africa illegally in November 1977 to join the ANC in exile.[28] He had participated in the 1976 student uprisings in Port Elizabeth and had been affected deeply by the murder of Steve Biko in September 1977. His departure for exile illustrates the odds the ANC faced in its attempts to build up an effective presence outside so that it could take on the South African state. Magxwalisa and three fellow recruits traveled by train from Port Elizabeth to Soweto, about 660 miles away. They lay low in Soweto and stayed with ANC sympathizers until November 1977, when the ANC arranged for a taxi to take Magxwalisa and his comrades, now joined by five other recruits, to Swaziland. An ANC scout took the group to a spot along the border post where they could cross into Swaziland. The group spent four days at the ANC "White House" in Manzini (the site noted by Phumla Williams in Chapter 8), before crossing illegally into Mozambique. Magxwalisa received military training in Angola. Early in 1979, the ANC sent Magxwalisa to the Soviet Union for advanced military training. The training course, which lasted ten months, included a three-day holiday to the Black Sea. Magxwalisa returned to Angola in February 1980. Magxwalisa served as a military instructor at an ANC camp in Pango, east of the Angolan capital Luanda, teaching recruits military tactics, from April to November 1980. In July 1982, Magxwalisa and six ANC colleagues, all traveling under false names on United Nations passports, went to Mozambique via Zambia. Aboobaker Ismail, also known as Comrade Rashid Patel, met Magxwalisa's group at the airport in Maputo. "This was the first that I saw Rashid Patel," Magxwalisa noted in his statement to the police. Ismail recruited Magxwalisa and six others into a special operations unit named after Solomon Mahlangu, an ANC insurgent hanged by the Pretoria government in 1979 for terrorism. Magxwalisa's unit attacked economic installations. Their first target was a bridge over the Orange River, near the Northern Cape town of Upington. The mission failed. In 1983, Comrade Rashid ordered the Solomon Mahlangu group to attack a train bridge over the Umfolozi River in Natal. In June 1983, the Security Police arrested Magxwalisa and members of his unit shortly after they crossed into South Africa from Lesotho on their way to their target.

"I have a strong suspicion that the police knew about our presence in the Republic of South Africa, but I am not sure who informed them," said Magxwalisa in his statement. Upon his arrest, he later recalled, "One of the security guys said, 'You must talk because we know everything about you.'"[29] Magxwalisa played dumb at first. This changed, however, when the police began torturing him: "The torture was not black bags over your head. You stand day and night for six days. There's no blood circulation. I had been involved in operations before, but I only admitted to this one."[30] Magxwalisa saw the album for the first time during his interrogation. His chief interrogator, the man who wrote down Magxwalisa's 170-page statement, complete with about fifty pages related directly to photographs in the album, was a former Rhodesian Intelligence Officer; Lieutenant Davidson had defected to the South African Security Police after Zimbabwe became independent in 1980.:

> He's the one who first came with the album. He introduced himself. He was from Pretoria. He even told me he was from Rhodesia. "I want you to identify each picture. Tell me who is this, what is his nom de guerre, where is he now, what is he doing."[31]

Magxwalisa identified hundreds of fellow ANC members, including Odirile Meshack Maponya, an ANC insurgent whose story we will hear in Chapter 11. Magxwalisa identified Maponya by his alias (Chibuku Mainstay) and then under the heading "Where trained and where last seen," answered cryptically:

> Novo Catengue + Russia
> Pango 1981

The first line referred to the ANC camp in Angola at which Maponya was trained. "Russia" indicated that Maponya also received specialized training in the Soviet Union. The second line meant that Magxwalisa last saw Maponya in the ANC's Pango camp in Angola in 1981.

Magxwalisa misidentified Aboobaker Ismail, with whom he had worked closely for three years, calling him Barry Gilder. Asked where Ismail was trained and when last he saw him, Magxwalisa told Davidson:

Unknown
Last seen: 1983-03-22

Magxwalisa gave many such accounts, identifying individuals and saying where and when he had last seen them. He talked about this to me in August 2017:

The hard thing was that you could not say you don't recognize anyone. You'll recognize the dead, ones in the frontline state, ones in Angola. They were interested in: What are they doing now? What operations are they involved in.[32]

When I showed Magxwalisa a copy of his mug shot, he replied: "This is me. This is the photo they had of me. No one would have recognized me."[33] As for what the album itself represented, "It's what the Security Branch used to identify and track the whereabouts of MK members: Where is he? What is he doing?" Asked what memories came to mind when he saw his mug shot, Magxwalisa replied, "I think of my mother. The first thing, I think of my mother."[34] She died in 1980, three years after Magxwalisa went into exile. In 1983, a court sentenced him to twenty-four years on Robben Island for terrorism. He served eleven years before F. W. De Klerk's government released him, following the onset of negotiations to end apartheid. We have no way of knowing how his mother would have responded to the news of his sentence. She had tried to shield him from the law by taking him to a labor office to get a dompas. She had tried to protect him from the systematic criminalization entailed by the pass laws. The photograph from that visit had ended up in the Security Police album, branding her son the worst form of criminal in apartheid South Africa: a terrorist. We cannot assume that Nellie Magxwalisa would have approved of her son's political choices. We cannot take it as given that she would have gone along with his decision to go into exile and to take up arms against apartheid.

Magxwalisa died in May 2018 of complications from diabetes. He had retired from the South African National Defense Force with the rank of brigadier-general. When he told me in August 2017 that his mug shot reminded him of his mother, I wondered what regrets, if any, were embedded in the memories of his mother. Magxwalisa responded emotionally and personally to seeing his mug shot, more than thirty-seven years after his mother died and more than twenty-three years after his release from prison. Magxwalisa's reaction was of history as lived experience. It showed how history haunts the present.

TEN

Capitol Drama

IN MARCH 1982, Capitol Hill hosted one of the strangest dramas in Washington, DC. The stage was Room 2228 in the Dirksen Senate Office Building, the cast an international array of actors, including a US assistant secretary of state for African affairs, a politics professor from Kansas, Namibian refugees, a former communist, and three self-described ex-terrorists from South Africa. Props included a rocket propelled grenade (RPG) launcher and an AK-47 assault rifle. Directing all this was Jeremiah Andrew Denton, a senator from Alabama and a retired rear-admiral in the US Navy who had spent eight years in a prisoner-of-war camp in North Vietnam. Denton chaired the US Senate Subcommittee on Security and Terrorism. The subcommittee was a subsidiary of the US Senate Committee on the Judiciary, chaired by Strom Thurmond, the veteran senator from South Carolina. To give it its full name, Denton's show was in fact a congressional hearing into "the role of the Soviet Union, Cuba, and East Germany in fomenting terrorism in Southern Africa."[1]

These were heady days in the world. President Ronald Reagan was in his second year in office, the Soviet Union was under the dying leadership of Leonid Brezhnev, and the Cold War was going through one of its frostiest phases. In Africa, Asia, and Latin America, where the Cold War had always been a hot war, thousands were dying in conflicts of various sorts. Like many hot wars around the world at the time, the conflict in South Africa had also assumed the divides of the Cold War, with the apartheid government aligned with the United States, the United Kingdom, and other members of what was referred to as the free world. The ANC supported the Soviet Union, the source of most of its military supplies.[2] But South Africa was an awkward ally for the United States. Following the collapse of the Portuguese Empire in 1974 and the demise of Rhodesia in 1980, South Africa was the only country in Africa still ruled by a white minority.

With the United States still dealing with its own history of racial oppression, South Africa presented both a problem in itself and a painful reminder of America's own sordid history. But South Africa was strategically important—or so said many in the US establishment, especially the military. It was mineral-rich and sited along one of the most important shipping routes in the world. How, then, to deal with an ally who exposed you to ridicule and to charges of hypocrisy by your biggest enemy, the Soviet Union? For Denton, the solution was simple: ignore South Africa's domestic policies and focus instead on the supposed strategic importance of South Africa to the United States. As Denton said in his opening remarks at the start of his show, "The purpose of these hearings is not to debate the appropriate US policy toward southern Africa. . . . Nor is it our purpose to analyze South African domestic policies. Surely no one on this subcommittee would condone or attempt to justify, in any respect, policies of racial discrimination in South Africa, the United States, or elsewhere."[3] Denton had to say that.

South Africa was the political skunk of the world.[4] Not even an ardent right-winger like Denton could openly support apartheid. He had to make the US public believe that the hearings were his production, an all-American affair driven by his concern for the spread of freedom around the world. He wanted Americans to think that he alone had scripted and cast the show—and that he had done this for their own good. American citizens had to know how important South Africa was to their freedom. As Denton put it in his opening remarks, "Americans have only recently begun to understand the strategic, economic, and political importance of [southern Africa] to the welfare, indeed the survival, of the free world."[5] The fate of the United States and the rest of the free world depended on southern Africa, but Americans were too ignorant to know this, Denton suggested. He would lift this veil of ignorance. But the show that came to be called the Denton hearings was anything but.

It was a co-production staged by Denton and the South African government, especially its intelligence agencies. The South Africans provided Denton with the actors who played the African parts. They decided for Denton which Namibians and South Africans could appear before his subcommittee, and what each witness could say. The four South Africans who testified before Denton were in fact employees of South Africa's security agencies. Nokonono Delphine Kave, Bartholomew Hlapane, Jeff Mthuthuzeli Bosigo, and Ephraim Tlhomedi Mfalapitsa were on the apartheid payroll.[6] Denton called them courageous souls who risked their lives to speak publicly about Soviet perfidy. In truth, the four were apartheid foot soldiers following orders. Kave, aged twenty-eight and the only woman in the group, claimed to have defected from the ANC. The ANC had sent Kave to the Soviet Union for specialized training. Instead of training her, however, Kave said that KGB officers had drugged and raped her.[7] Hlapane, age sixty-four, was a former executive member of the ANC and the South African Communist Party (SACP).[8] Hlapane said white communists had duped him in 1955 into joining the Communist Party. But he had seen the error of his ways. He had come to realize that white communists were not interested in the lot of black South Africans.[9] They were lackeys of the Soviet Union using blacks to hand South Africa over to the Soviet Union. Bosigo, aged twenty-three, was a former member of the ANC who had received military training in Angola and East Germany. Asked by Denton to demonstrate how the RPG worked, Bosigo replied, "Unfortunately, we do not have a rocket here."[10] Mfalapitsa, aged twenty-nine, was also an ANC defector. To demonstrate his training in East Germany and the Soviet Union, Mfalapitsa assembled and disassembled an AK-47 assault rifle for Denton's show.

To get a flavor of the kinds of questions that Denton asked his witnesses, here is Denton asking Mfalapitsa about the AK-47 used as a prop during the hearings: "It is my understanding that this weapon is made in Czechoslovakia, but you got it in East Germany. Is that right?"[11] What Denton did not say, what he could not say, was that at least two of his South African witnesses, Bosigo and Mfalapitsa, were members of an apartheid death squad responsible for the deaths of anti-apartheid activists.[12] Bosigo and Mfalapitsa were part of a secret group of former freedom fighters who had switched sides in the apartheid conflict and were working for the apartheid state. They were called *askaris,* the Arabic term for soldiers brought to South Africa via a network of counterinsurgencies stretching back to German and British colonialism in East Africa, and to the Zimbabwean war of independence in Rhodesia.[13] It is unlikely that Denton knew the details of what Bosigo and Mfalapitsa did in the service of the apartheid state. Not many South Africans knew, either. But did he know that these witnesses were not just simple folk who had been duped by white communists in the pay of the

Soviet Union, but had since abandoned communism's failed god? Did he know that these were not African innocents come to Washington, DC, to bear witness to the duplicity of the Soviet Union?

Not that one would know this from looking at the album, but Bosigo, Mfalapitsa, and Hlapane were apartheid collaborators. (Kave was a different case.) The three men were former freedom fighters who had changed sides and were now fighting for the apartheid government against former comrades.[14] They were like Gladstone Mose, whom we have already met. By *collaborator* I mean that these individuals began their political lives on one side of the conflict in South Africa and ended up on the other.[15] They switched sides. From having taken an oath to give their lives in pursuit of freedom, they had become defenders of apartheid. That defense took many forms. Overtly, askaris such as Bosigo and Mfalapitsa testified against former comrades in court and, as was the case with Denton's hearings, denounced them in public; covertly, they hunted down ex-colleagues for capture, torture, and assassination.[16]

Hlapane, the only one among the men who did not receive military training, served as a professional state witness for the apartheid state, testifying in a string of terrorism and treason trials against former colleagues. Hlapane had been active in the ANC and SACP underground before he was arrested on June 24, 1963, and placed in solitary confinement, under a ninety-day law passed a month earlier as part of a massive crackdown of opposition to apartheid. During his 172 days in solitary confinement, he was tortured so severely that he suffered serious psychological difficulties and had to seek counseling upon his release.[17] He was detained again in 1964 and placed in solitary confinement for two months. In 1966, he was again arrested under the ninety-day law and placed in solitary confinement for three months. This last stretch finally destroyed him. By the time he arrived in Washington to take part in Denton's show, he had been working for the South African security services for sixteen years. He helped put many of his former colleagues in jail. Among those he testified against was Braam Fischer, a celebrated lawyer and the scion of a prominent Afrikaner family, who had found common cause with South Africa's black majority.[18]

ANC assassins killed Hlapane and his wife in December 1982, nine months after his appearance before Denton's commission. While Hlapane came to Denton's show via detention and torture, Bosigo and Mfalapitsa took different routes. Bosigo defected in 1980 after falling out with his comrades in the ANC. Thanks to the Truth and Reconciliation Commission (TRC), we know how Mfalapitsa ended up disassembling and assembling an AK-47 in front of two US senators on Capitol Hill. When Mfalapitsa appeared before Denton in March 1982, he had been a defector for just three months. Mfalapitsa had abandoned his ANC post in Botswana in December 1982 and joined the South African Security Police. But because he was so new, he had to prove his loyalty to his new masters in the most lethal way possible: he betrayed a close family friend and two comrades to a police death squad.[19] Believing that Mfalapitsa was still a freedom fighter, the family friend and his two comrades asked Mfalapitsa to help them leave the country to join the ANC in exile. Thinking that this was a trap set by his new masters to test his loyalty, Mfalapitsa reported the three men to his new masters. His masters ordered Mfalapitsa to lure the boys to a disused mine shaft and to give them booby-trapped hand grenades. That is how askaris operated: pretending to be freedom fighters while in fact in the employ of the apartheid state. Mfalapitsa did as instructed. Two of the boys were killed instantly, the family friend survived. Mfalapitsa received a R1000 bonus and new clothes for the mission. In 2000, the truth commission rejected Mfalapitsa's application for amnesty for the mission.

About Looking (Again)

Kave seems to have been an apartheid agent all along, used by apartheid intelligence to infiltrate the activist circles around Steve Biko before the police killed him in 1977. Kave was related to Lennox Sebe, leader of the Bantustan of Ciskei, and his brother Charles Sebe—a fact she was only too happy to advertise at the Denton hearings.[20] Charles Sebe headed Ciskei's Intelligence Services and was a member of South Africa's intelligence services.[21] It would appear that, after working within Biko's network and, in the process, establishing her legend as an activist, Kave set out to infiltrate the anti-apartheid networks fast gaining strength outside South Africa, especially after June 1976. This was after thousands of young, mainly black, South Africans fled into exile to escape government's repression of a student uprising that had broken out in Soweto in June 1976 and then spread to other parts of South Africa. You will not glean any of this history, however, by being faithful to the album, the index, and their operating logic.

Go to the album in search of terrorists and that is what you will find—not complex characters whose presence in the album collapses the thin line between collaboration and resistance. Comb through the album with the help of the index and you will find Bosigo (mug shot 88), Kave (696), and Mfalapitsa (1331). Hlapane, the only one in the group who did not go into exile, is not in the album. Look blindly at the album for terrorists and that is what you will find.

Look more carefully at the index, however, and you will notice that appended to the names Kave, Bosigo, and Mfalapitsa is an asterisk. That is the only typographical hint that there might be more to the names so adorned than the mug shots suggest. It turns out that C2, the Security Police unit in charge of the album, used an asterisk to show when a name had been deleted from the album and the index.[22] Members of

C2 used an asterisk to indicate when a person was no longer of interest to the Security Police. The police did this when they arrested a person in the album, when they killed a suspected terrorist, or when, as was the case with Kave, Bosigo and Mfalapitsa, the person had begun working for the police. The practice was not consistent, however. We cannot simply look to the asterisks in the index for proof of collaboration or spying; and conversely, the album features many apartheid spies and collaborators whose names are not marked with an asterisk. How then to think about the album as a historical source and whether it succeeded in its objective to apprehend terrorists? Eugene Fourie responded in August 2015 to my question about why he and his colleagues in C2, the only unit in the Security Police allowed to alter the album and the index in any way, kept the mug shots of askaris, collaborators, defectors, and double agents in it:

> Not everyone in exile knew that these people were working with us. There was still a doubt [that] maybe they were sent to another camp or killed when they were arrested. Not everybody knew which askaris worked for us—there was always a doubt. That's why we kept them in the album. Some people didn't know [that these people] were working for us, if they see them in the album. . . . They think "he's still in MK somewhere, in another camp."[23]

Jan Potgieter, who served in the Security Police from 1973 to 1994, said the police kept the mug shots of defectors and informers in the album to keep tabs on them. "That way, you can also follow the movements of your agents. He can't bullshit you and say 'I was a commander in an ANC camp' when he was just a low-level guy," Potgieter said.[24] It helped to keep the agents' mug shots in the album, too, because the police could use captured insurgents to check in on the where-abouts of their agents. Asked how many of the people in exile the album captured, Fourie doubted it was the majority:

> I would say about 40 percent. We never knew the exact numbers of people who were in exile. [The] ANC told us twenty thousand—we doubted that. I would say there were about twelve thousand. You see, we also had files on persons that we didn't have photos about. So, if you start talking to a man about this photo and then he says, "but I was trained with this guy and he trained with that man and they were in this group of thirty who went to East Germany," you get all the names of the thirty people. And of the thirty people you might have ten photos. But then you write down all the info about the other people, as well, although you only have the MK name. This guy might know where he comes from. We also had info about the many people in exile that we didn't have photos of.[25]

The album gave the Security Police an edge they would not have en-joyed otherwise. It magnified their prowess and made them look more efficient than they were. Asked to imagine a police life without the album, Fourie said it would have been very difficult:

> You wouldn't know what people looked like. You wouldn't know who to look for. If you hear someone is coming, you just look in the index [for] this man and then you know who to look out for. If it wasn't for the album, we should have had three hundred askaris to identify people. We would have needed three hundred askaris to identify people coming in, if we didn't have the album. The album made everything easier.[26]

A notable feature of the album is the age of the mug shots. Yet Fourie said this did not blunt the usefulness of the album.

> These people stay in camps together for years so they know [one another] very well. It's amazing how they recognize people from old photos. It's amazing [but it's] because they live with them for so many years in the camps. They move around from Tanzania to Angola to Russia to Cuba. They all move in groups so they know each other very well. And they might also have old photos of themselves and their families that they carry with them. It was very amazing to see how they recognized old people from old photos. Or you give them a clue—"Do you know this and this guy, his MK name?" "No, I know him. We trained together in Cuba." Then he would look and look and say "that's him" or he would say "It's not him."[27]

Jan Potgieter, who was head of the Soweto Intelligence Unit by the time he left the Security Police in 1994, had a different explanation for why the age of the mug shots did not blunt their effectiveness. Potgieter said: "Because of their level of education, which wasn't very high. . . . That's one thing about the black people, they've got superb memories. They are able to observe much better than the white people."[28] The biggest surprise, said Fourie, was how eager most captured insurgents were to talk.

> If you come in with all those photos, it doesn't matter how stubborn this man is or how helpful he is, the biggest surprise for me was that everybody tried to show you how much they know about every person. It was for them a proud thing to say, "I know this man," and to give you all the information to show that he is a

clever man. Because you're a lonely man, only you and him, nobody else, only you and him, nobody listening, so he can talk.[29]

We cannot, however, measure the efficiency of the album solely by
what Fourie and his colleagues were able to make their captives do.
We cannot judge its efficacy by the ease with which the album elided
the categories collaborator and resister. Insurgents had their own ways
of measuring their efficiency against that of their enemies. This began
with how South Africa's security agencies dealt with ANC aliases. This
was no easy task. There was the case of Barry Gilder, the ANC insurgent that the Security Police mistook for Aboobaker Ismail / Comrade
Rashid. Sue Rabkin, an ANC operative high on the Security Police's
wanted list, is in the album—except that the mug shot in the album
belonged to her sister-in-law Hilary Rabkin.[30] This would be unremark-
able if not for the fact that Sue Rabkin was so extensively surveilled
that the Security Police even had floor plans of her apartment in
Maputo, Mozambique. They wanted to kill her. It cannot be that the
Security Police did not know what Sue Rabkin looked like. They had
arrested her in July 1976. She was sentenced to three years in prison for
furthering the aims of the ANC and the SACP in a much-publicized
trial, during which photographs of her were splashed across South African newspapers. Yet they put the wrong picture in the album. Why?

When I showed Joel Netshitenzhe a digital copy of the album in 2016,
he thought at first that it reflected a "ruthless efficiency," but then wondered how accurate such a reading was.[31] In fact, the story of how
Netshitenzhe went into exile raises doubts about the efficiency of the
Security Police. In August 1976, Netshitenzhe, then a second-year medical student at the University of Natal in Durban, decided to leave
South Africa to take up arms against apartheid. This was in the aftermath of the June 1976 student uprisings. Netshitenzhe and a friend

named Chris Pepane fled first to Matatiele, a town about two hundred miles west of Durban. Their plan was to connect with the Njongwes, a prominent family active in the ANC underground in the area. Zwelinzima Njongwe, the eldest of the Njongwe children, was an ANC operative responsible for taking recruits out of the country. It took Zwelinzima about six weeks to come up with a plan for Netshitenzhe and Pepane—since joined by Njongwe's younger brother Nkululo and a friend named Reggie Mpongo—to cross illegally into Lesotho. The recruits spent about six weeks in Lesotho while ANC operatives in that country organized travel documents for them. The documents and the attached photographs were genuine but Netshitenzhe and his friends had to assume fake Sotho names.

Because Lesotho is landlocked completely by South Africa, however, Netshitenzhe and his friends had to cross back into South Africa, travel through South Africa to Swaziland, and then cross from there to Mozambique and onward to Angola, where they underwent military training. To get to Swaziland, the group had to cross the South African border at two points and yet they were not hassled by the South African Security Police, which was responsible for the border posts in question. If the Security Police were as efficient as they liked to put out, they should have picked up information about the men during the three months it took the group to escape from Durban, cross into Lesotho, cross back into South Africa and then out again through Swaziland. The police did not. "Because if [the album] was of great use, then they would have identified us through the photos—not so much the names— they would have identified us as we crossed from Lesotho into South Africa or from South Africa into Swaziland, already when everyone knew that we had disappeared," Netshitenzhe said.[32] He wondered if framing questions about the album in terms of Security Police efficiency was perhaps the wrong way to go about examining the history of the album. "We are talking about it in terms of their [Security Police] efficiency and inefficiency. Shouldn't you also inversely use it as a reflection of the ANC's own efficiency, that the systems of concealment worked? The *noms de guerre* and whatever?"[33] Garth Strachan, an ANC insurgent who operated from Zimbabwe, echoed Netshitenzhe's observation:

> I personally can't recall ever being able to say "we're under surveillance." But we were. They had a sophisticated surveillance operation. In one year I moved house eighteen times. Sometimes people thought we were being overly cautious, but when I interviewed Guy Bowden [a South African agent arrested in Zimbabwe in 1988] I said, "thank God I was overcautious." They had a sophisticated surveillance capacity. But I don't think we should exaggerate the extent of their surveillance, because we were getting around. Their successes have to be measured against our successes, because we were successful.[34]

There is perhaps no better proof of the ANC's success than the decade-long confusion by the Security Police and South Africa's intelligence agencies over whether Barry Gilder and Aboobaker Ismail were one and the same person. Could it be because Gilder did not have a conventional mug shot, with head and shoulders prominently on display? Gilder described his initial response to his mug shot, which I had shown to him for the first time in 2015:

> My first impression was a question: Where and when was it taken? I think you and I sat here trying to work that out. That's why I had this memory of there being more background in the photo you showed me but that can't be it. But the hair and the beard [are] certainly from my student days, my NUSAS days. I'm looking into

the camera, so it wasn't a surreptitiously-taken photograph, unless they'd hidden the camera in my mirror or something. I can't tell what clothes I'm wearing because it's black and white. But that was my student days' hair length, as far as I can recall. So I don't know. It could have been Craig Williamson [the police officer who infiltrated NUSAS] saying he was taking photos for the NUSAS album. I don't know.[35]

Like Netshitenzhe, Gilder also went into exile in 1976. But he did so to avoid being drafted into the apartheid military a second time.[36] Gilder had accepted his first call-up in 1968, spending nine months in the army. When the army came calling again in 1976, however, ordering him to report to camp, he decided to flee into exile, going through Botswana. Gilder had served on the same NUSAS executive as Craig Williamson, so it would not have taken Williamson long to report to his police handlers that Gilder had fled the country. This meant that the Security Police probably added Gilder's mug shot to the album as early as late 1976. There is a puzzle in the tale, however. When Gilder fled to exile, he already had a passport and had in fact used it to visit England in the late sixties. So why not use in the album the formal photograph that Gilder had submitted with his passport application? Looking at the photograph that did make it into the album, Gilder said:

This one doesn't really trigger a memory. There's no context. It's me apparently looking into a camera. It doesn't look like an ID or passport photo. I don't know whether it's cut out from a bigger photo of me and other people. There is nothing in the memory except the look that I had, or very soon after. And of course the question is: Who took the photo? How did it get into the album? Does it surprise me that I was of interest? . . . I'm not surprised that I was in the album. I know the story about my photo being mistaken for Rashid. So I'm trying to see Rashid in this photo.[37]

Gilder laughed as he said this, showing that while his mug shot triggered questions in his mind, it also gave him pleasure.

Yes, I suppose there's a kind of perverse pride in being in the album. Kind of validates me as a genuine terrorist. . . . Ja, perverse. Honored to have been counted as a genuine terrorist by them, the apartheid regime. You know, it raises questions. It raises questions, too, about their efficiency. One, that they had such an old photo of me in their album. And then, of course, the story about accepting the mistaken identification of me as Rashid. They might have said to you that Africans couldn't tell the difference. But they lived on that piece of intelligence for years, even into the '90s, I'm told.[38]

If the album raises questions about the much-vaunted efficiency of the Security Police, what does it tell us about apartheid South Africa? An answer comes from Gilder:

You are asking me to get philosophical on this? It's an interesting but rather blurry window on our history. Blurry in the sense that it's photographs taken from people that, in many cases that you know or knew—kind of a frozen moment in their early lives in most cases. Context, like in my photograph, is not there. Blurry in the sense that it's a very unfocused snapshot of our history. Interesting in that it tells you to some extent how much apartheid security knew about us—but also the mistakes they made. They weren't infallible. They weren't all-seeing, all-powerful, intelligence [from a] tradecraft, proficiency point of view. We might have done the same thing, had photographs of our enemies. How useful were they? What would be interesting is to see what the photographs led to.[39]

What do you mean?

What intelligence they led to, if you have a captured guerilla or a
source and you show this photograph. "I know this person,
I last saw this person in Quibaxe [an ANC military camp in
Angola] in 1983." What intelligence came out of that? How
did they translate that to usable intelligence? In many cases,
I would imagine the fallibility of memory got them wrong
intelligence, bad intelligence. Somehow make many of these
people look so evil. Angry terrorists. So, I'm saying: To what
extent was this a reliable method of gaining good intelligence? If it was a captured guerilla shown a photograph of
someone they were in camp with, they would have known
that person by the MK name. So the cops would have had
to connect the MK name with the real name if they had it.
How many photos are in the album?[40]

While he took pleasure in the validation the album accorded him as a
"genuine terrorist," Gilder said he had questions about who was not
included in the album. Policeman Eugene Fourie speculated that the
album had only about 40 percent of the insurgents in exile. We also
know from Fourie that the police deliberately planted mug shots of
their agents and collaborators in the album. So who was *not* in the
album? There is no straight answer, it turns out, to that question.

There is a story told about Craig Williamson and the album. Shortly
after his unmasking as an apartheid spy in Europe in 1979, Williamson
returned to South Africa and was promptly promoted to colonel in the
Security Police. His brief included keeping tabs on white activists and
running agents within the white left. One day in 1981, Williamson

walked into a room to interrogate NUSAS president Andrew Boraine, held in solitary confinement. Williamson slapped a copy of the album on the table, pointed to a mug shot, and screamed at Boraine: "Who do you recognize?" As Boraine, aged twenty-two, struggled to identify the identikit, Williamson gloated: "That's me! That's me!"[41] To cover Williamson's tracks, his police handlers had also branded him a terrorist and put his mug shot in the album. When I first interviewed Williamson about the album in 2016, he told me that he first saw the album after his return to South Africa in 1980. Asked how he felt when he saw himself in the album for the first time, Williamson laughed:

> Well, you know, I'd been used to them [his Security Police colleagues] thinking, most of my colleagues thinking, I was a terrorist. And then, you know, at that time we were always on the intelligence side. It was used to identify people, either if we had an agent who'd, if we were debriefing someone, then we could go through the album. It was important to link real names to MK names and other *noms de guerre* that people were using. And some guys used more than one name. I, for example, had more than one name. Some ANC people knew me as Newman, others knew me as Colin. It was important to use the album to identify who was who. And then, obviously, if we got photographs, surveillance pictures of people, we could give it across to see one and them.[42]

Williamson said the album was torn between two functions, one investigative and the other intelligence-gathering.

> The typical policemen want to gather evidence and they want to arrest somebody, charge someone, convict someone and put them in prison. Whereas the intelligence guys are actually not very interested in that. They want to gather informa-

tion. They want to protect their sources. They don't want people to have to go and give evidence because it'll blow who they are, where they are getting their information. So there was a contradiction in the organization. So the album was also pulled between these two functions. The one lot wanted to have somebody who'd been arrested and say to him, "Who do you recognize? Who were you trained with? What were you doing?" But their idea was to, at some stage, have evidence against these people. But the intelligence function people. . . . I might ask very different questions: "Who are these guys?" But then I might ask: "Is he happy? Has he got family here? Is he homesick? Do his family have money problems?" Because I am looking for a way to hook him.[43]

How crucial was the album to the intelligence unit of the Security Police?

It was important, because it's pretty useless me putting in a report where somebody says "this MK operative came to Swaziland, his name is Joe Soap," and we have no idea who Joe Soap is. We need to know who Joe Soap is. The album came in [handy], because the way any underground or revolutionary or guerilla organization works is "need to know." One of the reasons I got away with what I got away with for so long was because of the compartmentalization.[44]

The album was, however, a work of human hands. It needed humans to come alive. Only humans could make it live. This meant it was subject to the vicissitudes of human memory. Human fallibility made the album itself fallible. That is how Williamson explained the confusion by the Security Police over whether Barry Gilder was Aboobaker Ismail.[45] But, as Gilder said when I relayed Williamson's story to him in May 2016, "If, indeed, Williamson had correctly identified the photo of me as not being Rashid, why were they still mistaking me for Rashid into the 1990s?"[46] There is, of course, one possible answer to Gilder's question, an answer that would be of a piece with the racism at the heart of apartheid: the Security Police held on to the idea that Rashid was in fact a white man because their racism would not let them accept that a black man could be as efficient and successful against the might of the apartheid state as Rashid was. The Security Police and their colleagues in the intelligence services were inclined to believe Rashid was Gilder because that would mean their nemesis was, like them, white, and therefore a worthy opponent. Just as they wanted to believe the stories of innocence told by Kave, Bosio, Mfalapitsa, and Hlapane—well-intentioned blacks led astray by white communists and their KGB masters—they wanted to believe Rashid was Gilder. That is why they held on to that belief right to the end of apartheid. The mix-up was not so much a fault of the album as a failure of looking and seeing. The album could only do so much for Williamson and his colleagues when they only saw what they wanted to see.

ELEVEN

Sins of History

I CANNOT SHOW you the photograph with which this chapter begins. But I can tell you about it.[1] A body lies on its side on a pavement.
Its left leg, severed at the knee from the rest of the body, is about a foot
away. The left shoe, its rubber sole burnt onto the pavement, stands *en*
pointe between the dismembered leg and the rest of the body. The shoe
is empty. The left thigh is missing. So are the forearms. What remains
of the left arm, from the elbow to the shoulder, lies next to a silver
parking meter. A man in a bluish-grey suit and grey shoes, visible only
from the waist down, stands behind the meter. To the man's right is
another man, he in a white, short-sleeved shirt, khaki pants, and khaki
shoes. The second man, whose face is the only one visible in the photograph, is on his haunches, leaning into the body on the sidewalk. His
fingers are bloody. To the second man's right stands another, in a light
brown, tweed coat with suede elbow patches, brown trousers, and a
brown pair of shoes. Only the right arm and leg of the man in brown
are visible. His left hand holds a blue denim jacket with a silver metal

star pinned to its left breast pocket—a clue to whose mutilated body this is.[2]

I can tell you about the man whose body lay in pieces on the ground and about the white-shirted man with the bloodied fingers. The dismembered body belonged to Odirile Meshack Maponya; the man in the white shirt was Deon Gouws. Maponya was black, Gouws white. Maponya was an insurgent, a member of the military wing of the ANC; Gouws was a member of the South African Security Police, an explosives expert attached to a secret unit formally called C1 but known colloquially as Vlakplaas. Maponya was in the process of planting a minilimpet mine outside Sterland Cinema, a whites-only movie house in Pretoria, on Friday evening, April 15, 1988, when the bomb exploded prematurely.

Maponya, who went by the *nom de guerre* of Mainstay Chibuku, wanted the bomb to go off at 7:30 PM, as moviegoers were leaving the cinema. It went off as he was priming it at 7:00 PM. I can also tell you that, sixteen years after the photograph described above was taken, Gouws himself became the victim of a bomb blast when, during the Iraq War, a suicide bomber drove an ambulance laden with explosives into the Baghdad hotel in which Gouws, retired from the South African Police on medical grounds, was staying, along with other mercenaries. The attack left Gouws with shrapnel in his brain, cost him fingers and a toe, but he lasted another twelve years before dying from his injuries. I can also tell you about Susan Purén, a photojournalist who happened to be staying at a hotel a few blocks from Sterland Cinema in April 1988 and who, upon hearing Maponya's limpet mine go off, reached instinctively for her camera, took out the black-and-white film already in the camera, put color film in, and ran in the direction of the blast. "Because if this was black-and-white," Purén told me years later as she pointed at a copy of the photograph mentioned above, "it was nothing. It wouldn't have the same impact."[3] Purén knew about the power of color because, five years earlier, on May 20, 1983, she and her husband, Lourens Purén, were the first journalists to respond to an ANC car bomb attack outside the headquarters of the South African Air Force in Pretoria. That attack, known as the Church Street bombing, killed nineteen people and injured more than two hundred others.[4] The Puréns worked for Armscor, the state-owned armaments corporation, and happened to be in the vicinity when the Church Street bomb exploded. They had in their car a company camera, loaded with black-and-white film, and used it to take pictures of the aftermath. The photographs made it into local newspapers but, devoid of color, did not have the impact that her 1988 photograph would have. They did not register in the public consciousness the way the 1988 photograph did.

I can also tell you about a man who, although key to the events captured by Purén's photograph, is absent from it. Rodney Baduza Toka, a fellow ANC insurgent who was with Maponya on the night of the incident, had chosen the cinema as, in his words, the "easiest target" to bomb following a reconnaissance mission the day before.[5] Toka and Maponya had decided to bomb the cinema in retaliation for the assassination on March 28, 1988, of an ANC comrade named Patrick Sandile Vundla. A team of South African special forces had killed Vundla, who went by the alias Naledi, during a raid on Botswana, where Vundla was based. "So, due to that thing of Naledi, then Mainstay decided we must carry [out] some operations in the city center in Pretoria," Toka told me.[6] Mainstay and Toka planned to hit a number of targets that April night and Toka himself had a mini-limpet mine that he planned to use after Maponya finished priming his. But as Maponya was on his knees on the sidewalk, fiddling with his bomb, trying to set the timer before attaching the explosive to the underside of a car parked outside the cinema, a group of boys standing across the street from the cinema took an interest in the two suspicious men. One of the boys approached. "This boy might have thought we were criminals. I don't think he might have felt that we were guerillas, [and that] we were planting something. He might have just been curious to say 'maybe they want to steal a car, maybe they want to do something,'" Toka recalled.[7] Toka walked towards the boy and, as a distraction, engaged him in small talk. A tree stood between Maponya, still busy with his bomb, and Toka and the boy. That tree saved Toka and the boy. The explosion was so sudden, so loud, that Toka thought Maponya had placed the bomb and left the scene. But as he regained his senses and noticed people running in all directions, screaming "it's a bomb, it's a bomb," he threw the limpet mine he had on him into a dustbin nearby, and fled the scene.

It was only the next day that Toka learned, from photographs taken by Purén and published in the Afrikaans daily *Beeld,* followed Sunday by the weekly *Rapport,* that Maponya was dead, that his bomb had "cut him in half."[8] When Toka visited the Maponyas that Sunday to tell the family what had happened, Purén's photographs had beaten him to it. "Already they had seen the newspapers, because that morning I found them crying."[9] That proved to be only the beginning of the Maponyas' encounter with Purén's photograph and, as it turned out, the last time the family would see Odirile Maponya in any form.[10] Out of spite, the Security Police buried him as a pauper in Pretoria and refused to show the family his grave. When Maponya's younger brother Itumeleng Maponya, himself an ANC insurgent, was arrested in June 1988 and placed in solitary confinement, his police interrogators taunted him with the photograph. Itumeleng, who spent a year in solitary confinement before being sent off to Robben Island for three years for terrorism, told me, "In solitary confinement there was two newspapers [even though security detainees] were not qualified to get a newspaper . . . but there were two newspapers they thought, psychologically, they are damaging to me."[11] One newspaper showed what Itumeleng remembered as "the scattered body of Mainstay;" the other carried a confession by Almond Nofomela, a member of a police death squad responsible for a litany of murders.[12] Nofomela, who was on death row at the time and trying to get a reprieve, said that he and his Vlakplaas colleagues had killed Odirile's and Itumeleng's brother, Japie Maponya, in May 1985, during a police search for Odirile. Itumeleng recalled seeing the two newspapers, "but I . . . did not take them and read them. I only looked at them out of the corner of my eye. But I left them [untouched] as I was exposed to them before I was arrested."[13] Like other members of the Maponya family, Itumeleng had already encountered Purén's photograph showing the "scattered body" of his brother.

Before Odirile Maponya's body was scattered across a Pretoria pavement and then dumped in an unmarked grave, however, he was to his family a devout Christian, a popular schoolteacher, keen karateka, bodybuilder, ballroom dancer, and talented musician. "He had four voices," said Itumeleng. "He could handle contralto; he could handle soprano; he could handle tenor; he could handle bass. That's the talent he had."[14] To the Security Police, however, before Maponya was a jumble of bloodied limbs, he was a terrorist (fig. 11.1).

He was one of apartheid's most wanted men in the 1980s, suspected of involvement in the 1985 killing of a policeman named Jacob Tswane. The police left a trail of destruction in their pursuit of Maponya. They turned his father, Joseph Maponya, into an informer paid to spy on his family, killed his brother Japie Maponya in 1985, murdered his ANC colleague Stanza Bopape in 1988, and arrested and tortured his brother Itumeleng and cousin Tiro Tumane.[15] During that pursuit, Maponya

1783

FIGURE II.I Mug shot of Odirile
Maponya in the Terrorist Album.
Courtesy of National Archives & Records
Service of South Africa.

was to the police a two-dimensional figure—a mug shot. But, as this
chapter shows, Maponya also had a life beyond the album, a life worth
examining if we want to understand why some rebelled against apartheid. By mentioning what Odirile Maponya meant to his family—his
devotion, his faith, his singing, his sportsmanship—I do not mean to
gloss over the terror of his actions. Indeed, I foreground his actions and
their aftermath to force us to think critically about the meaning of terrorism in apartheid South Africa. By presenting Maponya as he appeared to people other than the police, I "re-member" his body and do
so in ways that might allow us to understand why an individual like
Maponya made the choices he made. Resurrecting Maponya's paper cadaver also means calling into question the very status of the apartheid
security archive as a repository of truths whose supposed exemplary
recordkeeping testifies to its objectivity.

Reverberations

On April 16, 1988, a day after the bomb blast that killed Maponya, a police detective wrote the following in his investigation diary: "The
black man has been positively identified as trained ANC terrorist
Odirele [sic] Meshack Maponya. . . . He was identified by Senior Sergeant Modisane, who knew him personally."[16] The detective said
that colleagues from the forensics division had taken samples from
the scene, while a photographer from the local fingerprinting office
had taken pictures. The investigator had also found a piece of Odirile's
finger, to be used no doubt for fingerprint confirmation. The diary
brought it all together: an insurgent, the police, forensic investigators, a
crime scene photographer, and, of course, the policeman who knew the
dead insurgent. The detective did not mention the Terrorist Album, but
it is not difficult to imagine that it, too, had done its work. Photographs
had certainly done theirs. In fact, a day after the blast, a captured ANC
insurgent named Sipho Solly Mokwena confirmed Odirile's identity
for the police with the help of a photograph taken at the scene. Mokwena, arrested on April 5, 1988, described Odirile as the man he
"knew as Mainstay." But it took Modisane's physical identification of
Odirile's corpse to confirm that the man the police had been hunting
for ten years was dead. But how was it that Modisane, a career policeman, knew Odirile personally? It turns out that Modisane knew the
Maponya family well. Odirile's father Joseph was a registered police
informer and, between April 1979 and April 1981, Modisane had been
his handler. Joseph's career as an informer began on May 6, 1977, with
a letter by Lieutenant-Colonel L. J. Erasmus, divisional commander of
the Security Police in Krugersdorp, asking his superiors for permission
to register "Bantu man Joseph Maponya" as a paid informant at R15 a
month.[17] Joseph's informer reports began appearing on May 30, 1977,

with his first handler, "Bantu Lieutenant" N. J. Leshi, describing him as a "source [who] provides daily service" to the police.[18] It is important to note that Joseph began working for the Security Police eleven months after the June 1976 uprisings, but three months before his son Odirile fled into exile. It is not clear why Joseph, a postman in the West Rand township of Kagiso, began spying for the police (or why the police targeted him for recruitment) but it would appear that, from the beginning, his primary target was his own family, and especially his son Odirile. On August 30, 1977, Joseph received R15 for what his handler called daily service for the police.[19] Odirile had yet to go into exile. Joseph, who only had a Standard Six education, reported verbally to his handlers, who then wrote the reports down for submission to their superiors. On September 1, 1977, Joseph received R15 for informing on the work of the Young Christian Workers' Movement, to which his children belonged.[20] In October and November 1977, Joseph received R20 each month after reporting to his handler that a person, whose name is redacted from the report, was helping people flee South Africa for Botswana.[21] Even though Joseph's reports revolved around his son Odirile, there is no indication that Joseph was motivated by concern for his son. It is not evident from the reports, which are often no more than three sentences at a time, what Joseph thought about his son and about his son's decision to go into exile. In fact, one cannot even tell just by looking at the reports that Joseph and Odirile were father and son. Often, the police reports simply say that Joseph is trying to get as much information as he can about Odirile.

Chapter 10 revealed the taint of collaboration on the album and the pitfalls of taking the album at face value. This chapter explores the ways in which the drama of the struggle against apartheid and the tragedy of exile played out in one family. Rather than tie up the loose ends of stories chronicled above, it examines the ways in which the album bears mute testimony to the suffering of one South African family. Whereas Chapter 10 offered cautionary tales about the pervasiveness of betrayal and collaboration in the anti-apartheid struggle, this chapter looks at the relationship between the personal and the political in that struggle. Readers who have made it this far in the book have already discerned the rough outline of the album's history. They have picked up knowledge of photography in South Africa, the early development of policing and police photography in the country, and the origins of a dedicated Terrorist Album following the country's turn to violence after the banning of the ANC and other organizations in 1960. They have learned how the Security Police used the album, where and when they used it, and with what results. By paying attention to the interviews with the Security policemen mentioned in the book, they have learned how a small police unit managed the album, how and when the unit's members updated it, and what they did to ensure that, on the surface at least, the album stayed true to its official purpose of apprehending and branding as terrorists individuals who left South Africa without government permission. More importantly, readers now understand the relationship between the album and death. Policeman Craig Williamson killed Ruth First for no better reason than that she was in the album. This was an object filled with risk. To be on its pages was to be marked for death. As Williamson said, echoing the hunting metaphor beloved by the police, to be in the album was to be fair game.

By following the stories of the individuals framed by the album, however, readers have also learned about bravery and courage from tales of young South Africans thrust into a war they did not ask for. They have learned about the album's failures, deliberate and genuine. These ranged from misidentifications to obfuscations—such as mug shots placed in the album to obscure the presence of apartheid agents in the resistance.

The album was not an object to be trusted—not by its owners and certainly not by historians, who can only show up after the fact. By recounting the pain of one family, this chapter preempts any attempt to look at the album as a collective portrait of heroism. This is not to deny the courage of those individuals who gave up their youths and their lives in the fight against an authoritarian regime that was as racist as it was vicious. Although ANC members dominate the album, they were not the only ones in the album. Even though ANC defectors constituted the majority of the collaborators and defectors in the album, they were by no means the only ones. This, then, is not an ANC album. It is a collection of individual stories that speak to the complexity of life under apartheid. Many people ended up in the album because the police put them there for choosing to go into exile rather than live under apartheid; others ended up there for reasons we can only guess at. We cannot place all those reasons within a nationalist frame. But we can look at the story of one family for insight into a traumatic past.

Rather than knit together the different narrative strands pursued in this book to argue why the album matters for South African history, this chapter narrates a messy family story about paternal betrayal, domestic discord, torture, post-traumatic stress, spite, paupers' graves, and missing bones. This may resonate with families in South Africa and abroad. But it does not make the Maponyas representative of South African families. The Maponyas are no metonym for black South Africa. To treat them as such would be to fall for the fallacy that every black person was a freedom fighter and all blacks suffered similarly under apartheid. The Maponyas are not representative of anyone but themselves. If the reader finds something familiar in the Maponya story, let it be because their story is fashioned out of the most human of elements: betrayal, intergenerational disputes, divorce, envy, love, money, sibling rivalry, and many things besides.

By telling a story that has no neat ending, this book explodes the narrow view presented by the album as a way of suggesting critical ways of reading the album and other remnants of the apartheid security archive. This is not simply a book about individuals branded terrorists by the apartheid government. It is also a tale about the apartheid security archive and the violence that that archive continues to inflict on individuals and families. It has been more than thirty years since the Maponya family lost Japie and Odirile, and the family is no closer to finding their remains. Kagiso, their hometown, boasts two post-apartheid monuments to the men—a clinic and a school—but both are misnamed as a result of divisions in the family over how to remember them. For the family, the album remains open, as it were, to the page showing Odirile's mug shot. Their memory of Odirile remains suspended in Susan Purén's photographs, a jumble of bloodied limbs. Without Odirile here to tell us why and how he went into exile, we are left with family members' accounts and the informer reports that Joseph Maponya, the family patriarch, submitted between the 1970s and the 1980s. We cannot ignore those reports. To do that would be to leave out the intricacies—not to mention the twists and turns— of the Maponya story. At the same time, we cannot trust those reports, because to do that would be to give the last word to the white men who refused to let go of their apartheid worldview, even as they were asking Joseph and others like him to betray their families. From the black policemen who were the face of apartheid for most black South Africans to the apartheid agents and informers whose official anonymity could never mask their blackness, each bore the adjective *Bantu* more like a condition than an arbitrary description.[22] Each police report marked a black cop as a Bantu policeman, an agent as a Bantu informer, and a black witness as a Bantu witness. We cannot take such bureaucratic racism as proof, however, of generalized black oppression. Also, we cannot shun the apartheid security archive because it upsets cherished ideas about black solidarity. The struggle against apartheid was no less noble because of the betrayal of men such as Joseph Maponya; the fight for justice in South Africa was no less necessary because of the terrorism of men such as Odirile Maponya. Saul Dubow argues not only that the armed struggle was unnecessary but also that it delayed the end of apartheid—at great human cost.[23] This book does not intervene in that debate. It uses the album to understand why individuals framed by the album as terrorists made the choices they made, and the context under which they made those choices.

Family Fights and Flights

Given Joseph Maponya's work for the Security Police, it is not surprising that our account of how Odirile Maponya ended up in exile came from the father. On November 29, 1977, Joseph gave the police a sworn statement that not only explained how Odirile made his way into exile but also gave us a biographical sketch of his son.[24] Odirile had been born in 1952 in Krugersdorp, in the West Rand. He attended Lengau Primary School and Mosupatsela High School, both in Kagiso, and Herman Thebe High School in Rustenburg. Between January and June 1977, Odirile taught at Lengau Primary School. In July 1977, he left teaching for a job at the Plascon Paint Factory in Krugersdorp. Joseph's account of his son continues:

> At the end of September he told me he was going to visit his grandmother in Driefontein, Zeerust. A few days later, I visited Driefontein. After my arrival, I learnt from Bantu woman Kenemang Mokgwe [that] the grandmother had heard that Meshack had fled

to Botswana. He is a citizen of the Republic of South Africa. I do not know if he is in possession of valid travel documents. He was in possession of a reference book. To date, I have not heard from him.[25]

When Joseph signed that declaration, he had been on the Security Police payroll for seven months. Given that Joseph was informing daily for the police, we cannot rule out the possibility that he followed his son to Driefontein to check on his movements for the police. We can assume that Joseph's visit to the grandmother was no innocent family visit but a spying mission. It is, of course, possible that Joseph reported his son's disappearance to the police out of paternal concern. But the record of his spying and the associated payments suggest a different story. On June 1, 1978, the police paid Joseph R20 for a report in which he said he was looking for information about Odirile and two brothers from Kagiso named Lloyd Wellington Mmusi and Benjamin Mbulelo Mmusi. On June 29, 1978, the police paid Joseph R20 for informing on a group of blacks crossing illegally from Botswana into South Africa. In July and August 1978 he earned R20 and R25, respectively, for informing on a group infiltrating South Africa from Botswana. In October 1978, he received R25 for reporting his son's whereabouts. On November 1, 1978, the police paid him R25 for a report saying he was still looking for information about the whereabouts of his son and that of a neighbor named Benjamin Mbulelo Mmusi.[26] On April 30, 1979, we get the first signed informer note in which then-Constable M. Z. Modisane acted as Joseph's handler. In that report, for which Joseph earned R25, Modisane noted that "Source did not submit any reports but is still providing his services daily."[27] Modisane handled Joseph from April 1979 to April 1981, after which he ceased signing Joseph's reports.

On November 9, 1983, Lieutenant J. T. Mostert applied to his superiors in the Security Police in Krugersdorp to have Joseph scrapped (*geskrap*) as a registered informer. Mostert said, "Source is already very old and no longer interested in visiting his friends in order to get information." (Joseph was fifty six.)[28] By the police's own calculations, Joseph had earned R344.78 between May 1977 and September 1978, and R684 between October 1978 and February 1982. Tellingly, Joseph's scrapping as an informer came a year after Odirile, who had spent five years in Angola and East Germany undergoing military training, began operating inside the country. Were the two events connected? Did Joseph stop spying once he knew that his son, highly trained in the ways of war, was back in the country? Better yet, did he ever stop spying? The documentary evidence suggests otherwise. The evidence suggests that Joseph did not stop spying or looking for his son for the police. In November 1984 Joseph spotted his son at a house in Molatedi, a village in Bophuthatswana, near the border with Botswana. Joseph promptly informed the police about his sighting. Joseph, however, did not speak to the son he had not seen in seven years. As Captain Johannes Kleynhans said in a secret cable to his superiors:

> He did not speak to his son because of the enmity that exists between father and son as a result of Joseph's divorce from his wife Francis Maponya, who lives in . . . Bophuthatswana. Francis is Odirile Maponya's mother.[29]

This is the only report we have from Joseph's long association with the Security Police that speaks of discord between father and son. Joseph saw his son for the first time in seven years and yet did not say a word to him. Instead, he informed the police about his sighting. Not only that, Joseph ordered another of his sons, Japie, to visit his mother to see if Odirile was staying with her. Japie did as told and reported that their mother did not want Odirile staying with her. It would appear that Japie also met Odirile during that short visit. Kleynhans's report stated that "Since JAPIE MAPONYE's [sic] father JOSEPH MAPONYE was a reliable informer and Japie's loyalty was suspect, it was decided not to question him about his visit to his brother."[30] Kleynhans feared that Japie was torn between loyalty to his father, whom he respected, and loyalty to his brother Odirile, whom he idolized. But Kleynhans did not want Japie questioned about his meeting with Odirile, as that might have exposed the father.

Not only was Joseph spying on Odirile, he was pitting two sons against each other by getting Japie to inform on his fugitive brother. This was a dangerous move, as it turned out: when a Security Police death squad made up of askaris later kidnapped Japie, in September 1985 outside the Krugersdorp bank at which he was a security guard, it did so based on the West Rand Security Police's information that Japie was in contact with Odirile. Japie did not know where the police could find Odirile, but the police assumed he must. Worse, having used askaris to kidnap him and having tortured him severely during questioning, the Security Police worried that, if they let Japie go, he would expose their illegal activities and the identities of the askaris. To avoid that, they simply killed him, then dumped his body somewhere along the border with Swaziland. Could Joseph have anticipated this when he sent Japie to report on his brother's whereabouts in November 1984? We cannot say. Did Joseph know what danger he was exposing his family to? This we cannot say, either. But we can say that Joseph's spying on his son did not end in 1983. This raises questions about the reliability of police claims that they scrapped Joseph as a registered informer in November 1983.

It is possible, however, that the police meant to indicate that Joseph ceased being a registered informer and became instead a casual informer, called on by the police to give information when the need arose. On May 29, 1985, Joseph reported to Kleynhans, who seems to have become his handler, that Odirile was staying in Garankuwa and that he (Joseph) was trying to get the address for the police. This report came two days after Odirile allegedly killed a policeman named Jacob Tswane. According to the police, Odirile was part of an ANC unit that ambushed a team of police officers in Bophuthatswana. Kleynhans said, "I spoke to informer Joseph Maponye [*sic*] after the murder of Warrant / Officer Tswane about the possible involvement of his son O. M. Maponya in the murder but he could not provide any information other than what he provided in 1984."[31] Recall that in 1984 Joseph gave Kleynhans information that placed his son in Bophuthatswana. That information put Odirile near the scene of the crime—albeit a year before Tswane's murder. It is tempting to speculate about Joseph's motivations but that would be a futile exercise without the old man here to answer our questions. We can guess at his reasons but that too would be of limited use. How, then, do we make sense of this?

Was Kleynhans telling the truth when he said that Joseph did not get along with his son? And that this was because of Joseph's divorce from the mother? Did Joseph honestly get one son, Japie, to spy on another, Odirile? More than that, how do we reconcile the police claim that Joseph stopped spying for them in November 1983 with reports that Joseph was still working for the police in 1984 and 1985? What about Kleynhans's description of Joseph in 1984 as a reliable informer? It is worth mentioning that Kleynhans is the source of Joseph's informer reports and that he released these as part of an attempt to protect himself from possible prosecution for the police murder of Japie. Kleynhans submitted the reports in the form of an affidavit to the North Gauteng High Court in Pretoria in 1995 during the trial of Colonel Eugene De Kock, former head of a police death squad, for multiple murders, kidnapping, and robbery. The court sentenced De Kock in 1996 to two life terms and 212 years in prison for a string of convictions, including the kidnapping and murder of Japie. Kleynhans did not release these reports in the service of a greater good. He was afraid that De Kock might implicate him in the kidnapping and murder of Japie. Kleynhans, then a captain in the West Rand Security Police, was present when the police grabbed Japie from the streets and tortured him at the secret police farm called Vlakplaas.[32] So Kleynhans sought to spread the blame for police excesses as widely as he could, in hopes perhaps that if many were guilty then no one was guilty. His targets included Joseph Maponya, on whom he had leaned for information. That is why we cannot let Kleynhans have the last word on the matter of Joseph's spying, even as we use the reports that Kleynhans provided to the Pretoria High Court to enrich our story. What, for example, do Odirile's and Japie Maponya's surviving siblings have to say about the relationship between Joseph and Odirile? How do the siblings respond to the documentary evidence of Joseph's working for the police? These are difficult questions that take us beyond the album. By examining the relationship between Odirile and Joseph, we are able to go beyond the album and its affectations of omniscience. More than that, we are able to tell stories that the album cannot tell. The album cannot speak of the pain and tragedy behind Odirile's mug shot. It must be made to bear witness to that pain and tragedy.

Re-membering Odirile

Dithusang Jeremiah Maponya, six years younger than his brother Odirile, was the first person in the Maponya family to get involved in protest politics. In 1976, Dithusang spent six months in detention after the police accused him of burning down a school in Kagiso during the nationwide student uprisings that began that year. While the police let him go for lack of evidence, two of his colleagues, David Morake and Letsholo Ramokadi, wound up on Robben Island. Dithusang's escape from the clutches of the state did not spare him the wrath of his father. He told me during an interview in July 2018:

> The '76 thing destroyed my relationship with my father. He kicked me out of the house. I lived on the streets. [Odirile] tried to fight for me but he did not have any power. I returned home after a while but it was not pleasant.[33]

Dithusang said Joseph walked out on the family and their mother after Odirile left for exile in September 1977. "My father said he did not want to live in a house full of communists," recalled Dithusang. But Joseph did not just abandon the family; he took up with another woman in Kagiso. When I asked Dithusang about reports regarding his father's relationship with the police—reports, by the way, first made public during De Kock's trial in 1995 and repeated in 1999 during the truth commission's amnesty hearings into the murder of Japie—he expressed shock and surprise. "I'm hearing this for the first time. I don't feel right. It makes me sad." Recalling his father's reaction to the news of Odirile's death, Dithusang said, "He was not happy. He had lost two sons and was not happy about that. No parent would be happy about the way my brothers died." Itumeleng Maponya, the youngest of the Maponya sons, made a similar comment when I asked him in June 2018 about the father's links with the Security Police. "It's a lie," said Itumeleng. "There's no father who can sell his own son. How can a father do that? Have children, raise them, educate them, and then sell them out? That would never happen."[34] Itumeleng said he knew his father could not have been an informer, because the Security Police tortured him

FIGURE 11.2 Odirile
Maponya lifting a barbell.
By permission of the Maponya
family.

and harassed his family constantly: "They put him in a mine for three days, torturing him, wanting him to reveal the whereabouts of his children. He opposed amnesty [for the police officers and askaris responsible for Japie's death]. He was bothered by how they celebrated his death. . . . [He said,] 'We are dealing with people who have shown no remorse. They have not returned the remains. . . .' How can . . . such a person [sell out]?"[35]

Dire Moses Mochine began working with Odirile in the ANC underground in 1983. Mochine was sixteen. He ran errands for Odirile, such as storing arms and relaying messages between Odirile and his ANC colleagues in Botswana. Mochine's father owned a hardware store in Mabaalstad, a village about forty-nine miles north of Rustenburg. The village was close to the border with Botswana and Odirile would stay there on his way in and out of South Africa. The Mochines and Maponyas were close friends, and Odirile treated Mochine like a younger brother. This allowed Mochine to observe Odirile's relationships with various members of the Maponya family. "He had people in the family that he trusted," Mochine recalled, and "he had people in the family that he did not trust."[36] Joseph fell into the latter category. Mochine expressed concern about the old man's apparent obsession with money.

"He complained about De Kock and Nofomela," Mochine said, referring to two of the policemen involved in Japie's murder. "What preoccupied him was that they compensate him. He wanted money. That's what I did not understand. He wanted compensation. That I could not get."[37] Mochine found Joseph's stance confusing because, when the old man made his demands, apartheid had yet to end and the work of state assassins such as De Kock and Nofomela had yet to be exposed. While Dithusang said he was too young to notice anything amiss in the relationship between his father and Odirile, Tiro Tumane, a cousin who was close to Odirile and who grew up with the Maponya boys, told me why he believed Odirile abandoned teaching in July 1977 for a factory job at Plascon Paint in Krugersdorp:

> In those days, teachers had to fetch their pay packets and pay slips directly from the school principal's office. On payday, Odirile's father [who was well-known and respected in the community] would go to the principal and demand that Odirile's pay be given to him, saying he had paid for his education. Odirile got tired of that. So he quit and went to Plascon. He did not want his father confiscating his salary. That was the problem with the old man: he liked money.[38]

Could that have been the source of their discord? Could Odirile have fallen out with his father because he tired of his father commandeering his salary? Might that have driven Odirile into exile and the arms of the ANC? We cannot know that. Certainly the album cannot tell us that. All the album can do is show us Odirile's mug shot: a young man staring into the camera and an uncertain future. The family could not recall when Odirile posed for his mug shot. But they were certain that it was for his dompas and that he would have sat for it sometime in the late 1960s or early 1970s. When Odirile applied for his dompas, the Maponyas could not have known how his mug shot would travel: from being an official document of a so-called Bantu allowed to sojourn in so-called white South Africa to being the image of a wanted terrorist hunted for more than ten years by some of the worst killers in the apartheid state's ranks. Who Odirile was (a son and brother with a complicated family history) cannot be separated from what he became to the apartheid state (a wanted terrorist and suspected cop killer). For the community to whom Odirile and thousands of young people like him were freedom fighters, the celebration of Maponya as a hero has been thwarted by his missing bones and the fact that, after all these years, the family cannot agree on what to make of the relationship between Odirile and his father Joseph. The family cannot agree on how to deal with the loss of Japie, Odirile, and Joseph himself. Can the family celebrate Odirile without having, at the same time, to deal with questions about betrayal and collaboration at the heart of their family drama? Can the family take the memories of both Odirile and his father into post-apartheid South Africa without casting Joseph narrowly as a victim?[39]

That, in fact, is a question with which black South Africa has yet to grapple. How do we talk about the victims of apartheid violence without making it sound like every black person was a victim of that violence? How do we talk about black complicity with apartheid without making it sound like that complicity amounts to absolution for the crimes of apartheid? Do we need a new language to talk about the suffering caused by apartheid and by the complicity that made such suffering possible—a language that allows us to articulate both points without sinking into a morass of moral relativism? Or do we need to denaturalize race, together with all the moral and political assumptions built into the concept?

Conclusion

APARTHEID OPERATIVES set out to destroy *in toto* their security archive before the formal end of apartheid. They failed. Remnants of that archive remain. But those remnants do not remain simply as scraps of paper, informer reports, secret cables, discarded photographs, and the album and its index. They remain also as embodied memories, social memories, family stories, and missing human remains. The government task team set up in the aftermath of the truth commission to look for remains of the disappeared and bones of people like Odirile and Japie Maponya may yet find them. If my dealings with the Maponya family are anything to go by, however, such a discovery will not lead to a resolution. Far from bringing about closure, the bones of the two men are likely to raise difficult questions about who did what in the war against apartheid. What did you do in the war, Daddy?

Let us, in conclusion, return to the album and to another crime scene. Here is Sergeant Eugene Fourie testifying on July 19, 1999, before the truth commission's amnesty committee about the day that he and his colleagues kidnapped Japie Maponya:

> It was approximately lunchtime when we arrived [in Krugersdorp] and Col. de Kock went up to [West Rand Security Police head] Col. le Roux's office and he later came back down with Captain Kleynhans and . . . then he [De Kock] spoke to the black members [askaris] . . . Col. de Kock and Captain Kleynhans and I then climbed into Col. de Kock's vehicle and we went to the Krugersdorp central town area. When we climbed into the vehicle, Col. de Kock said that Col. le Roux and the others were having problems, that there was a man who they wanted to pick up and that his brother was a terrorist and that they wanted to monitor his movements and that this man who we were supposed to pick up was the brother of the terrorist and that he would know the where-abouts of his brother who was the terrorist . . . MK Mainstay.[1]

Was any mention made of who the terrorist was?

There was mention of it in the vehicle. I think that Mr. Kleynhans said—I can recall the name Mainstay. Mainstay Maponya. Later, I heard that his name was Orderele [*sic*].

Did the name Mainstay, or Mainstay Maponya, ring any bell for you at that stage, from within your own experience?

Yes, I knew MK Mainstay because he was in our terrorist photo album and it was my job to work with the terrorists' photo album during interrogation, so I knew him.

What Fourie meant was that he knew Odirile's mug shot. Fourie was familiar with what Maponya looked like. He knew the contents of the files the Security Police kept on Odirile. In truth, Fourie did not know

Maponya. All he knew about Maponya was a two-dimensional mug shot in black and white, and informer reports that could never give him the full story about the man.

This book has tried to give a fuller story about the man, as well as richer stories about some of the men and women framed as terrorists by the album. We cannot say we know these men and women the way that Fourie claimed to know them. But we can say that each one was more than the two-dimensional figure presented by the album. Crucially, each one came with a story that did not necessarily follow the dictates of a nationalist romance. These were not stories of little Davids toppling the apartheid Goliath. They were messier than that.

The romance and tragedy recounted in this book were not directly in the service of some greater cause. They were untidy dramas filled with the stuff of human life. As such, they do not lend themselves to a tidy conclusion. How then shall we conclude a book about histories that refuse closure? By thinking, I suggest, with four photographs. The first (fig. C.1) was taken on July 15, 1982, near the Botha's hoop border gate on South Africa's boundary with Swaziland.

The photograph, taken by Detective-Sergeant Jacobus Albertus Bierman of the local fingerprinting office (or PVAK) of the South African Police in Ermelo, shows a captured ANC insurgent by the name of Peter Mokaba pointing to the spot, along the barbed-wire fence between South Africa and Swaziland, where he and a comrade named Willie Madikoto had made their illegal crossing.[2] Mokaba, clad in a black leather jacket, is handcuffed.

The second photograph was taken by an unidentified PVAK photographer between January 6 and 7, 1988. It is not shown here, but it depicts ANC operative Chris Giffard, also handcuffed, pointing toward the border with Swaziland. Giffard is pointing toward the spot where he had collected fellow ANC operative Lumka Yengeni following her

FIGURE C.I Peter Mokaba. PVAK, National Archives, Pretoria, South Africa. Courtesy of PVAK of South African Police Service.

illegal crossing into South Africa in September 1987. In the photograph, Giffard stands between a Detective-Constable Manzini, to his left, and a Captain Jonker, to his right. Jonker, with his back to Giffard, is leaning over his car, taking down notes as Giffard tells the two Security policemen what he did in September 1987. To the Security Police, Giffard's and Mokaba's photographs are re-stagings of crimes already committed. As such, they follow a formula set by the Security Police and the police photographers whose vantage point we share as we look at the two images. As the Security Police said in a *Manual for the Investigation of Terrorist Cases,* "After a detainee is arrested, he must as soon as possible point out any evidence, for example, documents, weapons, arms caches, location of skirmish, places stayed, exit / entry corridors to South Africa, etc. Here a photographer must take photos of each point as it is identified."[3] Bierman, Jonker, Manzini, and the unnamed photographer who took Giffard's picture were playing it by the book, following the dictates of the manual.

The manual went on: "When someone is arrested, a photo of him must be bound in an album. It is not advisable to use this album for the investigation because it reveals who has been caught." But the manual was about more than the use of photographs. It was also about how Security Police investigators were supposed to handle themselves and their detainees during the course of their investigations:

> Before a detainee is questioned too much about his operations, he must be given a pen and paper so that he can write down his story, i.e. he must write about his activities and operations from start to finish. The paper should always be marked with the date and [be] in numerical order. If the detainee's report does not make sense, it must be torn up in his presence. After two or three times, he will come up with the right story. The detainee does it just to give his comrades a chance to leave the country. Inmates must be shackled to the chair at all times during interrogation to prevent escape. Interrogation must take place in a room equipped with burglar proofing. Every effort should be made to prevent suicide.[4]

The manual sought to give the Security Police a shared choreography for the investigation of terrorism. The only difference between Mokaba's and Giffard's photographs is in the way each man extends his handcuffed hands. Mokaba is pointing downward at the fence (to show where he crossed) while Giffard is pointing upward into the distance (to show the direction from which he and Yengeni came). If we accept the idea that there is always more to a photograph than what is inside its four corners, what bigger truth are these two men pointing us to? They are, I would suggest, directing our gaze to a past whose outline we can barely make out and a future whose shape we cannot yet discern. They are pointing us to a past that refuses to be settled. More importantly, the two men are directing our look beyond the frames of their photographs to histories of complexity and controversy. Peter Mokaba, who died in 2002, aged forty-three, was an apartheid agent and this photograph is a document not just of his arrest but, possibly, also of his betrayal of his comrades.[5] This photograph might mark not just his resistance to apartheid (for which he was arrested) but also his collaboration with apartheid (for which he was never called to account). When the news of Mokaba's spying first surfaced in the 1990s, he threatened to sue Gavin Evans, the journalist and ANC operative who made the claims. But he never did. When historian Padraig O'Malley confronted Mokaba in March 1997 about Evans's claims, Mokaba denounced Evans as a white hobo, a "reject from his community."[6] Tellingly, Mokaba did not once address the actual charge, that he spied for the Security Police. Instead of dealing with the charges against him, Mokaba only said that the ANC never questioned him or asked if he had ever worked for the Security Police. He went straight for the race card against Evans:

> I don't know how [Evans] was recruited into the ANC and that is why I am insisting today that if he was a member I want him to appear before the Disciplinary Committee of the ANC and he must be disgraced there. . . . I was never arrested [by the ANC], I never ever made a confession. [Evans] can never produce such confirmation. And who is he to be believed over and above what Mandela says, over and above what our own leaders say, the ANC, the intelligence structures of the ANC have said? And this is the type of role that we want the TRC to investigate, the role played by the press, the media, in violating our human rights during the apartheid era. They actually played a role.[7]

Rather than refute the serious charges against him, Mokaba chose to play the victim. He wanted the truth commission to investigate how the media violated his rights during the apartheid era. But none of this is in the photograph above. None of this raw history is in the staged photograph above.[8] It is only when we follow Mokaba's direction, look at where he is pointing, and imagine what else he might be showing us, that we come face to face with histories that refuse a simple telling. This refusal does not mean the absence of hope, however.

The third photograph (fig. C.2) was taken outside the Cape Supreme Court in 1990 shortly after the collapse of what the media had dubbed the "Rainbow trial" in reference to the diverse racial make-up of the accused.[9] The trial had started in 1989 as a treason case against fifteen accused, including Chris Giffard and Lumka Yengeni. Most of the accused had been detained for eighteen months before the trial started. Shortly before the proceedings began, however, the state changed its charge from treason to terrorism. But the accused refused to plead. Taking their cue from the legal move that Mandela made when he was charged with treason in 1963, they argued that it was in fact the apartheid government that should be in the dock to answer the charge of treason and terrorism: "As for the charge we now face, we again say that it is the State that stands accused. . . . It is terrorism when assassination squads, operating inside and outside this country, hunt for and eliminate opponents of apartheid. We think of Ruth First, Jeanette Schoon, Pat Ndzima, Cassius Make, Abram Tiro, and many others."[10] The photograph, taken on the eve of the dawn of freedom in South Africa, speaks of possibilities. It speaks of futures that these men and women had imagined. If the Terrorist Album atomized insurgents even as it labeled them all terrorists, this photograph brought insurgents together in ways that spoke of camaraderie, hope, and solidarity. This group portrait nullified the Terrorist Album. It is a portrait of freedom.

FIGURE C.2 Rainbow trialists, including Chris Giffard. By permission of Chris Giffard.

We arrive now at one last image—a photograph (fig. C.3) with which to think about histories that did and did not happen. It is my own first Pass photo, taken in Johannesburg sometime in 1991.

I am looking into the camera. My hair is in dreadlocks. I am wearing a round-neck, knitted sweater that, as I recall, was blue with a green chevron design running across the chest. Underneath the sweater is a light T-shirt whose outline I can barely make out and whose color I cannot remember. To be honest, I do not specifically remember the day I sat for that photograph. I know it was for a national identity document (ID) issued on September 16, 1991. At that time, I was a student at St. Barnabas College, an Anglican boarding school west of Johannesburg, getting ready to sit for my Matric, the final school examinations that would determine whether I went to university. That, perhaps, was the reason I sat for that mug shot. I had applied for an identity document because I wanted my ID number to show on my Matric certificate. St. Barnabas was a progressive school with a well-earned reputation

FIGURE C.3 Jacob Dlamini, 1991.

for opposition to apartheid. Two of my teachers had spent time in detention, and one had a brother in prison who had narrowly escaped assassination by a military death squad for spying on the South African Defense Force for the ANC. The school had also produced a fair number of student activists, some of whom had ended up in exile. When I sat for my ID photograph, the ANC had been unbanned for about a year and political exiles were returning home in their thousands.

But the spring of hope occasioned by the collapse of apartheid was also a winter of despair as a *de facto* civil war tore through communities, my hometown of Katlehong included, taking with it more than twelve thousand lives. In fact, more people died in that short bitter conflict during the last decade of apartheid than were killed in the preceding two decades of the struggle against apartheid put together. It was ugly. A war that, for some, had always been out there somewhere was suddenly here, turning my childhood friends into combatants and killers. With no exile to escape to, they took the streets on which, barely a few years before, we had played soccer and they turned them into trenches and killing fields.

One friend ended up in prison for the illegal possession of an AK-47 rifle; another died in a massacre blamed on rivalries between gangs of boys with too many guns and too little common sense—let alone political savvy. Many of these friends made it into the New South Africa, as political castaways in a place that had neither hope nor jobs for them. As I look at my Pass photo and recall the tales of bravado that my friends and I (already on the margins of the anti-apartheid insurgency) told one another about freedom fighters and about life in exile, I wonder what they would have made of my Pass-photo-turned-mug shot had apartheid not collapsed when it did and had we ended up in exile as freedom fighters. Would we have recognized one another's photographs in the album in the event of capture? In what contexts would we have

encountered the album—betrayal, collaboration, resistance or something along that continuum? What would we have told our interrogators about one another? These are questions about a history that
did not happen.

As for a history that did happen—an album that existed and was
used—this book has raised questions and offered answers. Readers
might find some answers more satisfying than others. Some might be
troubled by the realization that, despite the systematic destruction of
the apartheid security archive, enough remnants remain to pose difficult questions about the apartheid era and the ways in which individuals and families acted during that era. Having framed individuals as
terrorists in the past, the album now frames new questions about that
past. The album is a living object that can be made to speak of alternative histories. The trick, as this book shows, is to listen to its images
and to feel its content and history with every sense we can summon.
An album may constitute suspended conversations; a photograph may
be worth a thousand words. But those conversations and words have
to come from somewhere. They must have a history.

ABBREVIATIONS

NOTES

ACKNOWLEDGMENTS

INDEX

ABBREVIATIONS

ANC African National Congress
ARM African Resistance Movement
BOSS Bureau of State Security
IDAF International Defense Aid Fund
IUEF International University Exchange Fund
MK Umkhonto we Sizwe
NIS National Intelligence Service
NUSAS National Union of South African Students
PAC Pan Africanist Congress
SADF South African Defense Force
SAP South African Police
SB Special Branch

NOTES

Introduction

1. *The State,* published from 1909 to 1912, styled itself as a "South African national magazine" and was the first publication to imagine its audience in terms that were not only national but approximate to South Africa's current territorial boundaries. To be sure, Fayedwa's mug shots were not the first to be used in southern Africa. But they were certainly the first to be published in a magazine that saw itself as South African and imagined its audience to be South African. For a history of the journal, see Peter Merrington, "Pageantry and Primitivism: Dorothea Fairbridge and the 'Aesthetics of Union,'" *Journal of Southern African Studies* 21, no. 4 (December 1995): 643–656. See also Saul Dubow, "South Africa and South Africans: Nationality, Belonging, Citizenship," in *The Cambridge History of South Africa,* vol. 2, ed. Robert Ross, Anne Kelk Mager, and Bill Nasson (Cambridge: Cambridge University Press, 2011), 31.

2. The mug shot has generated excellent scholarship. See, for a sample, Sandra Phillips, "Identifying the Criminal," in *Police Pictures: The Photograph as Evidence,* ed. Sandra S. Phillips, Mark Haworth-Booth, and Carol Squiers, 11–32 (San Francisco: Chronicle Books, 1997); Giacomo Papi, *Under Arrest: A History of the Twentieth Century in Mug Shots,* trans. Jamie Richards (London: Granta Books, 2006); Raynal Pellicer, *Mug Shots: An Archive of the Famous, Infamous, and Most Wanted,* trans. Liz Nash (New York: Abrams, 2009); Jonathan Finn, *Capturing the Criminal Image: From Mug Shot to Surveillance* (Minneapolis: University of Minnesota Press, 2009); John Tagg, *The Burden of Representation: Essays on Photographies and Histories* (Minneapolis: University of Minnesota Press, 1993); Simon A. Cole, *Suspect Identities: A History of Fingerprinting and Criminal Identification* (Cambridge, MA: Harvard University Press, 2001); and, of course, the classic of the genre, Alphonse Bertillon, *Identification of Criminals,* trans. Gallus Muller (New York: AMS Press, 1889). For connections between mug shots and passports, see Jane Caplan and John Torpey, *Documenting Individual Identity: The Development of State Practices in the Modern World* (Princeton: Princeton University Press, 2001); John Torpey, *The Invention of the Passport: Surveillance, Citizenship and the State* (New York: Cambridge University Press, 2000); Martin Lloyd, *The Passport: The History of Man's Most Traveled Document* (Phoenix Mill: Sutton Publishing, 2003); and Craig Robertson, "Mechanisms of Exclusion: Historicizing the Archive and the Passport," in *Archive Stories: Facts, Fictions and the Writing of History,* ed. Antoinette Burton (Durham, NC: Duke University Press, 2005).

3. Martin Chanock makes this point eloquently: "One of the values of looking at policing, and at the administration of laws, is that it can show how the state was incomplete." Martin Chanock, *The Making of South African Legal Culture, 1902–1936: Fear, Favor and Prejudice* (Cambridge: Cambridge University Press, 2001), 52.

4. For insightful work on the album as object, see Martha Langford, *Suspended Conversations: The Afterlife of Memory in Photographic Albums* (Montreal: McGill-Queen's University Press, 2001); and Marianne Hirsch, *Family Frames: Photography, Narrative and Postmemory* (Cambridge, MA: Harvard University Press, 1997).

5. There is a rich literature on the use of objects to tell history. For a sample, see Steven Lubar, *Inside the Lost Museum: Curating Past and Present* (Cambridge, MA: Harvard University Press, 2017); Oivind Fuglerud and Leon Wainwright, eds., *Objects and Imagination: Perspectives on Materialization and Meaning* (New York: Berghahn, 2015); Amiria Henare, Martin Holbraad and Sari Westell, eds., *Thinking through Things: Theorizing Artefacts Ethnographically* (London: Routledge, 2007); and Elizabeth Edwards, Chris Gosden, and Ruth B. Phillips, eds., *Sensible Objects: Colonialism, Museums and Material Culture* (New York: Berg, 2006). More pertinent for this book is Elizabeth Edwards and Janice Hart, eds., *Photographs Objects Histories: On the Materiality of Images* (London: Routledge, 2004).

6. There is, of course, an extensive and very rich literature on power and surveillance, inspired by the work of Michel Foucault, notably Michel Foucault, *Discipline and Punish: The Birth of the Prison,* trans. Alan Sheridan (London: Penguin Books, 1977). Scholars working in the field of surveillance studies, however, have sought to move the field out of the shadow of Foucault. See, for example, Michael McCahill and Rachel L. Finn, eds., *Surveillance, Capital and Resistance: Theorizing the Surveillance Subject* (London: Routledge, 2014); and David Lyon, ed., *Theorizing Surveillance: The Panopticon and Beyond* (Devon: Willan Publishing, 2006).

7. For scholarship on the history of policing in South Africa, see John D. Brewer, *Black and Blue: Policing in South Africa* (Oxford: Clarendon Press, 1994); M. E. Brogden, "The Origins of the South African Police— Institutional versus Structural Approaches," *Acta Juridica* 1 (1989): 1–19; Marius De Witt Dippenaar, *The History of the SAP, 1913–1983* (Pretoria:

Promedia, 1988); Julia Hornberger, *Policing and Human Rights: The Meaning of Violence and Justice in the Everyday Policing of Johannesburg* (New York: Routledge, 2011); Jonny Steinberg, *Thin Blue: The Unwritten Rules of Policing South Africa* (Johannesburg: Jonathan Ball, 2008); Keith Shear, "Tested Loyalties: Police and Politics in South Africa, 1939–1963," *Journal of African History* 53, no. 2 (2012): 173–193; and Charles van Onselen, "Who Killed Meyer Hasenfus? Organized Crime, Policing and Informing on the Witwatersrand, 1902–8," *History Workshop Journal* 67, no. 1 (March 2009): 1–22. For much older but still relevant work on the history of policing in South Africa, see Lennox van Onselen, *A Rhapsody in Blue* (Cape Town: Howard Timmins, 1960).

8. I borrow the idea of the "social life" of objects from Arjun Appadurai, ed., *The Social Life of Things: Commodities in Cultural Perspective* (Cambridge: Cambridge University Press, 1986).

9. Hannah Arendt, *Responsibility and Judgment* (New York: Schocken Books, 2003), 147.

10. I borrow this phrase from Okwui Enwezor and Rory Bester, eds., *Rise and Fall of Apartheid: Photography and the Bureaucracy of Everyday Life* (New York: International Center of Photography, 2013).

11. By this I mean that these neglected objects might help us understand why complexity is not an argument in itself. To say that apartheid was complex should not be the end of the argument but its beginning.

12. For pathbreaking scholarship on the history of photography in Africa, see Wolfram Hartmann, Jeremy Silvester, and Patricia Hayes, eds., *The Colonizing Camera: Photographs in the Making of Namibian History* (Cape Town: University of Cape Town Press, 1998); Paul S. Landau and Deborah D. Kaspin, eds., *Images and Empires: Visuality in Colonial and Postcolonial Africa* (Berkeley: University of California Press, 2002); Jürg Schneider, "The Topography of the Early History of African Photography," *History of Photography* 34, no. 2 (2010): 134–146; and Terence Ranger,

"Colonialism, Consciousness and the Camera," *Past and Present,* no. 171 (May 2001): 203–215. For the history of photography in South Africa specifically, the standard works are Marjorie Bull and Joseph Denfield, *Secure the Shadow: The Story of Cape Photography from Its Beginnings to the End of 1870* (Cape Town: Terence McNally, 1970); and A. D. Bensusan, *Silver Images: History of Photography in Africa* (Cape Town: Howard Timmins, 1966). For authors who offer critical perspectives on the relationship between photography and surveillance in South Africa, see Lorena Rizzo, "Visual Impersonation: Population Registration, Reference Books and Identification in the Eastern Cape, 1950s–1960s," *History in Africa* 41 (June 2014): 221–248; Lorena Rizzo, "Visual Aperture: Bureaucratic Systems of Identification, Photography and Personhood in Colonial Southern Africa," *History of Photography* 37, no. 3 (2013): 263–282; Lorena Rizzo, "Shades of Empire: Police Photography in German South-West Africa," *Visual Anthropology* 26, no. 4 (2013): 328–354; Patricia Hayes, "Power, Secrecy, Proximity: A Short History of South African Photography," *Kronos,* no. 33 (November 2007): 139–162; Patricia Hayes and Andrew Bank, "Introduction," *Kronos,* no. 27 (November 2001): 1–14, and Andrew Bank, "Anthropology and Portrait Photography: Gustav Fritsch's 'Natives of South Africa,' 1863–1872," *Kronos,* no. 27 (November 2001): 43–76. For a comparative perspective, see William J. Maxwell, *F. B. Eyes: How J. Edgar Hoover's Ghostreaders Framed African American Literature* (Princeton: Princeton University Press, 2015); Simone Browne, *Dark Matters: On the Surveillance of Blackness* (Durham, NC: Duke University Press, 2015); and Alexander G. Weheliye, *Habeas Viscus: Racializing Assemblages, Biopolitics, and Black Feminist Theories of the Human* (Durham, NC: Duke University Press, 2014).

13. For more on the use of violence as an expression of a state's will to punish, see Didier Fassin, *The Will to Punish* (New York: Oxford University Press, 2018). For a treatment of policing as being by definition violent, see Micol

Seigel, *Violence Work: State Power and the Limits of Police* (Durham, NC: Duke University Press, 2018).

14. I am thinking here of the friend-enemy distinction as elaborated by that Nazi Carl Schmitt. See Carl Schmitt, *The Concept of the Political,* trans. George Schwab (Chicago: University of Chicago Press, 1996), 26.

15. Craig Williamson's testimony before the Amnesty Committee of the Truth and Reconciliation Commission, during Hearings into the Murders of Ruth First, Jeanette Schoon, and Katryn Schoon, September 16, 1998, http://www.justice.gov.za/trc/amntrans%5C1998/98090829_pre_2pretor7.htm, p. 38 of 90, hereafter Williamson testimony, September 16, 1998. Of course, apartheid agencies and their operatives killed many individuals not in the album. I quote Williamson here because his was the first truth commission testimony to connect the album to political assassinations. It is possible that Williamson and his colleagues might still have killed Ruth First, even if she was not in the album.

16. Craig Williamson, interview with author, Johannesburg, August 17, 2016.

17. Williamson testimony, September 16, 1998, page 39 of 90.

18. Williamson testimony, September 16, 1998, page 39 of 90.

19. For excellent work on the history of state surveillance in South Africa, particularly the monitoring of black bodies, see Keith Breckenridge, *Biometric State: The Global Politics of Identification and Surveillance in South Africa, 1850 to the Present* (New York: Cambridge University Press, 2014). On the role of photography in the production and management of racial difference, see Tina Campt, *Listening to Images* (Durham, NC: Duke University Press, 2017); and Tina Campt, *Image Matters: Archive, Photography, and the African Diaspora in Europe* (Durham, NC: Duke University Press, 2012); Andrew Bank, *Bushmen in a Victorian World: The Remarkable Story of the Bleek-Lloyd Collection of Bushman Folklore* (Cape Town: Double Storey Books, 2006); and Robert J. Gordon, *Picturing Bushmen: The Denver African*

Expedition of 1925 (Athens: Ohio University Press, 1997). For comparative work from other parts of the world, see Amos Morris-Reich, *Race and Photography: Racial Photography as Scientific Evidence, 1876–1980* (Chicago: University of Chicago Press, 2016); and Katherine Biber, *Captive Images: Race, Crime, Photography* (London: Routledge-Cavendish, 2007).

20. Williamson testimony, September 16, 1998, page 38 of 90.

21. Bessie Head, "Letter from South Africa: For a Friend, 'D. B.,'" *Transition,* no. 11 (November 1963), 40.

22. For work on the massacre, see Tom Lodge, *Sharpeville: An Apartheid Massacre and Its Consequences* (New York: Oxford University Press, 2011); and Phillip Frankel, *An Ordinary Atrocity: Sharpeville and Its Massacre* (Johannesburg: Wits University Press, 2001). For critical examinations of whether the massacre should have led to armed struggle against apartheid, see Saul Dubow, "Were There Political Alternatives in the Wake of the Sharpeville-Langa Violence in South Africa, 1960?" *Journal of African History* 56, no. 1 (March 2015): 119–142. See also Paul Landau, "The ANC, MK, and the 'Turn to Violence' (1960–1962)," *South African Historical Journal* 64, no. 3 (2012): 538–563; and Bernard Magubane, Philip Bonner, Jabulani Sithole, Peter Delius, Janet Cherry, Pat Gibbs, and Thozama April, "The Turn to Armed Struggle," in *The Road to Democracy in South Africa,* vol. 1: *1960–1970* South African Democracy Education Trust, 53–146 (Cape Town: Zebra Press, 2004).

23. Gillian Stead Eilersen, *Bessie Head: Thunder Behind her Ears: Her Life and Writing* (Johannesburg: Wits University Press, 2007), 53–55.

24. Karin A. Shapiro, "No Exit? Emigration Policy and the Consolidation of Apartheid," *Journal of Southern African Studies* 42, no. 4 (2016): 763–781, 764.

25. Shapiro, "No Exit?" 765.

26. Craig Williamson, interview, August 17, 2016; Eric Abraham, telephone interview with author, July 27, 2017.

27. For details of the killing and disappearance of Japie Maponya, see *Truth and Reconciliation Commission of South Africa Report,* vol. 2 (Cape Town: Juta & Co., 1998), 212 and 237.

28. Various branches of the apartheid security services destroyed tons of archival material as apartheid gave way to democracy. For an account of this orgy of destruction, see the *Truth and Reconciliation Commission of South Africa Report,* vol. 1 (Cape Town: Juta & Co., 1998), ch. 8. For a novel argument about how to use the senses (especially touch) in the apprehension of photographs, see Campt, *Listening to Images.*

29. See the final report of the *Truth and Reconciliation Commission of South Africa Report* (Cape Town: Juta & Co., 1998).

30. Saul Dubow, *Apartheid: 1948–1994* (New York: Oxford University Press, 2014), 276.

31. Ivan Evans, *Bureaucracy and Race: Native Administration in South Africa* (Berkeley: University of California Press, 1997).

32. Although I have changed the preposition, I owe this idea to Matthew Hull. See Matthew Hull, *Government of Paper: The Materiality of Bureaucracy in Urban Pakistan* (Berkeley: University of California Press, 2012).

33. For an excellent argument laying out the bureaucratic inconsistency and ideological incoherence of apartheid, see Deborah Posel, *The Making of Apartheid, 1948–1961: Conflict and Compromise* (Oxford: Clarendon Press, 1991).

34. See Nicky Rousseau, "Counter-revolutionary Warfare: The Soweto Intelligence Unit and Southern Itineraries," *Journal of Southern African Studies* 40, no. 6 (2014): 1343–1361, 1360.

35. Rousseau, "Counter-revolutionary Warfare," 1360.

36. *Truth and Reconciliation Commission Report, Vol. One,* 155.

37. See the *Truth and Reconciliation Commission Report, Vol. One,* 201.

38. See the *Truth and Reconciliation Commission Report, Vol. One,* 201.

39. See Anthony Richard Turton, *Shaking Hands with Billy: The Private Memoirs of Anthony Richard Turton* (Durban: Just Done Productions), 2010, 341–342.

40. *Truth and Reconciliation Commission Report, Vol. One,* 219.

41. *Truth and Reconciliation Commission Report, Vol. One,* 217.

42. *Truth and Reconciliation Commission Report, Vol. One,* 217.

43. *Truth and Reconciliation Commission Report, Vol. One,* 217.

44. *Truth and Reconciliation Commission Report, Vol. One,* 217.

45. Eugene Fourie, interviews with author, Free State, South Africa, August 27, 2015, and July 21, 2016.

46. For an example of this line of argumentation, see Vusi Pikoli and Mandy Wiener, *My Second Initiation: The Memoir of Vusi Pikoli* (Johannesburg: Picador Africa, 2013). To be fair, some scholars have given the TRC the credit it deserves. See, notably, Verne Harris, *Archives and Justice: A South African Perspective* (Chicago: Society of American Archivists, 2007); Sarah Nuttall and Carli Coetzee, eds., *Negotiating the Past: The Making of Memory in South Africa* (Oxford: Oxford University Press, 1998).

47. *Truth and Reconciliation Commission of South Africa Report,* vol. 2 (Cape Town: Juta, 1998), esp. ch. 3, "Appendix: State Security Forces: Directory of Organizations and Structures," 313–324. I give details of Joseph Maponya's relations with the Security Police in Chapter 11. Askaris were former insurgents turned, often through torture but sometimes through other inducements, into counterinsurgents. I write about one askari named Glory Sedibe in Jacob Dlamini, *Askari: A Story of Collaboration and Betrayal in the Anti-Apartheid Struggle* (New York: Oxford University Press, 2015).

48. For an elaboration of this point, see Verne Harris and Christopher Merrett, "Toward a Culture of Transparency: Public Rights of Access to Official Records in South Africa," in Harris, *Archives and Justice,* 269–288, 270.

49. Michael Ignatieff, Introduction to *Truth and Lies: Stories from the Truth and Reconciliation Commission in South Africa,* by Jillian Edelstein, 15–21 (London: Granta Books, 2001).

50. My interest in seeing the album as, at one level, representing a collective biography of a generation is inspired by my reading of R. F. Foster, *Vivid Faces: The Revolutionary Generation in Ireland, 1890–1923* (New York: W. W. Norton, 2015), as well as Luisa Passerini, *Autobiography of a Generation: Italy, 1968,* trans. Lisa Erdberg (Hanover, NH: University Press of New England, 1996). I thank David Atwell for bringing Foster's rich book to my attention.

51. I am, of course, echoing Ranajit Guha, "The Prose of Counter-Insurgency," in *Subaltern Studies II: Writings on South Asian History and Society* (New Delhi: Oxford University Press, 1983).

52. I owe this formulation to Nathan Arrington.

53. Lumka Yengeni, interview with author, Cape Town, September 8, 2017.

54. The documents in question come from the Department of Justice's Security Legislation Directorate and are the most complete records we have from the apartheid archive. Thankfully, the directorate ignored the orders issued in 1993 to destroy the apartheid archive. See the *Truth and Reconciliation Commission of South Africa Report, Vol. One,* 226–227.

55. For thoughtful examinations of this question, see Katherine Verdery, *My Life as a Spy: Investigations in a Secret Police File* (Durham, NC: Duke University Press, 2018); Katherine Verdery, *Secrets and Truths: Ethnography in the Archive of Romania's Secret Police* (New York: Central University Press, 2014); Istvan Rev, "The Man in the White Raincoat: Betrayal and the Historian's Task," in *Traitors: Suspicion, Intimacy and the Ethics of State-Building,* ed. Sharika Thiranagama and Tobias Kelly, 200–226 (Philadelphia: University of Pennsylvania Press, 2010).

56. See the *Truth and Reconciliation Commission Report, Vol. One,* 30.

57. Act No. 30 of 1950, quote at §5(1), p. 279, http://www.sahistory.org.za /sites/default/files/DC/leg19500707.028.020.030/leg19500707.028.020.030 .pdf.

58. For insight into the origins and operations of the act, see Keith Brecken-ridge, "The Book of Life: The South African Population Register and the Invention of Racial Descent, 1950–1980," *Kronos* 40, no. 1 (November 2014): 225–240; Keith Breckenridge, "Verwoerd's Bureau of Proof: Total Infor-mation in the Making of Apartheid," *History Workshop Journal* 59, no. 1 (Spring 2005): 83–108; Lorena Rizzo, "Visual impersonation: Population Registration, Reference Books and Identification in the Eastern Cape, 1950–1960s," *History in Africa* 41 (June 2014): 221–248.

59. Breckenridge, "Book of Life," 231.

60. Michelle Caswell, *Archiving the Unspeakable: Silence, Memory and the Pho-tographic Record in Cambodia* (Madison: University of Wisconsin Press, 2014); Kirsten Weld, *Paper Cadavers: The Archives of Dictatorship in Guate-mala* (Durham, NC: Duke University Press, 2014); Verdery, *My Life as a Spy*; Verdery, *Secrets and Truths*; Tina Rosenberg, *The Haunted Land: Facing Europe's Ghosts after Communism* (New York: Vintage Books, 1996).

61. Caswell, *Archiving the Unspeakable*, 8.

62. Caswell, *Archiving the Unspeakable*, 9.

63. Weld, *Paper Cadavers*, 2.

64. Weld, *Paper Cadavers*, 233.

65. Verdery, *Secrets and Truths*, 23.

66. Verdery, *Secrets and Truths*, 64.

67. See Ian Hacking, "Making Up People," *Historical Ontology* (Cambridge, MA: Harvard University Press, 2002), 107.

68. Finn, *Capturing the Criminal Image*, ix.

69. Alan Sekula, "Reading an Archive," in *Blasted Allegories: An Anthology of Writings by Contemporary Artists,* ed. Brian Willis, 114–129 (Cambridge, MA: MIT Press, 1987), 117.

70. For a treatment of the relationship between photographs and captions, see Robert Hariman and John Louis Lucaites, eds., *No Caption Needed: Iconic Photographs, Public Culture, and Liberal Democracy* (Chicago: University of Chicago Press, 2007).

71. Antoinette Burton, "Introduction: Archive Fever, Archive Stories," in *Archive Stories: Facts, Fictions and the Writing of History,* ed. Antoinette Burton, 1–24 (Durham, NC: Duke University Press, 2005), 6.

72. For a sample of this nonsense, see Hermann Giliomee, *The Afrikaners: Biography of a People* (Cape Town: Tafelberg, 2003).

73. See Jasper Ridley, *Mussolini* (London: Constable, 1997), 210–211.

1. From Racial Types to Terrorist Types

1. I draw for this chapter on Andrew Bank's insightful analysis of Gustav Fritsch's southern African travels, and on Patricia Hayes's pathbreaking work on the history of photography in southern Africa. Andrew Bank, "Anthropology and Portrait Photography: Gustav Fritsch's 'Natives of South Africa,' 1863–1872," *Kronos,* no. 27 (November 2001): 43–76; Patricia Hayes, "Power, Secrecy, Proximity: A Short History of South African Photography," *Kronos,* no. 33 (November 2007): 139–162, 139.

2. Bank, "Anthropology and Portrait Photography," 49–50. For a history of Robben Island, see Harriet Deacon, ed., *The Island: A History of Robben Island, 1488–1990* (Cape Town: Mayibuye Books, 1996).

3. For more on the cattle killings, see Jeff Peires, *The Dead Will Arise: Nongqawuse and the Great Xhosa Cattle-Killing Movement of 1856–7* (Bloomington: Indiana University Press, 1989).

4. Bank, "Anthropology and Portrait Photography," 50.

5. Prison photography in South Africa began in the first decade of the twentieth century. By 1916, prisons were photographing inmates as a matter

of course. But, this being South Africa, the prisons photographed only those whites sentenced to six months or more and only those blacks given a year or more in jail. By 1916, the prisons' photographic archive numbered 3,585 mug shots of black inmates and 828 of white inmates. *Report of the Commissioner of the South African Police for 1916* (Cape Town: Government Printers), 78. In 1918, Pretoria Central Prison, which seems to have contributed the bulk of the prison mug shots taken in South Africa at the time, transferred forty albums and 6,349 negatives to the Central Identification Bureau of the South African Police. *Report of the Commissioner of the South African Police for 1918* (Cape Town: Government Printers, 1919), 91. For more on the general history of prisons in South Africa and on the history of Pretoria Central Prison, founded in 1865, see S. Singh, "The Historical Development of Prisons in South Africa: A Penological Perspective, *New Contree,* no. 50 (November 2005), 15–38.

6.   For a detailed examination of Fritsch's career as a scientist, see the pathbreaking Andrew Zimmerman, *Anthropology and Antihumanism in Imperial Germany* (Chicago: University of Chicago Press, 2001). For additional insight into the intellectual trajectory of Fritsch, a recent graduate in medicine from the universities of Berlin, Breslau, and Heidelberg, see Bank, "Anthropology and Portrait Photography," 46.

7.   Bank, "Anthropology and Portrait Photography," 47. See also Patricia Hayes and Andrew Bank, "Introduction to the Special Issue on Visual History," *Kronos,* no. 27 (November 2001):1–14, 3.

8.   For a general account of the origins of photography, see the indispensable volume Alan Trachtenberg, ed., *Classic Essays on Photography* (New Haven: Leete's Island Books, 1980), 4.

9.   For a definitive account of the early history of photography in the Cape, see Marjorie Bull and Joseph Denfield, *Secure the Shadow: The Story of Cape Photography from Its Beginnings to the End of 1870* (Cape Town: Terence McNally, 1970), 32–36.

10. For an excellent study of missionaries and their use of photography in Africa, see the wonderful T. Jack Thompson, *Light on Darkness? Missionary Photography of Africa in the Nineteenth and Early Twentieth Centuries* (Grand Rapids, MI: William B. Eerdmans, 2012).

11. Missionaries such as John Kirk and Charles Livingstone were among the pioneers of photography in Africa. For a detailed history of this phenomenon, see especially Thompson, *Light on Darkness,* chs. 1–3.

12. A definitive account of the history of the Bleek-Lloyd collection is Andrew Bank, *Bushmen in a Victorian World: The Remarkable Story of the Bleek-Lloyd Collection of Bushmen Folklore* (Cape Town: Double Storey, 2006). For a more recent, excellent examination of the Bleek-Lloyd collection, see Tina Campt, *Listening to Images* (Durham, NC: Duke University Press, 2017), ch. 3.

13. T. Jack Thompson offers a thoughtful examination of Thiesson's image in Thompson, *Light on Darkness,* 23–26.

14. Bank, "Anthropology and Portrait Photography," 44. The Agassiz commission fell to daguerreotypist Joseph T. Zealy, who took the daguerreotypes of seven men and women from a plantation in Columbia—with the sitters naked and the images taken from the front and the side. For more on Agassiz, see Brian Wallis, "Black Bodies, White Science: Louis Agassiz's Slave Daguerreotypes," *American Art* 9, no. 2 (Summer 1995): 38–61.

15. Bank, "Anthropology and Portrait Photography," 59–60.

16. Andrew Bank writes of Fritsch: "He streamlined the collection in such a way that the evidence of racial mixing or fluidity of identity that can be read from his travel narrative and original photographs was excised." Bank, "Anthropology and Portrait Photography," 63.

17. Bank, "Anthropology and Portrait Photography," 63.

18. Bank, "Anthropology and Portrait Photography," 65.

19. Bank, "Anthropology and Portrait Photography," 65. On the subject of early criminology's fascination with human heads, see the perceptive

analysis in the classic essay, Allen Sekula, "The Body and the Archive," *October* 39 (Winter 1986): 3–64.

20. For pathbreaking scholarship on the history of photography in Africa, see note 12 in the Introduction.

21. Hayes, "Power, Secrecy, Proximity," 141.

22. Jens Jäger, "Photography: A Means of Surveillance? Judicial Photography, 1850 to 1900," *Crime, History and Societies* 5, no. 1 (2001): 27–51, 27. This section draws extensively on Jäger's essay for the history and the details mentioned here.

23. Jäger, "Photography: A Means of Surveillance?" 28.

24. A. Pinto Leite, "Report of Inspector in Charge of the Criminal Identification Bureau," in *Report of the Commissioner of the South African Police for 1916*, 82. (Hereafter, Leite, "Report of the Inspector, 1916.")

25. Allan Sekula offers a sophisticated reading of this phenomenon in Sekula, "The Body and the Archive," esp. 18, 19, and 37 on Francis Galton's and Cesare Lambroso's attempts to offer a biological reading of the so-called criminal type.

26. Jäger, "Photography: A Means of Surveillance?" 28.

27. Sekula, "The Body and the Archive," 6, makes this point eloquently.

28. Jäger, "Photography: A Means of Surveillance?" 29.

29. Bank, "Anthropology and Portrait Photography," 44.

30. Jäger, "Photography: A Means of Surveillance?" 30.

31. Jens Jäger writes: "This does not imply that portraits were never scrutinized with the application of physiognomic theories—this surely happened—but there was nothing decisively different in the staging of the sitters." Jäger, "Photography: A Means of Surveillance?" 30.

32. Jäger, "Photography: A Means of Surveillance?" 39.

33. Jäger, "Photography: A Means of Surveillance?" 39–40.

34. Sekula's "The Body and the Archive" offers one of the best examinations of Bertillon's career.

35. Jäger, "Photography: A Means of Surveillance?" 42.

36. I derive these details from Jäger, "Photography: A Means of Surveillance?"

37. The system had its first US showing at the World's Columbian Exposition in Chicago in 1893. The Chicago Police Department adopted Bertillonage in 1894 and the National Bureau of Criminal Identification followed suit in 1898. Sandra Phillips, "Identifying the Criminal," in *Police Pictures: The Photograph as Evidence,* ed. Sandra S. Phillips, Mark Haworth-Booth, and Carol Squiers, 11–32 (San Francisco: Chronicle Books, 1997).

38. Phillips, "Identifying the Criminal," 18–27.

39. Thomas Byrnes, *Professional Criminals of America* (New York: Cassell, 1886).

40. Keith Breckenridge, *Biometric State: The Global Politics of Identification and Surveillance in South Africa, 1850 to the Present* (New York: Cambridge University Press, 2014), 63.

41. Breckenridge, *Biometric State,* 63.

42. Francis Galton, quoted in Breckenridge, *Biometric State,* 63–64.

43. Breckenridge, *Biometric State,* 65.

44. Breckenridge, *Biometric State,* 66

45. Breckenridge, *Biometric State,* 67.

46. For more on the South African War, see Bill Nasson, *The War for South Africa: The Anglo-Boer War, 1899–1902* (Cape Town: NB Publishers, 2011).

47. Henry's deployment to South Africa was in fact short-term and he took extended leave of ten months from the Indian Colonial Service to fulfill it. Breckenridge, *Biometric State,* 68.

48. "These two little pockets of law geared to the requirements of the gold mines—the prohibition of alcohol for Africans and the criminalization of the simple possession of unwrought gold—each provided the focus for a special-purpose branch of Henry's new Criminal Investigation Department." Breckenridge, *Biometric State,* 71.

49. As Justin Willis points out, the state's interest in the prosecution of liquor laws was connected inextricably to the state's interest in the mobilization of African labor. Justin Willis, "Thieves, Drunkards and Vagrants: Defining Crime in Colonial Mombasa," in *Policing the Empire: Government, Authority and Control, 1830–1940*, ed. David Anderson and David Killingray. 219–235 (Manchester: Manchester University Press, 1991).

50. Breckenridge, *Biometric State*, 71.

51. Breckenridge, *Biometric State*, 72.

52. Breckenridge, *Biometric State*, 72. This phenomenon did not change, even after the founding of the national South African Police in 1913. By 1916, for example, only 284 members of the 7,572-strong force belonged to the detective branch of the police and 95 of these were probationers. To show the importance of the mining industry, however, the Transvaal CID had 341 detectives in its ranks. *Report of the Commissioner of the South African Police for 1916*, 4 and 18.

53. Breckenridge, *Biometric State*, 72.

54. Breckenridge, *Biometric State*, 74.

55. Breckenridge, *Biometric State*, 74.

56. Breckenridge, *Biometric State*, 74.

57. Breckenridge, *Biometric State*, 75–88. The Belgian Congo, Kenya, and Sierra Leone were among the colonies and states that sought South African advice.

58. "Annual Report of the Criminal Investigation Department of the South African Police for the year 1916," in *Report of the Commissioner of the South African Police for the year 1916*, 82.

59. Breckenridge, *Biometric State*, 75.

60. Breckenridge, *Biometric State*, 79.

61. For more on the history of Chinese labor on the Witwatersrand mines, see Rachel Bright, *Chinese Labor in South Africa, 1902–1910: Race, Violence and Global Spectacle* (Hampshire, UK: Palgrave Macmillan, 2013).

62. Breckenridge, *Biometric State,* 81.

63. Breckenridge, *Biometric State,* 90.

64. Breckenridge, *Biometric State,* 91.

65. Breckenridge, *Biometric State,* 103.

66. A careful examination of Gandhi's complicated relationship with the British empire is found in the fine book Ashwin Desai and Goolam Vahed, *The South African Gandhi: Stretch-Bearer of Empire* (New Delhi: Navayana, 2016).

67. See the 1919 annual report of the Central Identification Bureau by C. G. MacPherson, inspector in charge of the bureau, in *Report of the Commissioner of the South African Police for 1919* (Cape Town: Government Printers, 1920), 80.

68. For a rich history of policing in South Africa, see John D. Brewer, *Black and Blue: Policing in South Africa* (Oxford: Clarendon Press, 1994), 6.

69. This point is made well in David Anderson and David Killingray, "Consent, Coercion and Colonial Control: Policing the Empire, 1830–1940," in *Policing the Empire: Government, Authority and Control, 1830–1940,* ed. Anderson and Killingray, 1–17 (Manchester: Manchester University Press, 1991), esp. 2, 5.

70. John D. Brewer, a historian of policing in general and of the South African Police in particular, makes this point eloquently in Brewer, *Black and Blue,* 6.

71. For scholarship on the history of policing in South Africa, see note 7 in the Introduction.

72. *Report of the Commissioner of the South African Police for 1916,* 18.

73. Leite, "Report of the Inspector, 1916," 69.

74. Leite, "Report of the Inspector, 1916," 79.

75. In fact, the SAP was one of two national police forces formed on April 1, 1913. The other, the South African Mounted Rifles (SAMR), was an explicitly paramilitary force charged with the policing of rural areas, while

the SAP maintained order in the urban areas. It was only between 1920 and 1926 that the SAMR merged gradually into the SAP, and only in 1936 that the SAP became truly national, after the last of the municipal police forces (Durban) joined the national force. For the institutional history of the South African Police, see Marius De Witt Dippenaar, *The History of the SAP, 1913–1983* (Pretoria: Promedia, 1988); and Brewer, *Black and Blue*, 111–112.

76. For excellent work on the racism of the white working class in South Africa, see Jeremy Krikler, *White Rising: The 1922 Insurrection and Racial Killing in South Africa* (Manchester: Manchester University Press, 2005). The Industrial and Commercial Workers' Union (ICU), founded in Cape Town in 1919, was an early target of covert police action. Informer reports and accounts by undercover police officers are in the National Archives of South Africa, Pretoria, Department of Justice Collection, at, for example, TAB GNLB 359, 142 / 24. For a history of the ICU, see Helen Bradford, *A Taste of Freedom: The ICU in Rural South Africa, 1924–1930* (New Haven, CT: Yale University Press, 1987); see also P. L. Wickins, *The Industrial and Commercial Workers' Union of Africa* (Cape Town: Oxford University Press, 1978).

77. Brewer, *Black and Blue*, 130.

78. Jan Smuts, quoted in Brewer, *Black and Blue*, 93.

79. *Report of the Commissioner of the South African Police for 1916*, 92.

80. *Report of the Commissioner of the South African Police for 1916*, 92.

81. *Report of the Commissioner of the South African Police for 1927* (Pretoria: Government Printers, 1928), 22.

82. Brewer, *Black and Blue*, 131.

83. Brewer, *Black and Blue*, 159.

84. For an excellent examination of the depiction of Afrikaners as God's chosen people, see Andre Du Toit's timeless essay "No Chosen People: The Myth of the Calvinist Origins of Afrikaner Nationalism and Racial

Ideology," *American Historical Review* 88, no. 4 (October 1983): 920–952. Conveniently, this revisionism of South Africa's policing history also allowed Afrikaner nationalists not only to downplay the long history of pro-Nazi sympathies within their ranks but to ignore the complicated story of Afrikaner collaboration with the British. Albert Grundlingh, *The Dynamics of Treason: Boer Collaboration in the South African War of 1899–1902*, trans. Bridget Theron (Pretoria: Protea Book House, 2006).

85. Brewer, *Black and Blue*, 174–175. For an examination of Du Plooy's career in the South African Police, see Keith Shear, "Tested Loyalties: Police and Politics in South Africa, 1939–1963," *Journal of African History* 53, no. 2 (2012): 187–189.

86. Amery alerted the Governor-General to the availability of "periodical courses at New Scotland Yard for dominions police." These three-week courses covered organization, property, finance, and the basic training of recruits. Scotland Yard also offered more specialized training for members of Criminal Investigation Departments from the colonies and dominions. This included instruction on how to prepare a case, how to investigate a crime, how to take fingerprints, how to classify criminals and their methods, how to monitor aliens, how to conduct port duties, and how to carry out surveillance of suspects. The courses, offered in May, June, and July, cost ten guineas per trainee. British Colonial Secretary Leo Amery to the Governor-General of the Union of South Africa, the Earl of Athlone, February 3, 1925, SAP 12/19/48/1, Box 418, National Archives of South Africa.

87. As David Anderson and David Killingray point out, however, this policing common sense did not necessarily assure the diffusion of one policing model throughout the British empire. Far from it. Anderson and Killingray, "Consent, Coercion and Colonial Control."

88. The South African Police renamed the Special Branch the Security Police in 1960. See the self-published memoir Petrus Cornelius Swanepoel,

Really Inside Boss: A Tale of South Africa's Late Intelligence Service (and Something about the CIA) (Derdepoort Park, 2007).

89. Robert J. Palmer to Scotland Yard chief Harold R. Scott, August 15, 1947, in National Archives of South Africa, SAP 12/19/48/1, Box 418.

90. Robert J. Palmer to Scotland Yard chief Harold R. Scott March 1, 1948, National Archives of South Africa, SAP 12/28/48, Box 418.

91. It is not clear from the archival material if this May 1948 visit was the same one that Du Plooy undertook in 1947 or if it was a different visit. Palmer to Scott, August 15, 1947, and March 1, 1948.

92. James Sanders, *Apartheid's Friends: The Rise and Fall of South Africa's Secret Service* (London: John Murray, 2006), 9–11.

93. Sanders, *Apartheid's Friends,* 11.

94. Sanders, *Apartheid's Friends,* 11.

95. In March 1950, Prime Minister D. F. Malan informed George McGhee, the U.S. Assistant Secretary of State for Near-Eastern and African Affairs, that South Africa wanted to join NATO. B. C. Connelly, confidential Memorandum of Conversation, March 6, 1950, *Foreign Relations of the United States,* S1.1 1950, vol. 5, 1815–1817, "North Atlantic Pact," 1816.

96. McGhee told Malan that the United States' demurral "did not exclude the possibility of other similar arrangements for other areas." *Foreign Relations of the United States,* 1950, vol. 5, 1816. This rebuff might have driven South Africa, working with Argentina and Chile, to try and set up the South Atlantic Treaty Organization. For more on plans for this organization, see Andrew Hurrell, "The Politics of South Atlantic Security: A Survey of Proposals for a South Atlantic Treaty Organization," *International Affairs* 59, no. 2 (Spring 1983): 179–193.

97. Brewer, *Black and Blue,* 169.

98. Figures derived from the annual *Report of the Commissioner of the South African Police* (Pretoria: Government Printers) for the years 1952 to 1960.

99. Brewer, *Black and Blue,* 197.

100. Figures derived from the annual *Report of the Commissioner of the South African Police* for the years 1952 to 1960.

101. Brewer, *Black and Blue,* 203.

102. Figures derived from the annual *Report of the Commissioner of the South African Police* for the years 1951 to 1960.

103. I base this conclusion on the annual *Report of the Commissioner of the South African Police* for the years 1916 to 1926 and the years 1951 to 1960.

104. For a history of the pass laws, see Keith Shear, "At War with the Pass Laws? Reform and the Policing of White Supremacy in 1940s South Africa," *Historical Journal* 56, no. 1 (2013): 205–229; Michael Savage, "The Imposition of Pass Laws on the African Population in South Africa, 1916–1984," *African Affairs* 85, no. 339 (April 1986): 181–205. The pass laws were designed, first and foremost, to control the labor of Africans by regulating their mobility. According to the pass laws, Africans could not travel about the country without the written permission of a white overseer. See also Doug Hindson, *Pass Controls and the Urban African Proletariat in South Africa* (Johannesburg: Ravan Press, 1987).

105. For an excellent examination of apartheid plans to curb the so-called influx of blacks into the urban areas of South Africa, see Deborah Posel, *The Making of Apartheid, 1948–1961: Conflict and Compromise* (Oxford: Clarendon Press, 1991).

106. Brewer, *Black and Blue,* 207.

107. Brewer, *Black and Blue,* 215.

108. Brewer, *Black and Blue,* 216.

109. Brewer, *Black and Blue,* 216–217.

110. For a typical example of this kind of self-serving argument, see Maritz Spaarwater, *A Spook's Progress: From Making War to Making Peace* (Cape Town: Zebra Press, 2012).

111. For more on the event see Tom Lodge, *Sharpeville: An Apartheid Massacre and Its Consequences* (New York: Oxford University Press, 2011).

112. This is not to suggest that the turn to armed struggle was inevitable. As Saul Dubow argues, it is debatable whether the ANC and other anti-apartheid organizations needed to turn to violence. There are questions to be asked over whether these organizations had exhausted all their political options before taking up arms against the apartheid regime. Saul Dubow, "Were There Political Alternatives in the Wake of the Sharpeville-Langa Violence in South Africa, 1960?" *Journal of African History* 56, no. 1 (March 2015): 119–142. Nelson Mandela argued, of course, that they had no alternative. Nelson Mandela, *Long Walk to Freedom: The Autobiography of Nelson Mandela* (New York: Little, Brown, 1994), 271–272, 285.

113. For an examination of how the South African government sought to respond to decolonization in Africa, see Jamie Miller, *An African Volk: The Apartheid Regime and Its Search for Survival* (Oxford: Oxford University Press, 2016).

114. Brewer, *Black and Blue,* 246–247.

115. Brewer, *Black and Blue,* 250.

116. Brewer, *Black and Blue,* 250. For more on the militarization of white South African society, see Jacklyn Cock and Laurie Nathan, eds., *War and Society: The Militarization of South Africa* (Johannesburg: David Philip, 1989).

117. Brewer, *Black and Blue,* 255.

118. Dave Fell had this document declassified for his research on the history of military conflict in South Africa, and I am grateful to him for sharing this document with me.

119. General Constand Viljoen, interview by Hilton Hamann, in Hamann, *Days of the Generals: The Untold Story of South Africa's Apartheid-Era Military Generals* (Cape Town: Zebra Press, 2001), 9.

120. Constand Viljoen, interview, Hamann, *Days of the Generals,* 9.

121. For a poignant portrayal of the African Resistance Movement and its tragic failing, see the memoir Hugh Lewin, *Stones against the Mirror:*

Friendship in the Time of the South African Struggle (Cape Town: Umuzi, 2011). See also Jonty Driver, *The Man with the Suitcase: The Life, Execution and Rehabilitation of John Harris, Liberal Terrorist* (Cape Town: Crane River, 2015); and Eddie Daniels, *There and Back: Robben Island, 1964–1979,* (Cape Town: Mayibuye Books, 1998).

122. Brewer, *Black and Blue,* 254.

123. Brewer, *Black and Blue,* 248–258.

124. Leite, "Report of the Inspector, 1916," 78. As a rule, prison authorities photographed every white prisoner sentenced to six months or more in jail and every black inmate serving one year or more. In 1918, Pretoria Central Prison transferred forty photo albums and 6,349 negatives to the Central Identification Bureau as part of a drive to centralize the colonial state's use of mug shots for surveillance purposes. C. G. MacPherson, "Report of the Inspector in Charge of the Central Identification Bureau," in the *Report of the Commissioner of the South African Police for 1918,* 91.

125. Leite, "Report of the Inspector, 1916," 79.

126. Leite, "Report of the Inspector, 1916," 79.

127. C. G. MacPherson, "Report of the Inspector in Charge of the Central Identification Bureau, for the year 1919," 86.

128. C. G. MacPherson, "Report of the Inspector in Charge of the Central Identification Bureau, 1919," 86. The SAP renamed the Central Identification Bureau the South African Criminal Bureau in 1922. Brewer, *Black and Blue,* 89.

129. Leite, "Report of the Inspector, 1916," 82.

130. A. Pinto Leite, "Report of the Inspector in Charge of the Central Identification Bureau of the South African Police, in *Report of the Commissioner of the South African Police for 1917,* 94–95.

131. C. G. MacPherson, Report of the Inspector in Charge of the Central Identification Bureau, for the year 1918, 93. MacPherson repeated his plea in

his report for the year 1919. *Report of the Commissioner of the South African Police for 1919,* 87.

132. G. D. Gray, Deputy Police Commissioner of the South African Police, to all police stations, July 24, 1925, in National Archives of South Africa, SAP 148, 19/45/26, vol. 1, and 22/3/26, Box 418. Brewer claims the police began publishing the gazette in 1918. Brewer, *Black and Blue,* 89. But he is clearly wrong as in 1919 C. G. MacPherson was still pleading with government for just such a publication. As MacPherson put it in his report for the year 1919, "The issue of a monthly (or periodical) confidential photographic circular, containing photographs of classified expert forgers, burglars, swindlers, etc, to each station in the Union would serve a useful purpose." C.G. MacPherson, "Report of the Inspector in Charge of the Central Identification Bureau, 1919," 87.

133. Theodore Truter's remarks in the *Report of the Commissioner of the South African Police for 1926* (Cape Town: Government Printers, 1927), 29.

134. Karin A. Shapiro, "No Exit? Emigration Policy and the Consolidation of Apartheid," *Journal of Southern African Studies* 42, no. 4 (2016): 763–781, 764.

135. Shapiro, "No Exit?" 765.

136. Correspondence on the case is archived in the Wits Historical Papers, Alan Paton Papers, File AD1169–A16-001.

137. Alan Paton Papers File AD1169–A16-001.

138. Leite, "Report of the Inspector, 1916," 71; Brewer, *Black and Blue,* 87–88.

139. Brewer, *Black and Blue,* 88.

140. Supreme Court of South Africa, Criminal Cases, Witwatersrand Local Division, F1 (1921), Case number 100 / 121, 55–126, National Archives of South Africa.

141. For legal commentary on the case, see Elliot Goldstein, "Videotape and Photographic Evidence," *South African Law Journal* 102, no. 3 (1985): 485–496; and Elliot Goldstein, "Videotape and Photographic Evidence Update," *South African Law Journal* 106, no. 4 (1989): 718–723.

2. Apartheid's Mismeasure

1. Eugene Fourie, interview by author, Free State, South Africa, August 27, 2015.

2. The 1965 exiles list, dated October 6, 1965, is in the Wits Historical Papers.

3. Security Report No. 313, December 13, 1973, in Gladstone Silulami Mose file, Hennie Heymans Collection, Wits Historical Papers.

4. It is illuminating to read Head's case alongside those that William J. Maxwell considers in *F. B. Eyes: How J. Edgar Hoover's Ghostreaders Framed African American Literature* (Princeton: Princeton University Press, 2015).

5. See, for example, Frederick Cooper's analysis of apartheid South Africa in his brilliant Frederick Cooper, *Africa since 1940: The Past of the Present* (New York: Cambridge University Press, 2002), 144–154. Cooper describes South Africa as a "sophisticated police state" (149) that sought to protect apartheid through cooption and coercion. But the apartheid police were anything but sophisticated and South Africa itself was not a police state, a point I make in Chapter 1.

6. This is, of course, what apartheid apologists such as Hermann Giliomee and R. W. Johnson want us to believe. See the apartheid apologia in Hermann Giliomee, *The Afrikaners: Biography of a People* (Cape Town: Tafelberg, 2003); and the revisionist take on apartheid in R. W. Johnson, *How Long Will South Africa Survive? The Looming Crisis* (Johannesburg: Jonathan Ball, 2015). For illuminating examinations of the intellectual history of the notion of reason of state, see Pierre Bourdieu, "From the King's House to the Reason of State: A Model of the Genesis of the Bureaucratic Field," *Constellations* 11, no. 1 (2004): 16–36; David Armitage, "Edmund Burke and Reason of State," *Journal of the History of Ideas* 61, no. 4 (2000): 617–634.

7. For work that takes (perhaps too) seriously the idea of an existential threat to whites in South Africa, see Jamie Miller, *An African Volk: The Apartheid Regime and Its Search for Survival* (New York: Oxford University Press, 2016). This is a function, it seems to me, of Miller's overreliance on Giliomee's revisionist work. For an elaboration of the racist assumptions that underpin Afrikaner nationalist historiography, see F. A. van Jaarsveld, *The Afrikaner's Interpretation of South African History* (Cape Town: Simondium, 1964). Van Jaarsveld is considered the doyen of Afrikaner nationalist historiography.

8. I borrow the concept of slow violence from Rob Nixon. See the insightful Rob Nixon, *Slow Violence and the Environmentalism of the Poor* (Cambridge, MA: Harvard University Press, 2011). I also have in mind Mahmood Mamdani's critique of the tendency toward, not to mention the danger of, over-privileging the spectacular violence of apartheid at the expense of its more pervasive but slow variant. Mahmood Mamdani, "Amnesty or Impunity? A Preliminary Critique of the Report of the Truth and Reconciliation Commission of South Africa," *Diacritics* 32, no. 3 / 4 (Autumn-Winter, 2002): 33–59.

9. Dirk Coetzee offers a personal account of this type of barbarism in his unpublished memoir Dirk Coetzee, "Hit Squads: Testimony of a South African Security Policeman: The Full Story," 1990, rev. 1994, 81–84, Wits Historical Papers, A2790f, Dirk Coetzee, testimony. For another example of such gratuitous violence, see Peter Harris, *In a Different Time: The Inside Story of the Delmas Four* (Johannesburg: Umuzi, 2008).

10. The last apartheid president of South Africa made precisely this argument. F. W. De Klerk, *The Last Trek—A New Beginning: The Autobiography* (London: MacMillan, 1998).

11. I borrow the concept of the "cultural biography of things" from Igor Kopytoff, "The Cultural Biography of Things: Commoditization as Pro-

cess," in *The Social Life of Things: Commodities in Cultural Perspective,* ed. Arjun Appadurai, 64–94 (Cambridge: Cambridge University Press, 1986). It seems to me most productive to think of the album as having a cultural biography. As Kopytoff writes, "Biographies of things can make salient what might otherwise remain obscure" (67).

12. John Tagg, *The Burden of Representation: Essays on Photographies and Histories* (Minneapolis: University of Minnesota Press, 1993), 35.

13. Alan Sekula, "Reading an Archive," in *Blasted Allegories: An Anthology of Writings by Contemporary Artists,* ed. Brian Wallis, 114–129 (Cambridge, MA: MIT Press, 1987), 117.

14. Sekula, "Reading an Archive," 121.

15. This is not to suggest that the apartheid state was not pragmatic. As Saul Dubow points out, pragmatism was built into the marrow of apartheid. See, for example, the excellent Saul Dubow, *Apartheid: 1948–1994* (Oxford: Oxford University Press, 2014). Frederick Cooper says of apartheid South Africa, "This was not a state run by racist fanatics." Cooper, *Africa since 1940,* 145. Afrikaner nationalists might not have been fanatics but, *pace* Cooper, they were certainly racist.

16. Johan van der Merwe, email to Hennie Heymans, July 27, 2017. Email cited with permission of Hennie Heymans. , Van der Merwe is a former police commissioner.

17. Jac Büchner letter to author, November 17, 2016.

18. Hennie Heymans, interview with author, Pretoria, South Africa, July 22, 2016.

19. Hennie Heymans, interview, July 22, 2016.

20. It was only in 1972 that the South African Police accepted women as full members of the force. Marius De Witt Dippenaar, *History of the South African Police, 1913–1983* (Pretoria: Promedia, 1988).

21. It is worth recalling that when Nelson Mandela was sentenced to life in prison in June 1964, he was already in jail serving a five-year sentence for

incitement and for having left South Africa in 1961 without a passport. Nelson Mandela, *Long Walk to Freedom: The Autobiography of Nelson Mandela* (New York: Little, Brown, 1994).

22. On the killing of Mvemve, see Hugh Macmillan, "The African National Congress of South Africa in Zambia: The Culture of Exile and the Changing Relationship with Home, 1964–1990," *Journal of Southern African Studies* 35, no. 2 (June 2009): 303–329, 316; on the murder of Tiro, see Terry Bell and Dumisa Ntsebeza, *Unfinished Business: South Africa, Apartheid and Truth* (London: Verso, 2003), 157.

23. For the history of this university, see Anne Heffernan, "The University of the North and Building the Bantustans, 1959–1977," *South African Historical Journal* 69, no. 2 (2017): 195–214, 203–205.

24. *Truth and Reconciliation Commission of South Africa Report,* vol. 2 (Cape Town: Juta, 1998), esp. ch. 3, "Appendix: State Security Forces: Directory of Organizations and Structures," 313–324.

25. For Viktor's career as a police torturer, see Hugh Lewin, *Stones against the Mirror: Friendship in the Time of the South African Struggle* (Cape Town: Umuzi, 2011), 164–171.

26. For an account of British use of pseudo-gangs against the Mau Mau, see David Anderson, *Histories of the Hanged: The Dirty War in Kenya and the End of Empire* (New York: W. W. Norton, 2005). For another account of British tactics in Kenya, see Caroline Elkins, *Imperial Reckoning: The Untold Story of Britain's Gulag in Kenya* (New York: Henry Holt, 2005).

27. For an insider account of C1, see Coetzee, "Hit Squads."

28. *Truth and Reconciliation Commission of South Africa Report,* vol. 2, ch. 3, "Appendix: State Security Forces" 313–324

29. Eugene Fourie, interviews by author, Free State, South Africa, August 27, 2015, and July 21, 2016.

30. Eugene Fourie, interview, July 21, 2016.

31. See Index and Colonel Jac Büchner's memorandum to all section com-
    manders of the Security Police, July 30, 1985, Hennie Heymans Collec-
    tion, Wits Historical Papers.

32. Jac Büchner letter to author, November 17, 2016.

33. The year 1985 was one of the most repressive and violent in South Af-
    rican history. On July 20, 1985, President P. W. Botha declared a state of
    emergency. This led to the assassination of activists and the detention of
    thousands of South Africans. *Final Report of the Truth and Reconciliation
    Commission, Vol.* 2 (Cape Town: CTP Book Printers, 1998), 108–110. For
    an account of detentions during apartheid, see Terry Shakinovsky, Sharon
    Cort and Lauren Segal, *The Knock on the Door: The Story of the Detainees'
    Parents Support Committee* (Johannesburg: Picador Africa, 2018). Gerhardus
    Johannes Lotz, the security policeman from whom the index came,
    committed suicide in 2016. He had been implicated in a number of po-
    litical assassinations linked to police death squads in the 1980s. These
    assassinations included the notorious case of "the PEBCO Three."
    Gerhardus Johannes Lotz, testimony, Truth and Reconciliation Com-
    mission Amnesty Hearing, November 6, 1997, http://www.justice.gov.za
    /trc/amntrans%5Cpe/pebco3.htm.

34. Jacobus Büchner, testimony before Truth and Reconciliation Commis-
    sion, Section 29 hearing, Durban, South Africa, July 16, 1997. Transcript
    available from South African History Archive (SAHA), call number
    AL2878_B01.5.75.02.23. See especially pages 73–74. Büchner's and others'
    testimonies in Section 29 hearings were supposed to be sealed indef-
    initely. The courts lifted the seal in 2014, however, after SAHA, a non-
    governmental organization dedicated to increasing access to informa-
    tion, sued successfully for the lifting. "TRC's Secret Hearing Transcripts
    Handed over to SAHA," press release, March 24, 2015, http://www.saha
    .org.za/news/2010/March/trcs_secret_hearing_transcripts_handed
    _over_to_saha.htm. For general information on SAHA's Right to Truth

Project, see its website, http://www.saha.org.za/about_saha/right_to
_truth_project.htm.

35. Eugene Fourie, interview, August 27, 2015.

36. Eugene Fourie, interview, July 21, 2016.

37. Eugene Fourie, interview, August 27, 2015.

38. I write about Glory Sedibe in Jacob Dlamini, *Askari: A Story of Collaboration and Betrayal in the Anti-Apartheid Struggle* (New York: Oxford University Press, 2015).

39. It is not clear from the report if Sedibe was accusing Gilder or Rashid of
the affair. See *Uitkennings Lefoshie Glory Sedibe* [Identifications by Glory
Lefoshie Sedibe], internal police report, February 19, 1987, 15. Copy available from the Missing Persons task team of the National Prosecuting
Authority of South Africa.

40. *Uitkennings Lefoshie Glory Sedibe,* 109.

41. *Uitkennings Lefoshie Glory Sedibe,* 132.

42. *Uitkennings Lefoshie Glory Sedibe,* 115. For an intimate account of Slovo's
affair, see his daughter's poignant memoir, Gillian Slovo, *Every Secret
Thing: My Family, My Country* (London: Little, Brown, 1997).

43. Eugene Fourie, testimony before Truth and Reconciliation Commission's
Amnesty Committee, February 16, 2000, 7.

44. Eugene Fourie, interview, August 27, 2015.

45. Eugene Fourie, interview, August 27, 2015. Quatro was a notorious prison
camp run by the ANC in Angola. For an account of the horrors of the
camp, see Paul Trewhela, *Inside Quatro: Uncovering the Exile History of the
ANC and SWAPO* (Johannesburg: Jacana, 2009).

46. Eugene Fourie, interview, July 21, 2016.

47. Eugene Fourie, interview, August 27, 2015.

48. Eugene Fourie, interview, August 27, 2015.

49. Eugene Fourie, interview, August 27, 2015.

50. Eugene Fourie, interview, August 27, 2015.

51. Eugene Fourie, interview, August 27, 2015.

52. Eugene Fourie, interview, July 21, 2016.

53. In May 1984, the ANC published a thirty-page pamphlet, "Some Aspects of Enemy Counter-Guerilla Tactics Compiled from Our Own Experience," Wits Historical Papers, AG2510, F8. Zulu, as a senior ANC operative, would have been familiar with this document.

54. For a novel argument about photography and the haptic, see Tina M. Campt, *Listening to Images* (Durham, NC: Duke University Press, 2017).

55. Polaroid was a US company famous for its photography products and consumer electronics, and subjected to intense activist pressure for supplying photographic and other surveillance technology to apartheid South Africa. In 1971, black employees at its factory in Massachusetts founded the Polaroid Revolutionary Workers' Movement as part of a campaign to force the company to stop selling its photographic technology, which the South African government was using to produce passes for black South Africans. See the documentary film Connie Field, *Have You Heard from Johannesburg?* Clarity Films, Berkeley, CA, 2010. Also see Caroline de Crespigny, "The Polaroid Case: Blueprint for Action," *Sechaba* 5, no. 3 (March 1971), 4–7.

56. For more on the automation of apartheid South Africa, see Gabrielle Hecht and Paul Edwards, "History and the Technopolitics of Identity: The Case of Apartheid South Africa," *Journal of Southern African Studies* 36, no. 3 (September 2010): 619–639; Keith Breckenridge, "The Book of Life: The South African Population Register and the Invention of Racial Descent, 1950–1980," *Kronos* 40, no. 1 (November 2014): 225–240; and Keith Breckenridge, "Verwoerd's Bureau of Proof: Total Information in the Making of Apartheid," *History Workshop Journal* 59, no. 1 (Spring 2005): 83–108. See also Lorena Rizzo, "Visual Impersonation: Population Registration, Reference Books and Identification in the Eastern Cape,

1950–1960s," *History in Africa* 41 (June 2014): 221–248; and American Friends Service Committee, "Automating Apartheid: U.S. Computer Exports to South Africa and the Arms Embargo," pamphlet, 1982.

57. Eugene Fourie, interview, August 27, 2015.

58. Eugene Fourie, interview, August 27, 2015.

59. Eugene Fourie, interview, July 21, 2016.

3. The Uncertain Curator

1. I borrow this formulation from E. P. Thompson, who offers the following definition of history: "The discipline of history is, above all, the discipline of context; each fact can be given meaning only within an ensemble of other meanings." E.P. Thompson, "Anthropology and the Discipline of Historical Context," *Midland History* 1, no. 3 (1972): 41–55, 45. But, as the reader can see, I repurpose Thompson's formulation.

2. Jac Büchner, testimony, Section 29 hearing, Truth and Reconciliation Commission, Durban, July 16, 1997, 73, transcript available from South African History Archive (SAHA), call number AL2878_B01.5.75.02.23.

3. Mwezi Twala, *Mbokodo, A Soldier's Story: Inside MK* (Johannesburg: Jonathan Ball, 1994), 149.

4. Hugh Lewin, *Bandiet: Seven Years in a South African Prison* (Harmondsworth: Penguin Books, 1981), 25. It bears pointing out that the police were able to know so much about Lewin because his best friend Adrian Leftwich is the one who betrayed him. Hugh Lewin, *Stones against the Mirror: Friendship in the Time of the South African Struggle* (Cape Town: Umuzi, 2011).

5. Peter Jackson, "Introduction: Enquiries into the 'Secret State,'" in *Exploring Intelligence Archives: Enquiries into the Secret State,* ed. Gerald Hughes, Peter Jackson, and Len Scott, 1–11 (London: Routledge, 2008).

6. Jackson, "Introduction," 9.

7. Hughes and Scott take these questions from Hugh Trevor-Roper. Gerald Hughes and Len Scott, "'Knowledge is Never Too Dear:' Exploring Intelligence Archives," in *Exploring Intelligence Archives*, 13–29. 26.

8. Andreas Glaeser, *Political Epistemics: The Secret Police, the Opposition, and the End of East German Socialism* (Chicago: University of Chicago Press, 2011), xvi.

9. Silulami Gladstone Mose, affidavit, September 22, 1972, in the Hennie Heymans Collection, Wits Historical Papers.

10. Terry Bell and Dumisa Ntsebeza, *Unfinished Business: South Africa, Apartheid and Truth* (London: Verso, 2003), 196.

11. Timothy Gibbs, *Mandela's Kinsmen: Nationalist Elites and Apartheid's First Bantustan* (Johannesburg: Jacana, 2014), 125.

12. *Final Report of the Truth and Reconciliation Commission of South Africa, Vol. 2* (Cape Town: CTP Book Printers, 1998), 443.

13. Gladstone Mose, affidavit, September 22, 1972.

14. This point is made in a beautiful essay: David William Cohen, "A Curator's Fingers: Photographers, Subjects, and the Third Thing," in *Uncertain Curature: In and Out of the Archive*, ed. Carolyn Hamilton and Pippa Skotnes, 63–100(Johannesburg: Jacana, 2014), 64.

15. Cohen, "A Curator's Fingers," 64.

16. Security Report No. 313, December 13, 1973, Gladstone Silulami Mose file, Wits Historical Papers (hereafter "Mose file").

17. Security Report No. 450, January 22, 1974, in Mose file.

18. Carolyn Hamilton and Pippa Skotnes, "Introduction," in *Uncertain Curature: In and Out of the Archive.* ed. Carolyn Hamilton and Pippa Skotnes, 1–23 (Johannesburg: Jacana, 2014), 1.

19. Security Report No. 463, January 29, 1974, in Mose file.

20. Security Report No. 473, February 5, 1974, in Mose file.

21. Security Report No. 480, February 8, 1974, in Mose file.

22. Chris Nkosana was the *nom de guerre* used by Chris Hani.

23. Security Report No. 465, January 30, 1974, in Mose file. For more on the history of the ANC's radio broadcasts, see Stephen R. Davis, "Voices from Without: The African National Congress, Its Radio, Its Allies and Exile, 1960–84," in *Radio in Africa: Publics, Cultures, Communities,* ed. Liz Gunner, Dina Ligaga and Dumisani Moyo, 223–237(Johannesburg: Wits University Press, 2011).

24. For a thoughtful examination of exile as a political condition, see Edward Said, *Reflections on Exile and Other Essays* (Cambridge, MA: Harvard University Press, 2000).

25. Security Report No. 478, February 6, 1974, in Mose file.

26. Security Report No. 479, February 6, 1974, in Mose file.

27. Security Report No. 507, March 20, 1974, in Mose file.

28. Security Report No. 507, March 20, 1974, in Mose file.

29. Silulami Gladstone Mose, affidavit, April 23, 1974, in Mose file.

30. Security Report No. 610, January 9, 1975, in Mose file.

31. Security Report No. 510, April 2, 1974, in Mose file.

32. Security Report No. 511, April 2, 1974, in Mose file.

33. Security Report No. 554, December 2, 1974, in Mose file.

34. Security Report No. 631, January 21, 1976, in Mose file.

35. Security Report No. 537, August 1, 1974, in Mose file.

36. Security Report No. 545, August 22, 1974, in Mose file.

37. Security Report No. 635, May 20, 1976, in Mose file.

38. Security Report No. 452, January 23, 1974, in Mose file.

39. Barbara Miller makes this point about the relationship between informers and the Stasi in the German Democratic Republic in Barbara Miller, *Narratives of Guilt and Compliance in Unified Germany* (London: Routledge, 1999).

40. Miller, *Narratives of Guilt and Compliance,* 55.

41. Long the subject of ridicule and dismissal, homelands have come in for some innovative and much-needed reexamination. See, for a sample, "Homelands as Frontiers: Apartheid's Loose Ends," ed. Steffen Jensen and Olaf Zenker, special issue, *Journal of Southern African Studies* 41, no. 5 (2015). See also "Let's Talk about Bantustans," ed. Arianna Lissoni and Shireen Ally, special issue, *South African Historical Journal* 64, no. 1 (2012). For an illuminating study about the complicated relationship between the Transkei, South Africa's first bantustan, and the black nationalist movement, see Timothy Gibbs, *Mandela's Kinsmen: Nationalist Elites and Apartheid's First Bantustan* (Johannesburg: Jacana, 2014). For insight into how the apartheid regime understood its position in relation to the bantustans and to postcolonial Africa, see Jamie Miller, *An African Volk: The Apartheid Regime and Its Search for Survival* (New York: Oxford University Press, 2016). This new scholarship builds on such pioneering work as Nancy Jacobs, *Environment, Power and Injustice: A South African History* (New York: Cambridge University Press, 2003); and Isak Niehaus, *Witchcraft, Power and Politics: Exploring the Occult in the South African Lowveld* (London: Pluto Press, 2001).

42. Security Report No. 637, July 22, 1976, in Mose file.

43. For an account of this, see Nelson Mandela, *Long Walk to Freedom: The Autobiography of Nelson Mandela* (New York: Little, Brown, 1994), 521–522.

44. Security Report No. 467, January 30, 1974, in Mose file.

45. Security Report No. 467, January 30, 1974, in Mose file.

46. For a detailed examination of the memorandum, see Hugh MacMillan, "The 'Hani Memorandum'—Introduced and Annotated," *Transformation: Critical Perspectives on Southern Africa* 69 (2009): 106–129.

47. For excellent analysis of the conference, see Nhlanhla Ndebele and Noor Nieftagodien, "The Morogoro Conference: A Moment of Self-Reflection,"

in *The Road to Democracy in South Africa*, vol. 1: *1960–1970*, South African Democracy Trust, 573–600 (Cape Town: Zebra Press, 2004).

48. Security Report No. 467, January 30, 1974, in Mose file.

49. For an elaboration of this argument, see Mahmood Mamdani, *Citizen and Subject: Contemporary Africa and the Legacy of Late Colonialism* (Princeton: Princeton University Press, 1996).

50. This line of thinking was inspired in part by Samuel Huntington, the Harvard political scientist, who visited South Africa in 1982 to give the South Africans advice about how to reform apartheid. See Samuel P. Huntington, "Reform and Stability in South Africa," *International Security* 6, no. 4 (Spring 1982): 3–25.

51. Security Report No. 548, August 28, 1974, in Mose file.

52. Tambo was, by all accounts, a self-effacing man. This quality and his lack of a military bearing helped him keep the fractious ANC together during its thirty years in exile. Luli Callinicos, *Oliver Tambo: Beyond the Engeli Mountains* (Johannesburg: David Philip, 2004).

53. For the history of the idea of the Zulu as a martial race, see Carolyn Hamilton, *Terrific Majesty: The Powers of Shaka Zulu and the Limits of Historical Invention* (Cambridge, MA: Harvard University Press, 1998).

54. I take this heading from the title of Breyten Breytenbach's memoir, *The True Confessions of an Albino Terrorist* (New York: Farrar, Straus, Giroux, 1985).

55. Security Report No. 633, January 29, 1976, in Mose file.

56. Security Report No. 633, January 29, 1976, in Mose file.

57. For a good examination of this phenomenon within Afrikanerdom, see Irina Filatova and Apollon Davidson, *The Hidden Thread: Russia and South Africa in the Soviet Era* (Johannesburg: Jonathan Ball, 2013). See also Lindie Koorts, *DF Malan and the Rise of Afrikaner Nationalism* (Cape Town: Tafelberg, 2014).

58. Security Report No. 632, January 22, 1976, in Mose file.

59. Security Report No. 632, January 22, 1976, in Mose file.

60. To be fair to Breytenbach, these are not the only political reports he ever wrote. In 1970, he published an essay in the ANC journal *Sechaba* offering a withering assessment of Afrikaner politics. In it, he concludes that "Afrikanerdom is doomed and it will be for a free South Africa to decide how it can best integrate the Afrikaner." Breyten Breytenbach, "A Crack in the White Wall," *Sechaba* 4, no. 4 (April 1970): 14–17, 17.

4. Perusals

1. Report no. 10, letter from Kompol to Divisional commanders, October 3, 1975. Letter in Cosmos Aloys Sechaba Setsubi's police file, V41563. hereafter "Setsubi file." The file is housed in the National Archives in Pretoria. I use it here with the kind permission of Setsubi's widow, Yvonne Nompumelelo Setsubi.

2. Constable Van Vuuren, letter, October 27, 1975, in Setsubi file.

3. There is a rich literature on "the file" as both a material object and an instrument of coercion and surveillance. For a sample of this literature, see Katherine Verdery, *My Life as a Spy: Investigations in a Secret Police File* (Durham, NC: Duke University Press, 2018); Warwick Anderson, "The Case of the Archive," *Critical Inquiry* 39, no. 3 (Spring, 2013): 532–547; Timothy Garton Ash, *The File: A Personal History* (London: Atlantic Books, 2009); Matthew Hull, "The file: Agency, Authority, and Autobiography in an Islamabad Bureaucracy," *Language and Communication* 23 (2003): 287–314; and, for a classic statement of how to read "the file," see Robert Darnton, *The Great Car Massacre and Other Episodes in French Cultural History* (New York: Vintage Books, 1985), esp. 157.

4. See the marvelous essay Luise White, "Telling More: Lies, Secrets, and History," in *History and Theory* 39, no. 4 (2000): 11–22, 22. See also, for a brilliant examination of the power of rumor in southern Africa's liberation politics, the pathbreaking Luise White, *The Assassination of Herbert Chitepo: Texts and Politics in Zimbabwe* (Bloomington: Indiana University Press, 2003).

5. White, "Telling More," 22.

6. I borrow this point from Istvan Rev, "The Man in the White Raincoat," in *Past for the Eyes: East European Representations of Communism in Cinema and Museums after 1989,* ed. Oksana Sarkisova and Peter Apor, 3–56 (Budapest: Central University Press, 2008).

7. I am thinking here of the observation by Max Weber: "The individual bureaucrat cannot squirm out of the apparatus in which he is harnessed." *From Max Weber: Essays in Sociology,* ed. H. H. Gerth and C. Wright Mills (1948; London: Routledge, 1991), 228. Weber is of course trying to make the argument that modern bureaucracies are impersonal by design and nature. Apartheid's security apparatus disproves Weber's claim, however. Far from being a "dehumanized" structure, the apartheid bureaucracy was very much a personalized apparatus driven by human caprice.

8. To be fair to the Security Police and their unnamed source, the ANC was not much of a force—let alone a threat—in the 1970s. See, for example, Stephen R. Davis, *The ANC's War against Apartheid: Umkhonto we Sizwe and the Liberation of South Africa* (Bloomington: Indiana University Press, 2018); Hugh MacMillan, *The Lusaka Years: The ANC in Zambia, 1963 to 1994* (Johannesburg: Jacana, 2013); and Stephen Ellis, *External Mission: The ANC in Exile, 1960–1990* (Johannesburg: Jonathan Ball, 2012).

9. Natal Division, letter to Kompol and to Matatiele and Umtata divisions, November 10, 1975, in Setsubi file.

10. Constable Van Vuuren's history report, November 18, 1975, in Setsubi file.

11. I borrow the idea of thinking of the Security Police as authors or biographers from Verdery, *My Life as a Spy*; and Cristina Vatulescu, *Police Aesthetics: Literature, Film, and the Secret Police in Soviet Times* (Stanford: Stanford University Press, 2010).

12. Major J. J. Diedericks, Natal Divisional Commander, letter dated December 8, 1975, in Setsubi file.

13. Lieutenant-Colonel H. W. McDonald to Secretary of Internal Affairs, December 10, 1975, in Setsubi file.

14. Lieutenant-Colonel H. W. McDonald to Commanding Officer of South African Criminal Bureau, December 10, 1975, in Setsubi file. The C26 was a card containing the biographical details of every South Africa and held by the Department of the Interior.

15. Lieutenant G. Van Rooyen to Police Commissioner, January 30, 1976, in Setsubi file.

16. Lieutenant-Colonel Q. Grobler, stationed at Kompol, to the Natal Division, February 23, 1976, in Setsubi file.

17. Lieutenant-Colonel G. N. Erasmus to Kompol, June 28, 1978, in Setsubi file.

18. Secret extract from Bloemfontein Security Police report, October 22, 1978, in Setsubi file.

19. Lieutenant-Colonel G. N. Erasmus to Kompol, November 9, 1978, in Setsubi file.

20. Security Police report LB.4 / 405A / 7, December 13, 1978, in Setsubi file.

21. For an account of how the South Africans targeted the UN for infiltration, see Dirk Coetzee, "Hit Squads: Testimony of a South African Security Policeman: The Full Story," 1990, rev. 1994, Wits Historical Papers, A2790f, Dirk Coetzee, testimony.

22. Coetzee, "Hit Squads," 50.

23. Coetzee, "Hit Squads," 50.

24. Mark Orkin, "'Democracy Knows No Color': Rationales for Guerilla Involvement among Black South Africans," *Journal of Southern African Studies* 18, no. 3 (1992): 642–669, 643.

25. Peter Gill, *Policing Politics: Security Intelligence and the Liberal Democratic State* (London: Frank Cass, 1994), 155.

26. Report number LB.4 / 405A / 7, March 12, 1979, in Setsubi file.

27. See the boastful official history of the South African Police, Marius de Witt Dippenaar, *History of the South African Police, 1913–1988* (Silverton: Promedia, 1988).

28. Report number LB.4 / 848A / 7, "Bewegings: Opgeleide terroris" [Movements: Trained Terrorists], March 17, 1980, in Setsubi file.

29. Diarra S. Boubacar to O. T. Sefako, March 13, 1980, in Setsubi file

30. Secret extract, May 17, 1979, in Setsubi file.

31. Secret extract, July 24, 1979, in Setsubi file.

32. Secret extract, May 7, 1980, in Setsubi file.

33. Secret extract, October 6, 1980, in Setsubi file.

34. Secret extract, April 7, 1981, in Setsubi file.

35. Secret extract, July 9, 1982, in Setsubi file.

36. Secret extract, December 8, 1983, in Setsubi file.

37. Secret extract, January 2, 1985, in Setsubi file.

38. Security report numbered 84030213, July 23, 1984, in Setsubi file.

39. Security report numbered 84036077, August 15, 1984, in Setsubi file.

40. Security report numbered 84038295, September 12, 1984, in Setsubi file.

41. Report numbered 02.02.1984, February 17, 1984, in Setsubi file.

42. Security report numbered 84011436, March 7, 1984, in Setsubi file.

43. Security report numbered 87086041, November 12, 1987, in Setsubi file.

44. Security report numbered 88001860, December 9, 1987, in Setsubi file.

45. Chris Barron, "Sechaba Setsubi: Quiet Teacher Who Carried Out an MK Assassination, 1948–2018," obituary, *Sunday Times* [South Africa], March 18, 2018.

5. The Petty State

1. Paula Ensor, interview with author, Cape Town, South Africa, August 13, 2016.

2. Stephen Kotkin, *Magnetic Mountain: Stalinism as a Civilization* (Berkeley: University of California Press, 1995), 367.

3. Terry Bell and Dumisa Ntsebeza, *Unfinished Business: South Africa, Apartheid and Truth* (London: Verso, 2003), 9.

4. For more on the directorate, see *Truth and Reconciliation Commission of South Africa Report,* Vol. One, Chapter Eight, "The destruction of records," pp. 201–243. On the directorate specifically, see pages 226–227.

5. See *Truth and Reconciliation Commission of South Africa Report,* Vol. One, p. 218.

6. Katherine Verdery, *Secrets and Truths: Ethnography in the Archive of Romania's Secret Police* (New York: Central University Press, 2014), 52.

7. Paula Ensor interview, August 13, 2016.

8. Paula Ensor interview, August 13, 2016.

9. Clippings of these newspaper articles are contained in Ensor's Directorate of Security Legislation file, no. 2965, hereafter "Ensor file."

10. Secret police report to Secretary of Justice titled "Restrictions," March 8, 1978, Ensor file.

11. Secret memorandum by Bureau of State Security regarding Paula Ensor, February 23, 1973, Ensor file.

12. Ensor disputes this periodization. Email exchange with author, April 1, 2019.

13. Not mentioned in the memorandum is that Neville Curtis was the brother of Ensor's best friend, Jeanette Curtis. The security police killed Jeanette and her six-year-old daughter Katryn in June 1984, using a letter bomb sent by Craig Williamson, the police agent who had pretended to be a friend of the family. Jeanette was also in the album.

14. For Ensor's reflections on her friendship with Steve Biko, see Xolela Mangcu, *Biko: A Life* (Cape Town: Tafelberg, 2012; New York: I. B. Tauris, 2014), chapter 5, 138–144.

15. Paula Ensor, email to author, December 1, 2018.

16. Police Commissioner's report to Secretary of Justice about warning issued in terms of Act 44 of 1950, Section 10(i), Ensor file.

17. Paula Ensor interview, August 13, 2016.

18. Eckie Ekhart, who went on to become a highly-regarded musician in South Africa, confessed his spying to his friends. Roger Lucey, *Back in from Anger: The Story of a South African Troubadour Who Lost His Voice and Then Set Out on an Unbelievable Journey to Find It* (Johannesburg: Jacana, 2012), 172.

19. Secret memorandum from Secretary of Justice to Magistrate Goodhead, March 15, 1971, Ensor file.

20. Secret letter from Magistrate Goodhead to Secretary of Justice, March 26, 1971, Ensor file.

21. Francis Stock to Minister of Justice, March 31, 1971, Ensor file.

22. O. A. Meyer to Francis Stock, May 28, 1971, Ensor file.

23. Paula Ensor interview, August 13, 2016. I am grateful to Ensor for sharing with me her copy of the transcripts of the hearings of the Schlebusch "Commission of Inquiry into Certain Organizations."

24. Paula Ensor email, December 1, 2018.

25. Paula Ensor to Chief Magistrate of Cape Town, April 2, 1973, Ensor file.

26. Richard Luyt to Chief Magistrate of Cape Town, March 28, 1973, Ensor file.

27. Secret memorandum from Police Commissioner, May 16, 1973, Ensor file.

28. Paula Ensor to Chief Magistrate of Cape Town, June 11, 1973, Ensor file.

29. Secret memorandum from Department of Justice, July 23, 1973, Ensor file.

30. Secret memorandum from Department of Justice, July 23, 1973, Ensor file.

31. For more on Ensor's work in NUSAS, Glen Moss's memoir, *The New Radicals: A Generational Memoir of the 1970s* (Johannesburg: Jacana, 2014).

32. Paula Ensor to Chief Magistrate of Cape Town, November 13, 1973, Ensor file.

33. Secret BOSS memorandum, December 5, 1973, Ensor file.

34. Secret BOSS memorandum, December 5, 1973, Ensor file.

35. Cape Town Chief Magistrate to Paula Ensor, July 19, 1974, Ensor file.

36. Cape Town Chief Magistrate to Paula Ensor, November 28, 1974, Ensor file.

37. Cape Town Chief Magistrate to Paula Ensor, November 19, 1975, Ensor file.

38. Ivan Evans, *Bureaucracy and Race: Native Administration in South Africa* (Berkeley: University of California Press, 1997).

39. I borrow the idea of living as if authoritarianism did not exist from Tina Rosenberg, *The Haunted Land: Facing Europe's Ghosts after Communism* (New York: Vintage Books, 1996), 162.

6. The Embarrassed State

1. Terry Bell and Dumisa Ntsebeza offer an account of this episode in *Unfinished Business: South Africa, Apartheid and Truth* (London: Verso, 2003), 110–111.

2. Craig Williamson, interview with author, Johannesburg, South Africa, August 17, 2016. According to apartheid spy Gordon Winter, the Bureau of State Security considered Eric Abraham a "problem child" because he refused to spy for the bureau. See Gordon Winter, *Inside BOSS: South Africa's Secret Police* (London: Allen Lane, 1981), 223.

3. Extract drawn from secret memorandum from Department of Justice, November 2, 1976, in Eric Abraham's file, no. 3625 from the Directorate Security Legislation, hereafter "Abraham file."

4. Jeremy Thorpe was a committed opponent of apartheid and a sworn enemy of South Africa. But his political career ended in ignominy in

1979 following a scandal in his personal life. There is some suggestion that South African security agencies, especially the Bureau of State Security (BOSS), helped publicize the scandal. For an account of BOSS's involvement in the "Thorpe affair," see Winter, *Inside BOSS*, 394–410.

5. Eric Abraham, email to author, November 26, 2018.

6. Secret memorandum from Department of Justice, November 2, 1976, Abraham file.

7. Eric Abraham email, November 26, 2018. For an account of South Africa's invasion of Namibia, see Joseph Hanlon, *Beggar Your Neighbors: Apartheid Power in Southern Africa* (London: James Currey, 1986).

8. For a critical biography of Williamson, see Jonathan Ancer, *Spy: Uncovering Craig Williamson* (Johannesburg: Jacana, 2017); see also Bell and Ntsebeza, *Unfinished Business*, 82–124.

9. For a history of the fund, see Denis Herbstein, *White Lies: Canon Collins and the Secret War against Apartheid* (Pretoria: HSRC Press, 2004).

10. For an account of McGiven's story, see P. C Swanepoel, *Really Inside BOSS: A Tale of South Africa's Late Intelligence Service* (South Africa: Derdepoortpark, 2007), 56–57.

11. I borrow the idea of thinking of the Security Police as authors / biographers from Katherine Verdery, *My Life as a Spy: Investigations in a Secret Police File* (Durham, NC: Duke University Press, 2018); and from Cristina Vatulescu, *Police Aesthetics: Literature, Film, and the Secret Police in Soviet Times* (Stanford: Stanford University Press, 2010).

12. Secret memorandum from Department of Justice, November 2, 1976, Abraham file.

13. "Schoolchildren in Multi-race City Talks," *The Cape Argus,* December 6, 1971. The union was a truly nonracial organization. Bill Nasson, who went on to become a prominent historian of twentieth-century South African history, served on the executive, as did Nafisa Hansrod, David

Guma and the Graaf sisters (Tessa and Janet), and Laura Levetan, who herself would be banned.

14. Eric Abraham email, November 26, 2018. Abraham recounts the story of his betrayal by his father in Eric Abraham, *Betrayal,* BBC Radio 4, produced by John Murphy, broadcast August 1, 2005, available through Portobello Pictures, London, https://archive.portobellopictures.com/About/Eric-Abraham/Betrayal. For another account of George Abraham's betrayal of his son, see Roslyn Sulcas, "Interview with a Torturer," *New York Times,* June 6, 2014.

15. Eric Abraham email, November 26, 2018.

16. For a history of the ARM, see Hugh Lewin, *Stones against the Mirror: Friendship in the Time of the South African Struggle* (Cape Town: Umuzi, 2011).

17. Eric Abraham email, November 26, 2018.

18. Secret memorandum from Department of Justice, November 2, 1976, Abraham file.

19. For more on Moumbaris and Hosey, see Ken Keable, ed., *London Recruits: The Secret War against Apartheid* (Pontypool, Wales: Merlin Press, 2012).

20. Secret memorandum from Department of Justice, November 2, 1976, Abraham file.

21. Secret memorandum from Department of Justice, November 2, 1976, Abraham file.

22. For more on Morris, see Winter, *Inside BOSS,* 320–321.

23. For a history of South Africa's Intelligence services, see James Sanders, *Apartheid's Friends: The Rise and Fall of South Africa's Secret Service* (London: John Murray, 2006); Bell and Ntsebeza, *Unfinished Business;* and Kevin A. O'Brien, *The South African Intelligence Services: From Apartheid to Democracy, 1948–2005* (New York: Routledge, 2011).

24. Bell and Ntsebeza, *Unfinished Business,* 110.

25. With his career as a spy over, Morris reinvented himself as an expert on terrorism. For a sample of his expertise, see Michael Morris, *Terrorism: The First Full Account in Detail of Terrorism and Insurgency in Southern Africa* (Cape Town: Howard Timmins, 1971). See also Michael Morris, *Special Review: Republic of South Africa's Law and Order. Key Issues in Parliament* (Cape Town: Terrorism Research Associates, 1986).

26. Secret memorandum from Department of Justice, November 2, 1976, Abraham file. Abraham disputes this account. "This sounds like a fabrication from an informant. Not my language and not something I would have said." Eric Abraham email, November 26, 2018.

27. Eric Abraham email, November 26, 2018.

28. Bell and Ntsebeza, *Unfinished Business*, 110.

29. Gerhard Maré confirmed the meeting to me, Stellenbosch, July 27, 2017.

30. Eric Abraham email, November 26, 2018.

31. "Work for Us, Police Ask Student," *Sunday Tribune*, April 30, 1975.

32. Secret memorandum from Department of Justice, November 2, 1976, Abraham file. Abraham disputes this account.

33. Eric Abraham email, November 26, 2018.

34. Abraham disputes this police account. "I don't think this is correct. I shared a student flat with Gordon Young at the time and was with him when Security Police detained him having ransacked the apartment for several hours taking books and documents of his and mine. Apparently, Gordon had only spoken to Breytenbach on the telephone. Anyone and everyone who came into contact with Breytenbach either directly or indirectly was detained and spent months in solitary. It seemed that the Security Police monitored Breytenbach the moment he arrived in South Africa incognito and used the opportunity to round up as many activists as possible." Eric Abraham email, November 26, 2018.

35. Secret memorandum from Secretary for Justice, November 2, 1976, Abraham file.

36. Eric Abraham email, November 26, 2018.

37. For the story of Rick Turner, see Billy Keniston, *Choosing to Be Free: The Life Story of Rick Turner* (Johannesburg: Jacana, 2013).

38. Eric Abraham email, November 26, 2018.

39. Transcripts of the interviews, published in Abraham's news agency, The Southern African News Agency (SANA), are in Abraham file.

40. Winnie Mandela gives a moving account of her harassment and torture in her prison memoir: Winnie Mandela, *491 Days: Prisoner Number 1323 / 69* (Johannesburg: Picador Africa, 2013).

41. Transcripts of the interviews are in Abraham file.

42. Transcripts of the interviews are in Abraham file.

43. For more on the history of censorship in South Africa, see Peter D. McDonald, *The Literature Police: Apartheid Censorship and Its Cultural Consequences* (Oxford: Oxford University Press, 2009); and J. M. Coetzee, *Giving Offense: Essays on Censorship* (Chicago: University of Chicago Press, 1996).

44. Secret memorandum from secretary for justice, November 2, 1976. All the quotes and paraphrases in this section come from the memorandum, Abraham file.

45. Eric Abraham email, November 26, 2018. Mowbray is a suburb twenty minutes' drive south of the center of Cape Town.

46. Letter from Buchanans Law firm to Chief Magistrate of Cape Town, December 2, 1976, Abraham file.

47. Secret Police memorandum to secretary for justice, December 23, 1976, Abraham file. Abraham explained: "This was to be able to break the isolation of weekend solitary confinement in my own one roomed home. The only contact with the clergy I had had before was with those who

were dissidents. I am Jewish but not religious." Eric Abraham email, November 26, 2018.

48. "Complaint by Banned Man," *Eastern Province Herald,* December 9, 1976, Abraham file.

49. Eric Abraham email, November 26, 2018.

50. Amnesty International paid for the bodyguard, who did not last. See, for details, Eric Abraham *Betrayal,* BBC Radio 4 documentary, 2005.

51. Eric Abraham email, November 26, 2018.

52. "'Spite' Claim Rubbish, Say Police," *The Citizen,* December 10, 1976, Abraham file.

53. Abraham cable to UN General Secretary's office, December 7, 1976. See also letter from secretary of foreign affairs to secretary of justice, BOSS and police commissioner, January 13, 1977, Abraham file.

54. Hanekom letter to South African government, January 6, 1977, Abraham file.

55. Eric Abraham email, November 26, 2018.

56. Abraham said: "Pressured by the *Guardian,* BBC, and Amnesty International, the British High Commission in Gaborone arranged for me to leave as soon as possible to London via Rome to a press conference at Heathrow, political asylum in Britain, a Nansen stateless person's identity document and travel document and fifteen years of exile. I didn't see Williamson again but for a brief meeting at the Russell Hotel in Russell Square where he tried to dissuade me from taking a job in Geneva for an international NGO." Eric Abraham email, November 26, 2018.

57. Williamson quoted in "Two in Dash across the Border," *Rand Daily Mail,* January 6, 1977, Abraham file.

58. Williamson quoted in "Two in Dash across the Border," Abraham file.

59. Williamson quoted in "Two in Dash across the Border," Abraham file.

60. Bell and Ntsebeza, *Unfinished Business,* 90, 123.

61. Eric Abraham, telephone interview with author, July 27, 2018.

62. Eric Abraham email, November 26, 2018.

63. Craig Williamson interview, August 17, 2016.

7. Comrade Rashid

1. Eugene Fourie, interviews with author, Free State, South Africa, August 27, 2015, and July 21, 2016.

2. Eugene Fourie interviews, August 27, 2015, and July 21, 2016.

3. See Security Report by Silulami Gladstone Mose, November 29, 1974, in the Hennie Heymans Collection, Wits Historical Papers, hereafter "Mose file."

4. See Security Report by Silulami Gladstone Mose, November 29, 1974, Mose file. For an account of Amin Cajee's life and defection from the ANC, see his memoir, Amin Cajee, *Fordsburg Fighter: The Journey of an MK Volunteer* (Cape Town: Face2Face, 2016).

5. See Security Report by Silulami Gladstone Mose, December 4, 1974, Mose file.

6. See Security Report by Silulami Gladstone Mose, October 4, 1976, Mose file.

7. Properly speaking, Ismail was not a commander but commissar (meaning political head) of the Special Operations Unit but he was de facto its leader. For an account of his experience, see Aboobaker Ismail, "The ANC's Special Operations Unit," *The Thinker* 58 (2013), 32–35.

8. Aboobaker Ismail, interview with Padraig O'Malley, December 11, 2002, https://omalley.nelsonmandela.org/omalley/index.php/site/q/03lv00017 /04lv00344/05lv01405/06lv01431.htm. I tried for three years (2016–2019), either directly or through intermediaries, to secure an interview with Ismail. But he never responded to any of my questions, despite promising numerous times to do so.

9.   Aboobaker Ismail, interview with Padraig O'Malley, December 11, 2002.

10. For an account of Timol's death, see Imtiaz Cajee, *Timol: A Quest for Justice* (Johannesburg: STE Publishers, 2005).

11. Aboobaker Ismail, interview with Padraig O'Malley, December 11, 2002.

12. Aboobaker Ismail, interview with Padraig O'Malley, December 11, 2002.

13. See secret police memorandum about Lungile Magxwalisa dated July 19, 1983. Copy in Hennie Heymans Collection, Wits Historical Papers.

14. See secret police memorandum about Lungile Magxwalisa, p. 117.

15. See page 15 of a secret police report titled *Uitkennings Lefoshie Glory Sedibe*. Copy available from the Missing Persons Task Team of the National Prosecuting Authority of South Africa.

16. Barry Gilder, email to author, April 10, 2014. Gilder writes about this misidentification in his wonderful memoir. Barry Gilder, *Songs and Secrets: South Africa from Liberation to Governance* (Johannesburg: Jacana, 2012).

17. Trewits (an Afrikaans acronym that means Counter-revolutionary Information Target Center in English) was a secret security task team set up in January 1987 to identify targets for assassination. See *Final Report of the Truth and Reconciliation Commission* (Cape Town: CTP Book Printers, 1998), 275–284.

18. Craig Williamson, interview with author, Johannesburg, South Africa, August 17, 2016.

19. Barry Gilder, email to author, September 5, 2016.

20. Eugene Fourie interview, July 21, 2016.

21. Eugene Fourie interview, July 21, 2016.

22. Eugene Fourie interview, July 21, 2016.

23. See Naidu's cross-examination of Moni in *State vs Maseko and two others*, National Archives of South Africa, HGH 319 / 87, 3684–3700.

24. Rayman Lalla, interview with author, Pretoria, South Africa, September 10, 2017.

25. Rayman Lalla interview, September 10, 2017.

26. Eugene Fourie interview, July 21, 2016.

27. Rayman Lalla interview, September 10, 2017.

28. For more on the Matola raid to which Lalla is referring, see Joseph Hanlon, *Beggar Your Neighbors: Apartheid Power in Southern Africa* (London: James Currey, 1986).

29. Rayman Lalla interview, September 10, 2017.

30. Rayman Lalla interview, September 10, 2017.

31. For more on Operation Vula, see Conny Braam, *Operation Vula* (Johannesburg: Jacana, 2004).

32. Rayman Lalla interview, September 10, 2017.

8. The Family Bible

1. Chris Giffard, email to author, April 21, 2015. Giffard also gives a detailed account of his encounter with the album in an unpublished diary, titled *Surviving Section 29: A Detention Diary,* that he kept while in solitary confinement from December 16, 1987, to March 15, 1988. Copy in possession of author and excerpts from diary used with Giffard's kind permission.

2. Chris Giffard email, April 21, 2015; Chris Giffard, interview with author, Cape Town, South Africa, July 26, 2017.

3. Chris Giffard email, April 21, 2015.

4. Chris Giffard email, April 21, 2015.

5. Chris Giffard email, April 21, 2015.

6. Phumla Williams, email to author, August 2, 2016.

7. For more on the June 1976 protests, see Anne Heffernan and Noor Nieftagodien, eds., *Students Must Rise: Youth Struggle in South Africa before and beyond June '76,* (Johannesburg: Wits University Press, 2016); and Ali Khangela Hlongwane, Sifiso Ndlovu and Mothobi Motloatse, eds., *Soweto*

'76: Reflections on the liberation struggles. Commemorating the 30th Anniversary of June 16, 1976 (Houghton: Motloatse Arts Heritage, 2006). See also Helena Pohlandt-McCormick, "In Good Hands: Researching the 1976 Soweto Uprising in the State Archives of South Africa," in *Archive Stories: Facts, Fictions and the Writing of History,* ed. Antoinette Burton, 299–324 (Durham, NC: Duke University Press, 2005); Sifiso Ndlovu, *The Soweto Uprisings: Counter-memories of June 1976* (Johannesburg: Ravan Press, 1998).

8. For the intellectual history of the black consciousness movement in South Africa, see Daniel Magaziner, *The Law and the Prophets: Black Consciousness in South Africa, 1968–1977* (Athens: Ohio University Press, 2010); see also Xolela Mangcu, *Biko: A Life* (Cape Town: Tafelberg, 2012; New York: I. B. Taurus, 2014).

9. For an account of the generational efflux after the 1976 uprisings, see Stephen R. Davies, *The ANC's War against Apartheid: Umkhonto we Sizwe and the Liberation of South Africa* (Bloomington: Indiana University Press, 2018); Stephen Ellis, *External Mission: The ANC in Exile, 1960–1990* (New York: Oxford University Press, 2013); and Hugh Macmillan, *The Lusaka Years: The ANC in Exile in Zambia, 1963 to 1994* (Johannesburg: Jacana, 2013). For an insightful account of how the Rhodesian security services dealt with students fleeing into exile, see Luise White, "Students, ZAPU, and Special Branch in Francistown, 1964–1972," *Journal of Southern African Studies* 40, no. 6 (November 2014): 1289–1303.

10. For first-rate reflections on the methodologies of oral history, see Philippe Denis and Radikobo Ntsimane, eds., *Oral History in a Wounded Country: Interactive Interviewing in South Africa* (Scottsville: University of KwaZulu-Natal Press, 2008); see also Luise White, Stephan F. Miescher, and David William Cohen, eds., *African Words, African Voices: Critical Practices in Oral History* (Bloomington: Indiana University Press, 2001).

11. Phumla Williams email, August 2, 2016.

12. Phumla Williams email, August 2, 2016.

13. Phumla Williams, email, August 5, 2016.

14. Phumla Williams, email, August 17, 2016.

15. Phumla Williams, email, January 24, 2017.

16. See the documentary "Ms. Phumla Williams Tells Her Story," GovernmentZA, September 16, 2014, https://www.youtube.com/watch?v=B5 Hs2fu9aQM.

17. An account of Williams's kidnapping by a band of askaris is found in Jacob Dlamini, *Askari: A Story of Collaboration and Betrayal in the Anti-apartheid Struggle* (New York: Oxford University Press, 2015), 56, 185–187, 236.

18. Williams's biographical account to Security Police, June 30, 1987. See State vs Phumla Mirriam Williams, AK 2385, Boxes A-B, Wits Historical Papers, hereafter "Williams's statement."

19. See Williams's statement.

20. See Williams's statement.

21. See Williams's statement.

22. See Williams's statement.

23. Phumla Williams, email to author, November 10, 2013; also quoted in Dlamini, *Askari,* 187.

24. "Ms. Phumla Williams Tells Her Story."

25. "Ms. Phumla Williams Tells Her Story." Williams was released in 1991.

26. Lumka Yengeni, interview with author, Cape Town, South Africa, September 8, 2017.

27. Lumka Yengeni interview, September 8, 2017.

28. Lumka Yengeni interview, September 8, 2017.

29. Lumka Yengeni interview, September 8, 2017.

30. Lumka Yengeni interview, September 8, 2017.

31. Lumka Yengeni interview, September 8, 2017.

32. For an account of the prison, see Bridget Hilton-Barber, *Student Comrade Prisoner Spy: A Memoir* (Cape Town: Zebra Press, 2016).

33. Lumka Yengeni interview, September 8, 2017.

34. Lumka Yengeni interview, September 8, 2017.

35. Lumka Yengeni interview, September 8, 2017.

36. Lumka Yengeni interview, September 8, 2017.

37. Lumka Yengeni interview, September 8, 2017.

38. Lumka Yengeni interview, September 8, 2017.

39. Lumka Yengeni interview, September 8, 2017.

40. Lumka Yengeni interview, September 8, 2017.

9. The Dompas

1. Personal details come from Lungile Magxwalisa, interview with author, Pretoria, South Africa, August 29, 2017. I am glad I was able to interview Magxwalisa, who died on May 15, 2018, of complications from diabetes.

2. For more on pass books, see Keith Breckenridge, "The Book of Life: The South African Population Register and the Invention of Racial Descent, 1950–1980," *Kronos* 40, no. 1 (November 2014): 225–240; and Keith Breckenridge, "Verwoerd's Bureau of Proof: Total Information in the Making of Apartheid," *History Workshop Journal* 59, no. 1 (2005): 83–108. See also Lorena Rizzo, "Visual Impersonation: Population Registration, Reference Books and Identification in the Eastern Cape, 1950–1960s," *History in Africa* 41 (June 2014): 221–248; Michael Savage, "The Imposition of Pass Laws on the African Population in South Africa, 1916–1984," *African Affairs* 85, no. 339 (April 1986): 181–205; and Dough Hindson, *Pass Controls and the Urban African Proletariat in South Africa* (Johannesburg: Ravan Press, 1987). For a comparative international perspective on the workings of documentary identification in the management of the black diaspora, see Rebecca J. Scott and Jean M. Hébrard, *Freedom Papers: An Atlantic Odyssey in the Age of Emancipation* (Cambridge, MA: Harvard University Press, 2012).

3. Lungile Magxwalisa interview, August 29, 2017.

4. For the workings of influx control, see Deborah Posel, *The Making of Apartheid, 1948–1961: Conflict and Compromise* (Oxford: Clarendon Press, 1991).

5. Savage, "The Imposition of Pass Laws," 181–183

6. For a useful account of South Africa's economic downturn, see Nicoli Nattrass and Jeremy Seekings, *Class, Race and Inequality in South Africa* (New Haven, CT: Yale University Press, 2005).

7. See Posel, *Making of Apartheid.*

8. Steve Biko, "Let's Talk about Homelands," in *I Write What I Like,* ed. Aelred Stubbs (Oxford: Heinemann, 1987), 83.

9. The quote comes from a statement made in 1978 by the Minister of Bantu Development in apartheid South Africa. The statement is cited in an amicus curiae brief in a case involving South Africa's attempts to cede the homeland of KaNgwane to Swaziland. Lawyers' Committee for Civil Rights Under Law, "The Commission of Inquiry into Kangwane (The Rumpff Commission): in re the matter of the cession of Kangwane to Swaziland: Brief of the Lawyers' Committee for Civial Rights Under Law, USA, as amicus curiae," March 13, 1984 (Washington, DC, The Committee, 1984), 3–4.

10. See Savage, "Imposition of Pass Laws," 181.

11. For some black South Africans, there was also an element of pride attached to their passes because passes symbolized belonging and bureaucratic acceptance of their presence in so-called white South Africa. See Lily Saint, "Reading Subjects: Pass Books, Literature and Apartheid," *Social Dynamics: A Journal of African Studies* 38, no. 1 (2012): 117–133.

12. On forced removals, see Cherryl Walker, *Landmarked: Land Claims and Land Restitution in South Africa* (Johannesburg: Jacana, 2008); Lauren Platzky and Cherryl Walker, *The Surplus People: Forced Removals in South Africa* (Johannesburg: Ravan Press, 1985).

13. Jonny Steinberg, *Thin Blue: The Unwritten Rules of Policing South Africa* (Johannesburg: Jonathan Ball, 2008), 70–71.

14. Serote, "City Johannesburg."

15. See Stanley Manong, *If We Must Die: An Autobiography of a Former Commander of Umkhonto we Sizwe* (Johannesburg: Nkululeko, 2015), 8.

16. For more on Joe Mamasela and his murderous reign as an apartheid killer, see Lukhanyo Calata and Abigail Calata, *My Father Died for This* (Cape Town: Tafelberg, 2018); Antjie Krog, *Country of My Skull: Guilt, Sorrow and the Limits of Forgiveness in the New South Africa* (New York: Times Books, 1998); and Jacques Pauw, *In the Heart of the Whore: The Story of Apartheid's Death Squads* (Halfway House: Southern Book Publishers, 1991).

17. Manong, *If We Must Die*, 12.

18. Stanley Manong, interview with author, Cape Town, South Africa, July 28, 2017.

19. Manong, *If We Must Die*, 20.

20. For more on Calata, see Calata and Calata, *My Father Died for This*.

21. For more on the assassination of Goniwe and three of his colleagues, Christopher Nicholson, *Permanent Removal: Who Killed the Cradock Four?* (Johannesburg: Wits University Press, 2004).

22. Stanley Manong interview, July 28, 2017.

23. Stanley Manong interview, July 28, 2017.

24. Stanley Manong interview, July 28, 2017.

25. Stanley Manong interview, July 28, 2017.

26. Stanley Manong interview, July 28, 2017.

27. Stanley Manong interview, July 28, 2017.

28. Secret police memorandum about Lungile Magxwalisa by Lt. Davidson, NN 7/18/12/1 (1 / 13), July 19, 1983, in Hennie Heymans Collection, Wits Historical Papers.

29. Lungile Magxwalisa interview, August 29, 2017.

30. Lungile Magxwalisa interview, August 29, 2017.

31. Lungile Magxwalisa interview, August 29, 2017.

32. Lungile Magxwalisa interview, August 29, 2017.

33. Lungile Magxwalisa interview, August 29, 2017.

34. Lungile Magxwalisa interview, August 29, 2017.

10. Capitol Drama

1. See Report of the Hearings before the Subcommittee on Security and Terrorism of the Committee on the Judiciary, United States Senate, Ninety-seventh Congress, Second Session, on "The Role of the Soviet Union, Cuba, and East Germany in Fomenting Terrorism in Southern Africa," Serial no. J-97-101, vol. 1, hearings of March 22, 24, 25, 31, 1982 (Washington DC: U.S. Government Printing Office, 1982); hereafter the "Denton Hearings Report."

2. For an examination of the Cold War in relation to South Africa, see Stephen Ellis, *External Mission: The ANC in Exile, 1960–1990* (New York: Oxford University Press, 2013); Irina Filatova and Apollon Davidson, *The Hidden Thread: Russia and South Africa in the Soviet Era* (Johannesburg: Jonathan Ball, 2013); and Vladimir Shubin, *ANC: A View from Moscow* (Cape Town: Mayibuye Books, 1999).

3. Denton Hearings Report, 3.

4. This did not stop the South Africans from trying to sell the unpalatable to the world. See, for example, Ron Nixon, *Selling Apartheid: South Africa's Global Propaganda War* (Johannesburg: Jacana, 2015); Ryan Irwin, *Gordian Knot: Apartheid and the Unmaking of the Liberal World Order* (New York: Oxford University Press, 2012). For information on the epic corruption that this propaganda campaign brought about, see Hennie van Vuuren, *Apartheid Guns and Money: A Tale of Profit* (Johannesburg: Jacana, 2017).

5. Denton Hearings Report, 2.

6. See, for more on these apartheid agents, the *Truth and Reconciliation Commission of South Africa Report,* Vol. Two, Cape Town: Juta & Co., 1998. See also Terry Bell and Dumisa Ntsebeza, *Unfinished Business: South Africa, Apartheid and Truth* (London: Verso, 2003).

7. For Kave's testimony, see Denton Hearings Report, 350–387.

8. For more on Hlapane, see Madeleine Fullard, "State Repression in the 1960s," in *The Road to Democracy in South Africa,* vol. 1: *1960–1970,* South African Democracy Education Trust, 341–390 (Cape Town: Zebra Press, 2004);; Michael Dingake, *My Fight against Apartheid* (London: Kliptown Books, 1987).

9. For Hlapane's testimony, see Denton Hearings Report, 528–558.

10. For Bosigo's testimony, see Denton Hearings Report, 484–527.

11. For Mfalapitsa's testimony, see Denton Hearings Report, 454–527.

12. I write about Bosigo and Mfalapitsa in Jacob Dlamini, *Askari: A Story of Collaboration and Betrayal in the Anti-apartheid Struggle* (New York: Oxford University Press, 2015), 61, 43–45, 213–216. My account there is based on a reading of the archives of the truth commission, especially the statements that the men gave when they appeared before the commission to apply for amnesty for their misdeeds.

13. For an insightful account (different from South African attitudes towards askaris, see Michelle Moyd, *Violent Intermediaries: African Soldiers, Conquest and Everyday Colonialism in German East Africa* (Athens: Ohio University Press, 2014).

14. For an account of Bosigo's and Mfalapitsa's defections from the ANC, see Stanley Manong, *If We Must Die: An Autobiography of a Former Commander of Umkhonto we Sizwe* (Johannesburg: Nkululeko Publishers, 2015), 144–146, 165–167.

15. Collaboration around the world has generated a lot of literature. See, for a sample, Dlamini, *Askari;* Leigh Payne, "Collaborators and the Politics

of Memory in Chile," *Human Rights Review* 2, no. 3 (April-June 2001): 8–26; Jean-Paul Sartre, *The Aftermath of War*, trans. Chris Turner (Calcutta: Seagull Books, 2008); Timothy Garton Ash, *The File: A Personal History* (London: Atlantic Books, 2009); Betsy Konefal, *For Every Indio Who Falls: A History of Maya Activism in Guatemala, 1960–1990* (Albuquerque: University of New Mexico Press, 2010); Michael J. Lazzara, ed., *Luz Arce and Pinochet's Chile: Testimony in the Aftermath of State Violence,* trans. Michael Lazzara and Carl Fischer (New York: Palgrave Macmillan, 2011); and Timothy Brook, *Collaboration: Japanese Agents and Local Elites in Wartime China* (Cambridge, MA: Harvard University Press, 2005).

16. In fact, that is how the Security Police captured Phumla Williams in 1987. See Ch. 7.

17. Fullard, "State Repression in the 1960s," 375.

18. For an excellent biography of Fischer, see Stephen Clingman, *Braam Fischer: Afrikaner Revolutionary* (Johannesburg: Jacana, 2013).

19. The evidence is found in Mfalapitsa's testimony. Amnesty Hearing, Thaledi Ephraim Mfalapitsa, in the matter of the murder of Themisile Tuku, Case Number AM3592 / 96, before the Amnesty Committee, Truth Commission, Pretoria, July 25, 2000, http://sabctrc.saha.org.za/documents/amntrans/pretoria/54370.htm.

20. For Kave's testimony, see Denton Hearings Report, 350–387.

21. For more on Charles Sebe, see the *Truth and Reconciliation Commission of South Africa Report,* Vol. Two, Chapter Seven.

22. For an explanation of how the Asterix worked, see Colonel Jac Büchner's memorandum about the handling of the album and its index, July 30, 1985, in the Hennie Heymans Collection, Wits Historical Papers.

23. Eugene Fourie, interview with author, Free State, South Africa, August 27, 2015.

24. Jan Potgieter, interview with author, Edenvale, South Africa, July 4, 2018.

25. Eugene Fourie interview, August 27, 2015.

26. Eugene Fourie interview, August 27, 2015.

27. Eugene Fourie, interview, August 27, 2015.

28. Jan Potgieter, interview, July 4, 2018.

29. Eugene Fourie, interview, August 27, 2015.

30. Sue Rabkin, interview with author, Johannesburg, South Africa, June 10, 2018.

31. Joel Netshitenzhe, interview with author, Johannesburg, August 2, 2016.

32. Joel Netshitenzhe interview, August 2, 2016.

33. Joel Netshitenzhe interview, August 2, 2016.

34. Garth Strachan, interview with author, Johannesburg, South Africa, August 19, 2017.

35. Barry Gilder, interview with author, Johannesburg, South Africa, July 13, 2016.

36. Gilder recounts the story of his exile in his memoir, Barry Gilder, *Songs and Secrets: South Africa from Liberation to Governance* (Johannesburg: Jacana, 2012). He also gives a fictional account of the legacy of betrayal and collaboration in post-apartheid South Africa in a wonderful novel: Barry Gilder, *The List* (Johannesburg: Jacana, 2018).

37. Barry Gilder interview, July 13, 2016.

38. Barry Gilder interview, July 13, 2016.

39. Barry Gilder interview, July 13, 2016.

40. Barry Gilder interview, July 13, 2016.

41. Jonathan Ancer, *Spy: Uncovering Craig Williamson* (Johannesburg: Jacana, 2017), 139.

42. Craig Williamson, interview with author, Johannesburg, South Africa, August 17, 2016.

43. Craig Williamson interview, August 17, 2016.

44. Craig Williamson interview, August 17, 2016.

45. Craig Williamson interview, August 17, 2016.

46. Barry Gilder, email to author, May 9, 2016.

11. Sins of History

1. The refusal here to display the image itself, settling instead for a description of it, is inspired by those wise scholars who decry what is too often an easy and uncritical depiction of mutilated black bodies. See Saidiya Hartman, "Venus in Two Acts," *Small Axe* 12, no. 2 (2008): 1–14; Brian Wallis, "Black Bodies, White Science: Louis Agassiz's Slave Daguerreotypes," *American Art* 9, no. 2 (Summer 1995): 38–61: and Anne Fausto-Sterling, "Gender, Race, and Nation: The Comparative Anatomy of 'Hottentot'Women in Europe, 1815–1817," in *Deviant Bodies: Critical Perspectives on Difference in Science and Popular Culture,* ed. Jennifer Terry and Jacqueline Urla (Bloomington: Indiana University Press, 1995). Although Maponya's death was not a result of lynching, the display of his mutilated corpse begs comparison with photographs of lynchings. For more on black bodies and spectacular death, see Jacqueline Goldsby, *A Spectacular Secret: Lynching in American Life and Literature* (Chicago: University of Chicago Press, 2006); Amy Louise Wood, *Lynching and Spectacle: Witnessing Racial Violence in America, 1890–1940* (Chapel Hill: University of North Carolina Press, 2009).

2. Students of photographic theory might be tempted at this point to think about Roland Barthes's *punctum* and *studium*. I am, however, trying to present a slightly different photographic reading project from that offered by Barthes. I am interested in the political, social, and oral histories of police photography in South Africa. See Roland Barthes, *Camera Lucida: Reflections on Photography,* trans. Richard Howard (New York: Hill and Wang, 2010).

3. Susan Purén, interview with author, Pretoria, South Africa, September 10, 2017. The classic statement on the spectacular mutilation of black bodies remains C. L. R. James, *The Black Jacobins: Toussaint L'Ouverture and the San Domingo Revolution* (New York: Vintage Books, 1989).

4. Aboobaker Ismail (Comrade Rashid) applied for and received amnesty for his role in the bombing. See *Truth and Reconciliation Commission of South Africa Final Report,* Vol. Six, Cape Town: Juta & Co., 1998, 282, paragraph 71.

5. Rodney Baduza Toka, interview with author, Pretoria, South Africa, September 10, 2017. Toka writes about his experience as an insurgent and a fugitive in Rodney Baduza Toka, *Escape from Modderbee: A True Story of an Ex-MK Soldier* (Pretoria: Bheki Zungu, 2012).

6. Rodney Baduza Toka interview, September 10, 2017.

7. Rodney Baduza Toka interview, September 10, 2017.

8. Rodney Baduza Toka interview, September 10, 2017.

9. Rodney Baduza Toka interview, September 10, 2017.

10. For work on the relationship between photography and violence, see Susie Linfield, *The Cruel Radiance: Photography and Political Violence* (Chicago: University of Chicago Press, 2012); John Berger, *Understanding a Photograph,* ed. Geoff Dwyer (London: Penguin Books, 2013); Susan Sontag, *On Photography* (New York: Penguin Books, 2008); Ariella Azoulay, *The Civil Contract* (New York: Zone Books, 2008); David Levi Strauss, *Between the Eyes: Essays on Photography and Politics* (New York: Aperture, 2003); and Elizabeth Edwards, *Raw Histories: Photographs, Anthropology and Museums* (New York: Berg, 2001).

11. Itumeleng Maponya, interview with author, Garankuwa, South Africa, August 27, 2015.

12. For more on Nofomela's confession, see Jacques Pauw, *In the Heart of the Whore: The Story of Apartheid's Death Squads* (Halfway House: Southern Book Publishers, 1991).

13. Itumeleng Maponya interview, August 27, 2015.

14. Itumeleng Maponya interview, August 27, 2015.

15. Confirmation of Joseph Maponya's work for the Security Police can be found in a signed affidavit that Maponya submitted to the Krugersdrop Security Police as part of their inquest into the disappearance of Japie Maponya. In the report, written in Afrikaans, Maponya states: "Ek is 'n bron van die Veiligheidspolisie te Krugersdorp." [I am a source for the Krugersdorp Security Police.] See Maponya's affidavit in Japie Maponya Murder Docket, no. MR 245/12/94 Krugersdorp, July 23, 1990. For additional confirmation of Maponya's association with the Security Police, complete with verbatim reports and payment receipts for services rendered, see affidavit by Captain Johannes Kleynhans. The Kleynhans affidavit was made in December 1989 following Almond Nofomela's revelations about the killing of Japie Maponya and it forms part of Exhibit P (Bew P) in Inquest GO 824 / 90 (GO is Afrikaans for Geregtelike Ondersoek which means Inquest) into the disappearance of Japie Maponya. These reports now form part of the court record from the trial against former Security Police commander Eugene De Kock. See Exhibit 118H (Kleynhans affidavit) in *State v. Eugene Alexander de Kock*, Case No. CC 266 / 94, National Archives of South Africa, hereafter "Kleynhans affidavit."

16. South African Police investigation diary, Sunnyside Police Station, Pretoria, Inquest number 250-4-88, April 16, 1988.

17. Secret letter by Lieutenant-Colonel L. J. Erasmus, May 6, 1977, Kleynhans affidavit.

18. Secret report and receipt by Bantu Lieutenant N. J. Leshi, May 30, 1977, Kleynhans affidavit.

19. Secret report and receipt by Bantu Lieutenant N. J. Leshi, August 30, 1977, Kleynhans affidavit.

20. Secret report and receipt by Bantu Lieutenant N. J. Leshi, September 30, 1977, Kleynhans affidavit.

21. See Kleynhans affidavit.

22. Saul Dubow makes the telling point that half the police officers responsible for the Sharpeville massacre in March 1960 were black. See Saul Dubow, *Apartheid: 1948–1994* (New York: Oxford University Press, 2014), 76–77.

23. Dubow, *Apartheid,* 299.

24. Signed Joseph Maponya affidavit, November 29, 1977, Kleynhans affidavit.

25. Signed Joseph Maponya affidavit, November 29, 1977, Kleynhans affidavit.

26. Kleynhans affidavit.

27. Secret report and receipt by Constable M. Z. Modisane, April 30, 1979, Kleynhans affidavit.

28. Lt. Mostert report, November 9, 1983, Kleynhans affidavit.

29. Copy of Kleynhans's statement, Kleynhans affidavit.

30. Excerpt from Kleynhans's statement, Kleynhans affidavit.

31. Excerpt from Kleynhans's statement, Kleynhans affidavit.

32. For details of the killing and disappearance of Japie Maponya, see *Truth and Reconciliation Commission of South Africa Report,* Vol. Two, Cape Town: Juta & Co., 1998, p. 212 and p. 237.

33. Dithusang Maponya, interview with author, Kagiso, South Africa, July 4, 2018.

34. Itumeleng Maponya, interview with author, Garankuwa, South Africa, June 17, 2018.

35. Itumeleng Maponya interview, June 17, 2018.

36. Dire Moses (Lucky) Mochine, interview with author, Krugersdorp, South Africa, June 30, 2018.

37. Dire Moses (Lucky) Mochine interview, June 30, 2018.

38. Tiro Tumane, interview with author, Kagiso, South Africa, August 16, 2016.

39. It might be illuminating to think of this point in light of David Rieff's argument about the need to forget. See David Rieff, *In Praise of Forgetting: Historical Memory and Its Ironies* (New Haven, CT: Yale University Press, 2016).

Conclusion

1. Eugene Fourie, Amnesty Hearing, before the Amnesty Committee, Truth Commission, Pretoria, July 19, 1999, http://sabctrc.saha.org.za /hearing.php?id=53549&t=Eugene+Fourie&tab=hearings.

2. The photograph is part of a PVAK file numbered PR 129 / 82. The file includes an affidavit signed by Detective-Sergeant Jacobus Albertus Bierman, July 15, 1982.

3. "Handleiding oor die ondersoek van terroristiese sake" [Guide to Investigating Terrorism], 1. The manual is undated but probably dates from the period 1979–1980 because the most recent court case it cites is from November 1979. Copy in possession of author.

4. "Handleiding oor die ondersoek van terroristiese sake," 3.

5. Gavin Evans, a journalist and underground operative of the ANC, was part of an ANC team that investigated and confirmed Peter Mokaba's spying for the Security Police. Evans documented his findings in a number of places. See Gavin Evans, "Two Faces of Mokaba," *Mail & Guardian*, June 14, 2002, https://mg.co.za/article/2002-06-14-two-faces-of -mokaba; Gavin Evans, "Secret Histories," *Leadership* 13, no. 5 (1994).

6. Peter Mokaba, interview by Padraig O'Malley, March 25, 1997, https:// omalley.nelsonmandela.org/omalley/cis/omalley/OMalleyWeb /03lv00017/04lv00344/05lv01092/06lv01122.htm.

7. Peter Mokaba, interview by Padraig O'Malley, March 25, 1997.

8. Elizabeth Edwards, *Raw Histories: Photographs, Anthropology and Museums* (New York: Berg, 2001).

9. In the photograph are, left to right, Mthetheleli JJ Titana, Colleen Lombard, Alpheus Ndude, Gary Kruser, Zurayah Abass and, foreground, Chris Giffard (l) and Charles Captain Mahlali. I am grateful to Chris Giffard for sharing this photograph with me.

10. "The Rainbow Trial Plea." I am grateful to Chris Giffard for sharing his copy of the plea with me.

ACKNOWLEDGMENTS

Teju Cole is reported to have described landing in South Africa as akin to arriving in the aftermath of some great disaster. Cole was on to something. South Africa has certainly been the scene of disasters—not all of them natural. But the country has also been blessed. If one of these disasters—apartheid violence—accounts for this book's subject matter, the blessings that define South Africa account for the book's very existence. Call this mix of disaster and blessing a negative dialectic. A number of individuals blessed me with their generosity and, in the process, made this book possible.

Eric Abraham, Paula Ensor, Barry Gilder, Chris Giffard, Ray Lalla, Lungile Magxwalisa, Stanley Manong, Itumeleng Maponya, Dithusang Maponya, Joel Netshitenzhe, Sue Rabkin, Garth Strachan, Yvonne Nompumelelo Setsubi and her daughters Lerato, Moelo and Masechaba, Cyprian Setsubi, Tiro Tumane, Rodney Baduza Toka, Phumla Williams, and Lumka Yengeni shared their stories in a manner that recalled the anti-apartheid movement at its best. Jac Büchner, Eugene De Kock, Eugene Fourie, Andre Gouws, Hennie Heymans, Jan Potgieter, and Craig Williamson will not agree with much of what I say in this book. Still, they spoke to me in expectation of nothing more than a fair hearing. I thank them. The indefatigable Kumayl Molantoa covered ground that I could not, dug up archival gems that I could not get to, and connected me to people I might have missed otherwise. Gabby Mohale at Wits Historical Papers believed in this book long before I knew what I was doing. She helped me find archival material that turned out to be the spine this book needed.

Despite the odds, Gerrit Wagener, Natalie Skomolo, and Zahira Adams have made the National Archives in Pretoria a mandatory stop in any journey toward South Africa's recent past, while Sello Hatang, Razia Saleh, and Verne Harris have turned the Nelson Mandela Center of Memory into a place from which to understand the past better and to imagine possible futures. Dave Fell, whose research promises to add immeasurably to our understanding of South Africa's recent military history, shared his contacts and allowed me to use some of the material he had managed to get declassified by South Africa's notoriously opaque Defense Archive. Getting that material declassified was no small feat; sharing it with another scholar was a big gesture of collegiality.

David Atwell, Gabeba Baderoon, Barbara and Terry Bell, Madeleine Fullard, Tamar Garb, Nelson Kasfir, Kopano Ratele, Nicky Rousseau, James Sanders, and Piers Pigou embody the scholarly commons to a degree that puts many of us to shame. Gerhard Maré and Thembisa Waetjen are exemplars of what committed living and scholarship mean and look like. Jacklyn Cock and Luise White have, each in their own way and from places far and near, provided mentorship through their counsel and scholarship. Jonny Steinberg has been a steadfast supporter. So has Princeton University's History Department, my intellectual home for the past five years. I must mention Brooke Fitzgerald, Kelly Lin-Kremer, Pamela Long, Sorat Tungkasiri, Max Siles, and Carla Zimowsk. Emily Osborn, W. J. T. Mitchell, and their colleagues at the University of Chicago gave valuable feedback, as did Anna-Maria Makhulu, Karin Shapiro, and audiences at Duke, Johns Hopkins, and NYU.

Sharmila Sen, my editor at Harvard University Press, has been with *The Terrorist Album* from its beginnings as a proposal to its status now as a book. She has championed it every step of the way and, together with Associate Editor Heather Hughes, handled it with the utmost care and rigor. Sharmila and Heather not only shepherded the book, they also found anonymous readers whose astute readings made this a better book. Julia Kirby, Senior Editor at Harvard University Press, and her colleague Anne McGuire gave the manuscript the kind of copyediting attention that most writers can only dream of. Elaine Scarry saved me from ethical and moral embarrassment by reminding me of the importance of language, especially in any discussion of torture. The Stellenbosch Institute for Advanced Study gave me the time and the place from which to begin sorting through the research presented here; the Institute for Advanced Study at Princeton gave me the time and the place to begin writing this book.

Achal Prabhala made this book possible in ways that only he could. Patty, Mbali, Evie, and Khaya have lived with this book in its many iterations. I can never thank them enough for everything they have done and continue to do for me. They are my life.

INDEX

Page numbers in italics refer to figures.